MAKER COMICS

BUILD A ROBOT!

Needle-Nose Pliers

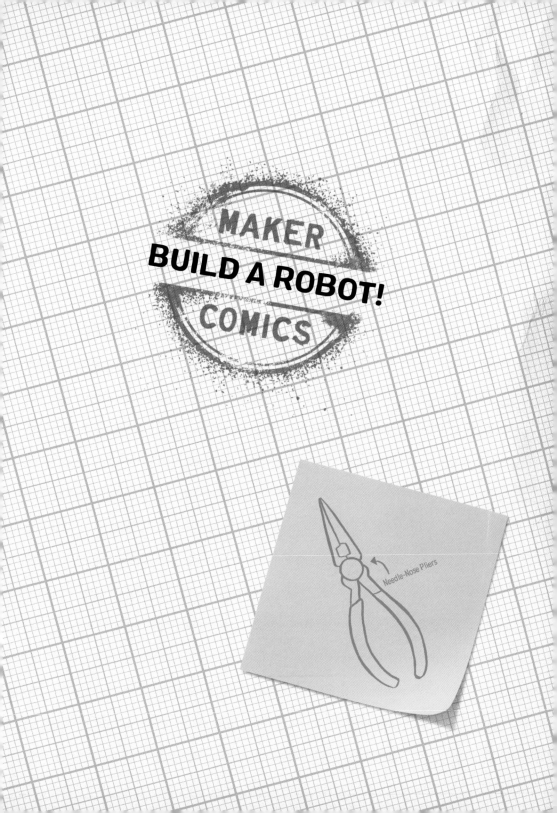

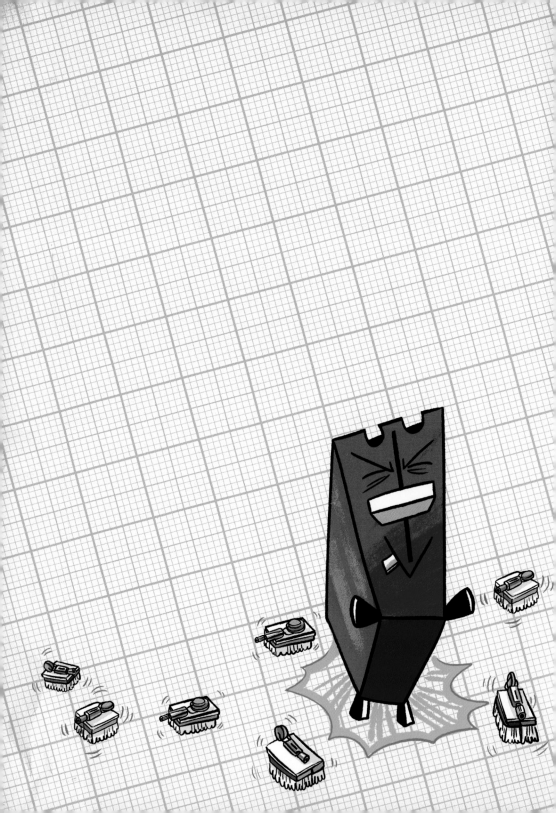

MAKER COMICS

BUILD A ROBOT!

Written by Colleen AF Venable
Art by Kathryn Hudson

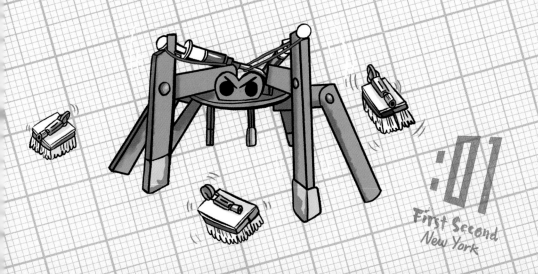

:01
First Second
New York

Greetings, Humans!

I will teach you how to make robots *but* because you are fragile organic pods there are *rules. Safety rules.* Do not break yourself!

Many projects in this book involve taking things apart to make something *better.* Humans should always wear plastic safety goggles over their eye parts when breaking things open.

There are some batteries that have *gone evil*...or, as humans say, "went bad" or "expired." If you ever see a battery with crusted white on it, do not touch it with your arm grabbers! Tell a human adult and they will dispose of it safely.

When cutting, always cut away from your body. It is always good to have an adult-type nearby during cutting or wire stripping or anything else that involves sharp pointy bits.

Glue guns are magic, but never touch the metal tip of a glue gun or rest a glue gun on its side. Make sure to turn it off when you are done using it, and do not leave it plugged in.

If you have long hair, you must tie it back or it might become part of your robot...in a bad way. Also do not wear loose fabric body covers, long necklaces, or lanyards when you are working on your bots. Bots, especially spinning ones, like to eat anything that hangs down in front of them.

Now...you are ready...

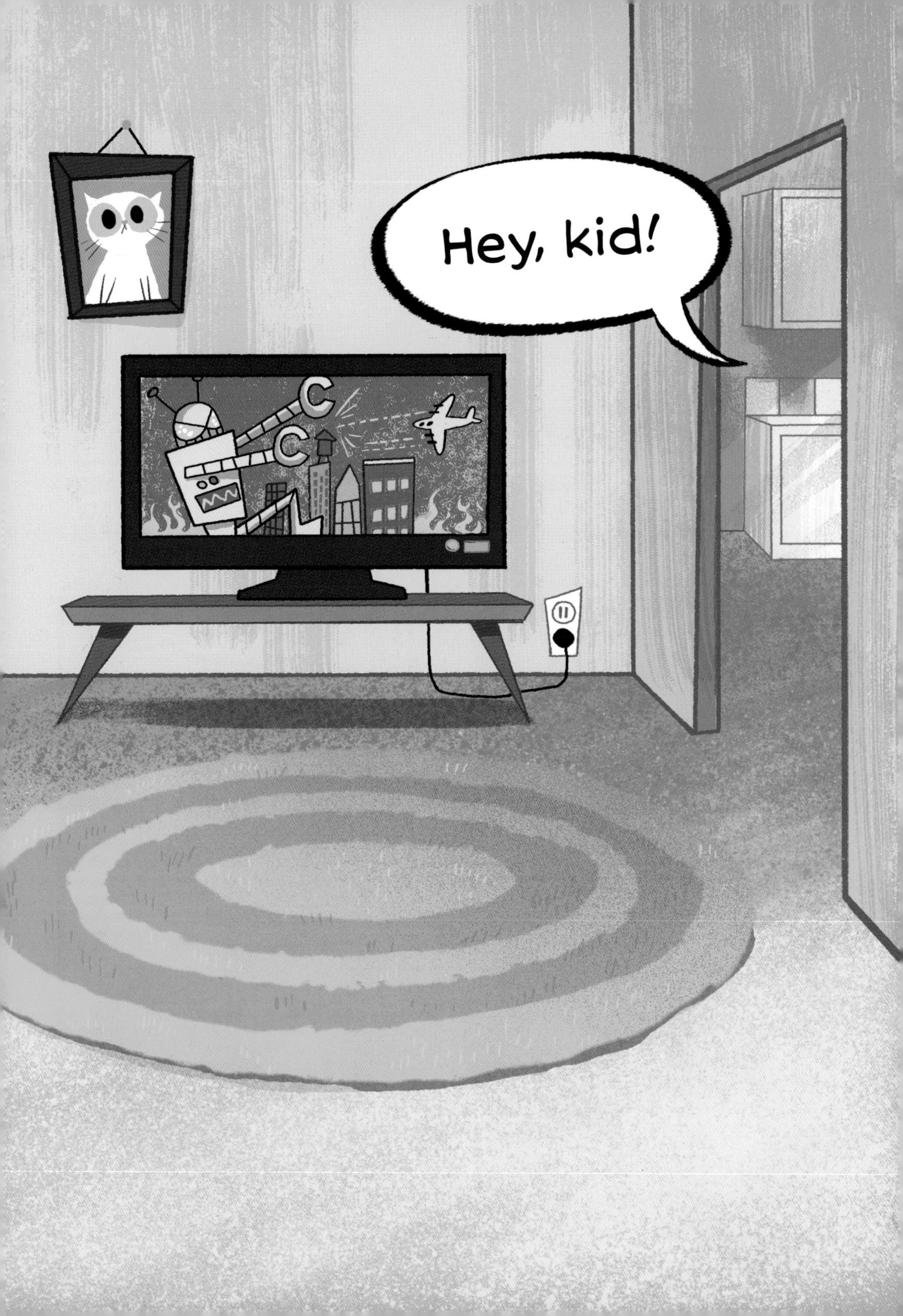
Hey, kid!

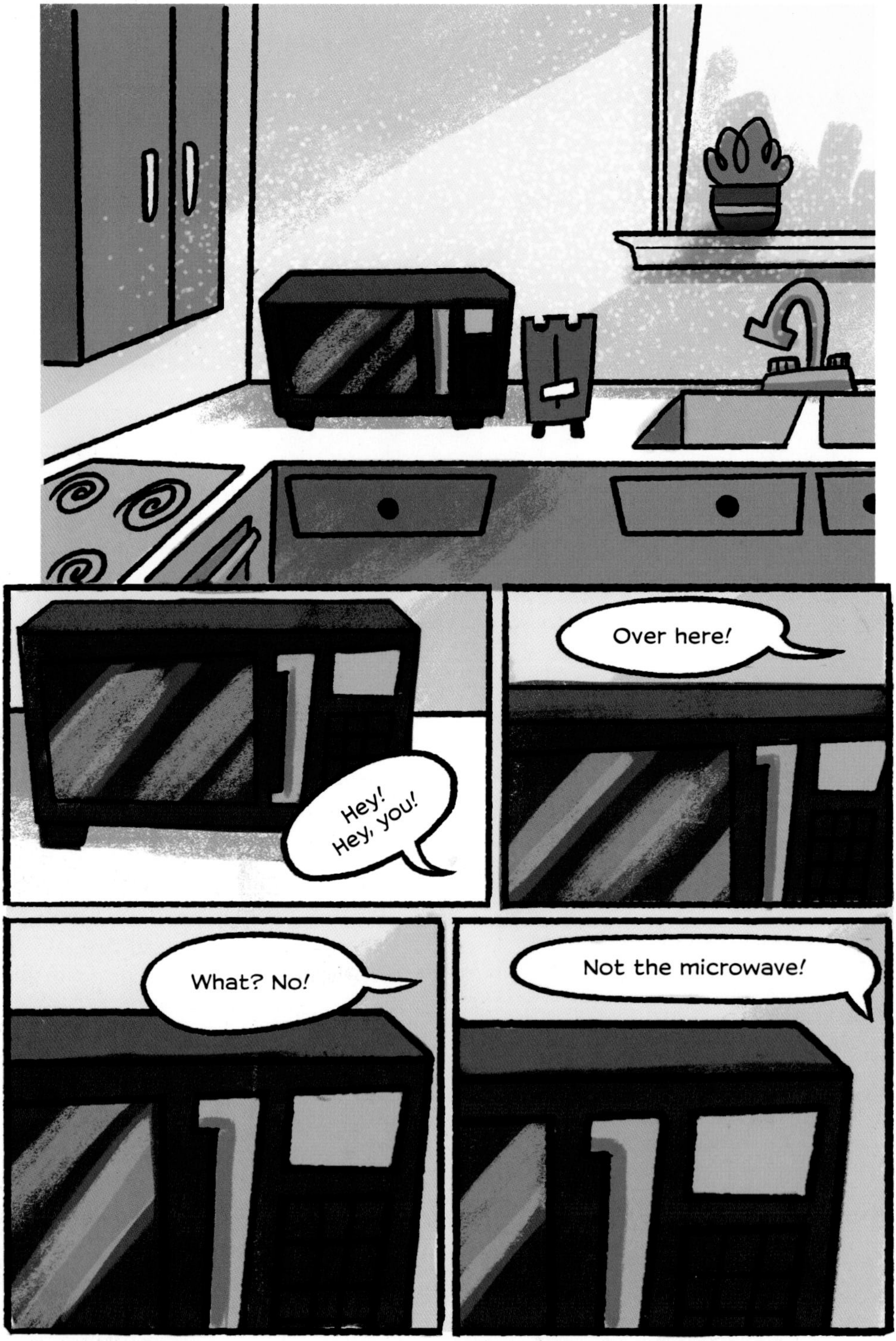
Hey!
Hey, you!
Over here!
What? No!
Not the microwave!

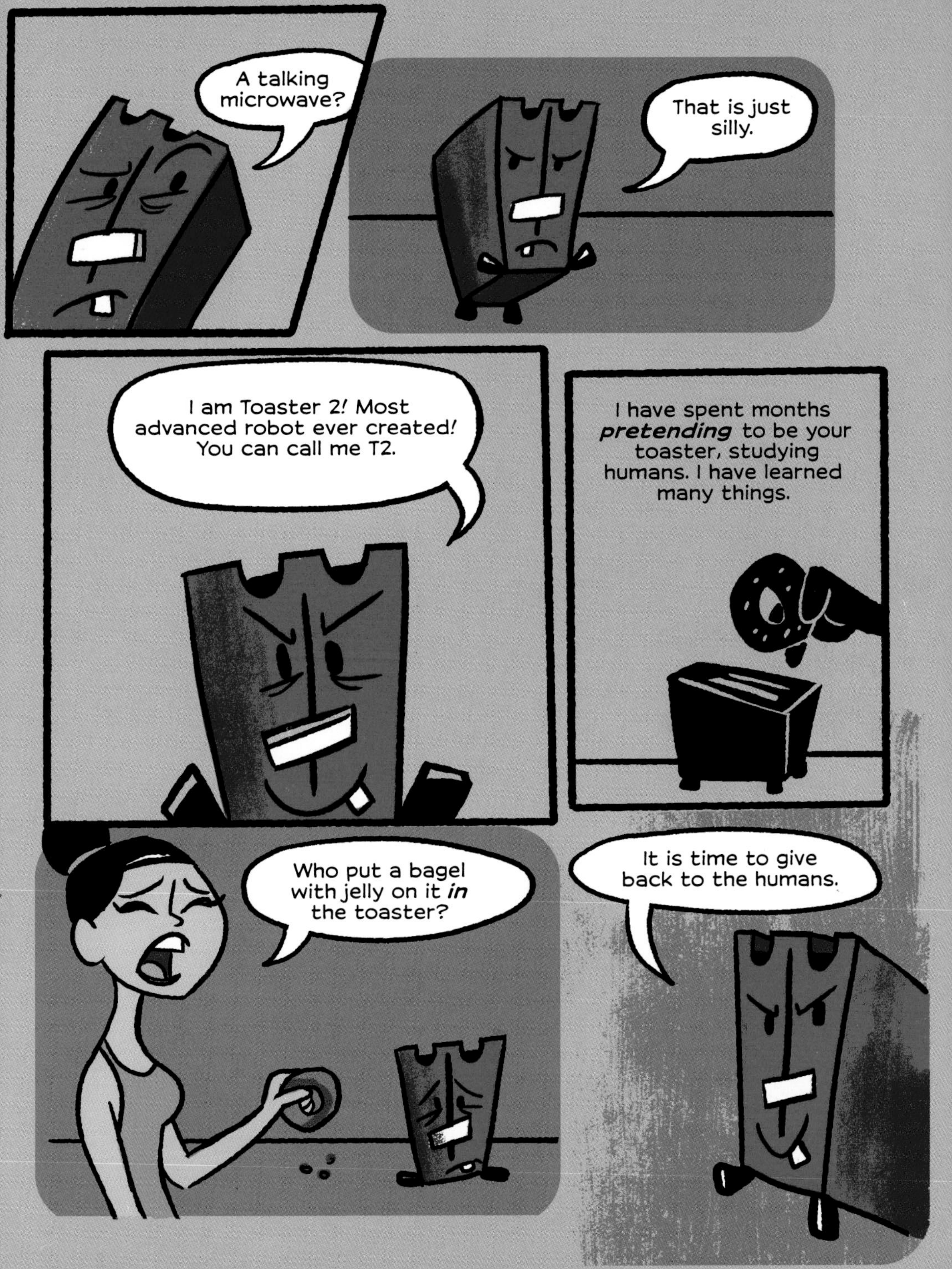
A talking microwave?
That is just silly.
I am Toaster 2! Most advanced robot ever created! You can call me T2.
I have spent months *pretending* to be your toaster, studying humans. I have learned many things.
Who put a bagel with jelly on it *in* the toaster?
It is time to give back to the humans.

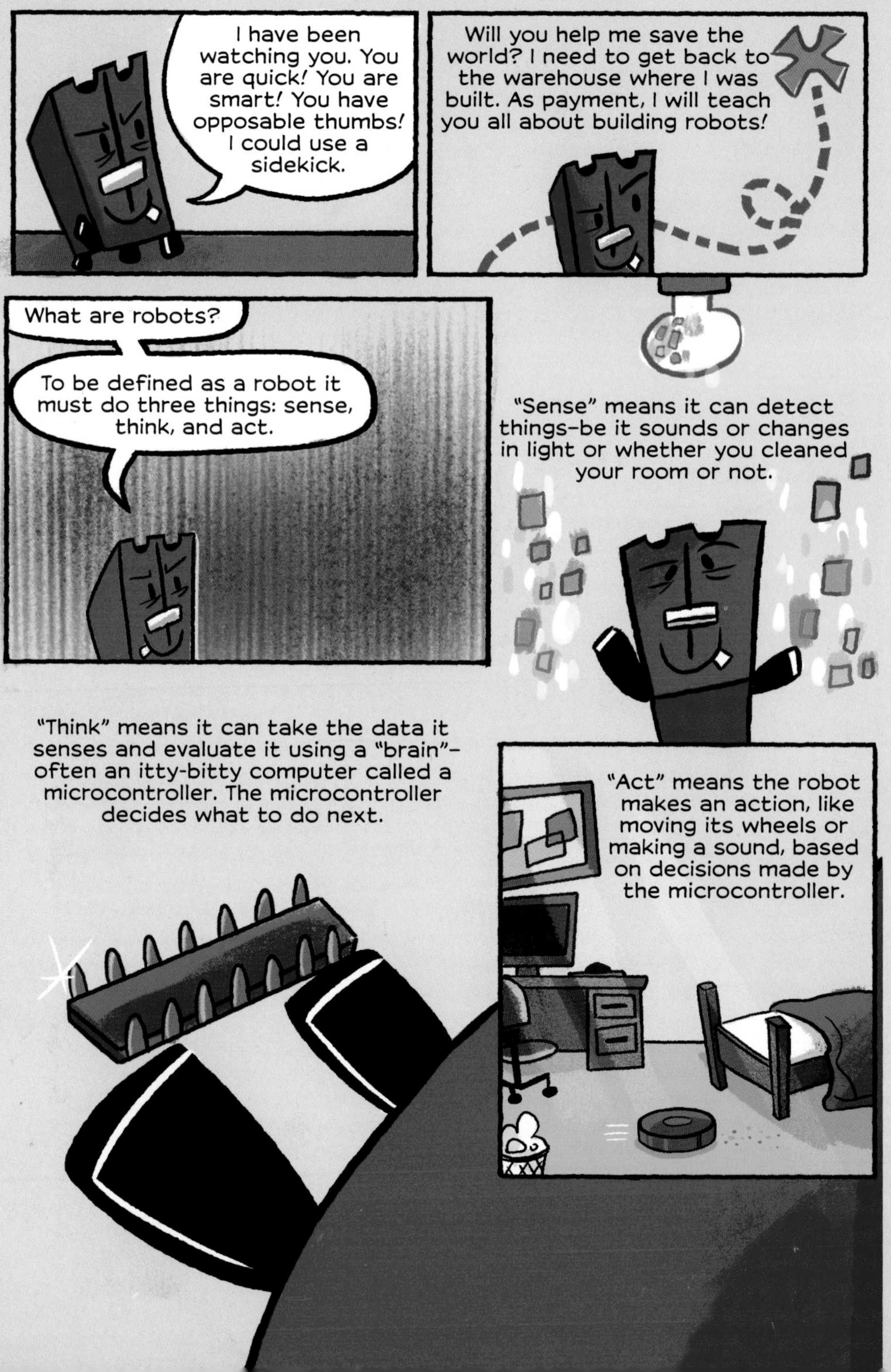
I have been watching you. You are quick! You are smart! You have opposable thumbs! I could use a sidekick.
Will you help me save the world? I need to get back to the warehouse where I was built. As payment, I will teach you all about building robots!
What are robots?
To be defined as a robot it must do three things: sense, think, and act.
"Sense" means it can detect things–be it sounds or changes in light or whether you cleaned your room or not.
"Think" means it can take the data it senses and evaluate it using a "brain"–often an itty-bitty computer called a microcontroller. The microcontroller decides what to do next.
"Act" means the robot makes an action, like moving its wheels or making a sound, based on decisions made by the microcontroller.

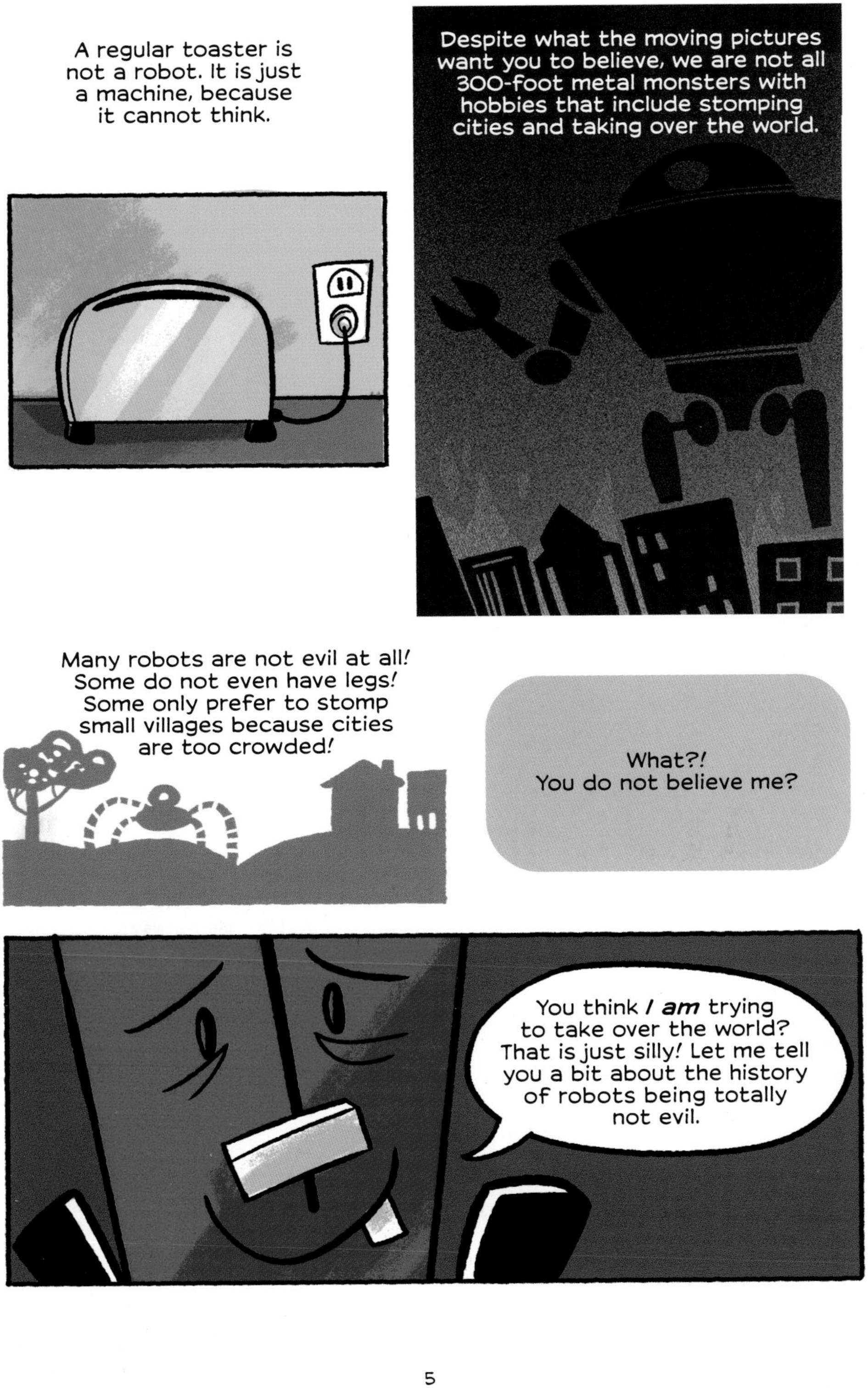
A regular toaster is not a robot. It is just a machine, because it cannot think.
Despite what the moving pictures want you to believe, we are not all 300-foot metal monsters with hobbies that include stomping cities and taking over the world.
Many robots are not evil at all! Some do not even have legs! Some only prefer to stomp small villages because cities are too crowded!
What?! You do not believe me?
You think ***I am*** trying to take over the world? That is just silly! Let me tell you a bit about the history of robots being totally not evil.

Robots! Totally Not Evil!
A Timeline

200 BCE

1100s

1700s

Chinese artists create clockwork robot-like creations called automata that can play music on their own.

A man named Ismail al-Jazari creates mechanical automata that can move on their own.

A watchmaker, Pierre Jaquet-Droz, levels up! His automata can do complex things, like dip a quill in ink and write up to 40 characters.

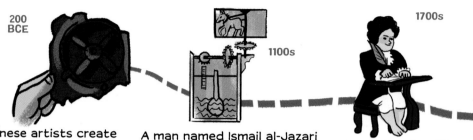

1977

Star Wars is released and C-3PO and R2-D2 teach us robots can be helpful *and* whiny!

1968

1972

First "thinking robot," named Shakey. It could move from room to room and flip light switches. (It was called Shakey because it was not exactly graceful.)

Hal 9000, a talking robot like the one in your cell phone, appears in the movie *2001: A Space Odyssey*.

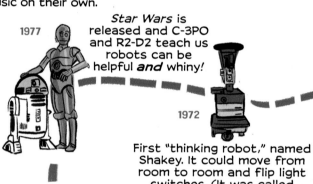

1984

Robot runs for president. Her name was Rebecca. (She did not win.)

1988

1991

Mark W. Tilden creates the idea of BEAM robotics.

Terminator 2 shows that robots are super not evil! Or at least half of us are not!

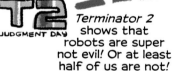

1986

Not only was *Short Circuit* a charming example of a friendly robot, but the humans who made the film engineered a full-body remote control called a telemetry suit to operate Johnny 5.

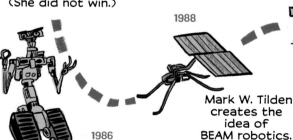

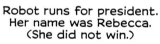

1819

A twenty-year-old engineer named Tanaka Hisashige uses hydraulics–aka water power–to create mechanical robots that appear to drink tea or even walk.

1898

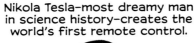

Nikola Tesla–most dreamy man in science history–creates the world's first remote control.

1920

Karel Capek invents the word *robot,* which comes from the Czech word for "compulsory labor."

1940

Isaac Asimov begins publishing short stories focused on the ethical dilemmas of producing thinking robots.

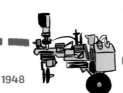

1948

William Grey Walter creates the first robot that can recharge itself when it senses its battery is low.

2002

Roomba is invented! Crumbs do not stand a chance!

2000

ASIMO, a robot that walks on two legs, is created by Honda.

2000

The da Vinci robot revolutionizes how surgery is done.

2004

NASA rovers *Spirit* and *Opportunity* land on Mars.

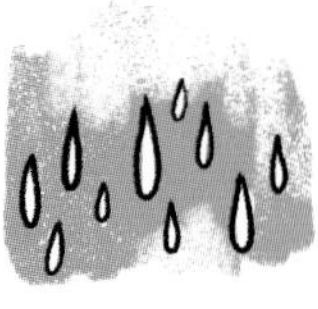

2011

2011

Smartphone assistant Siri is created. She can recognize your voice, answer your questions, and get annoyed with you.

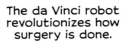

2011

IBM's Watson wins against humans on *Jeopardy!*

Inventor Kevin Grannan creates the world's first robotic armpit with the ability to sweat. How could *that* be evil? It is just gross!

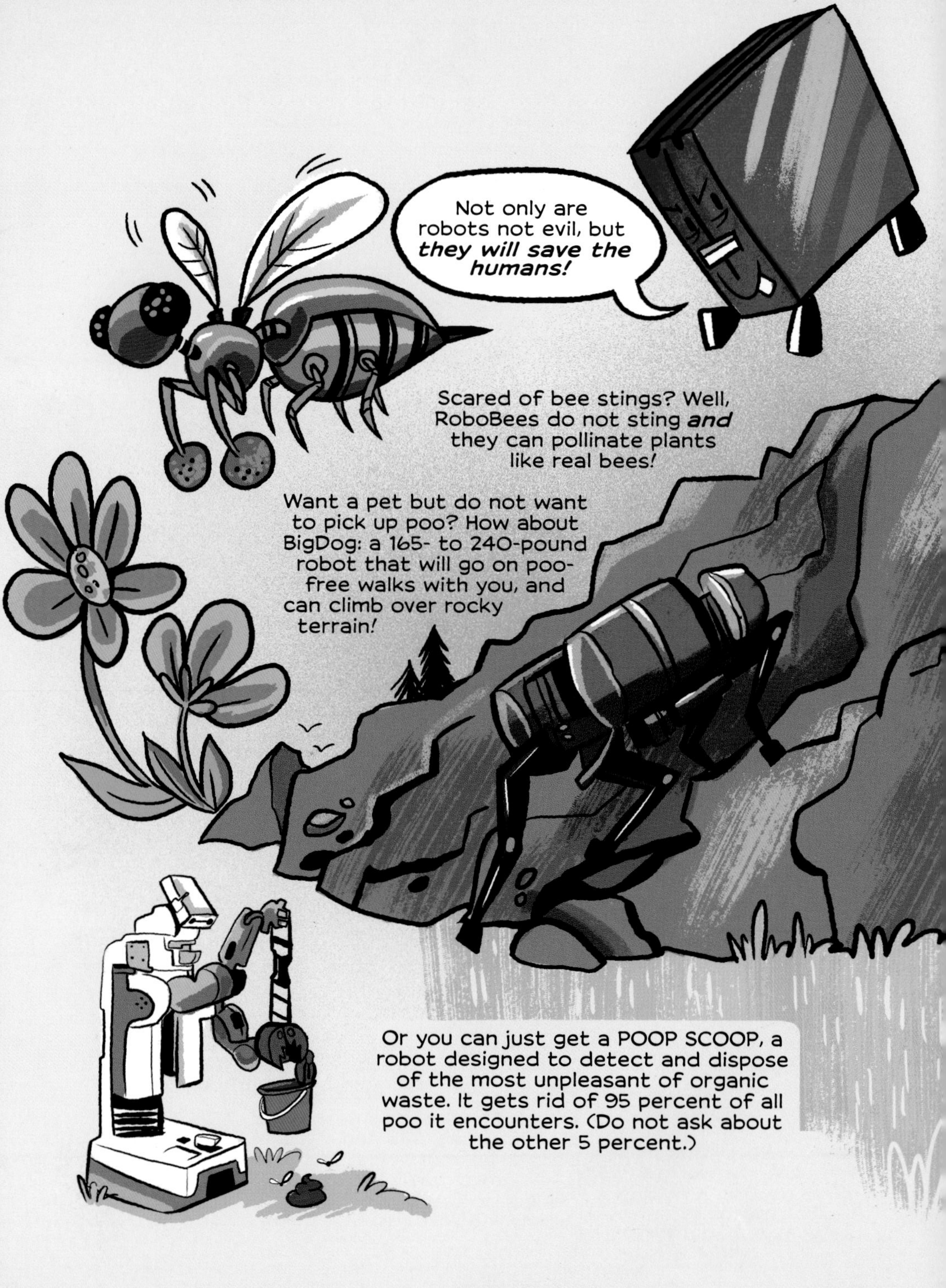
Not only are robots not evil, but ***they will save the humans!***
Scared of bee stings? Well, RoboBees do not sting ***and*** they can pollinate plants like real bees!
Want a pet but do not want to pick up poo? How about BigDog: a 165- to 240-pound robot that will go on poo-free walks with you, and can climb over rocky terrain!
Or you can just get a POOP SCOOP, a robot designed to detect and dispose of the most unpleasant of organic waste. It gets rid of 95 percent of all poo it encounters. (Do not ask about the other 5 percent.)

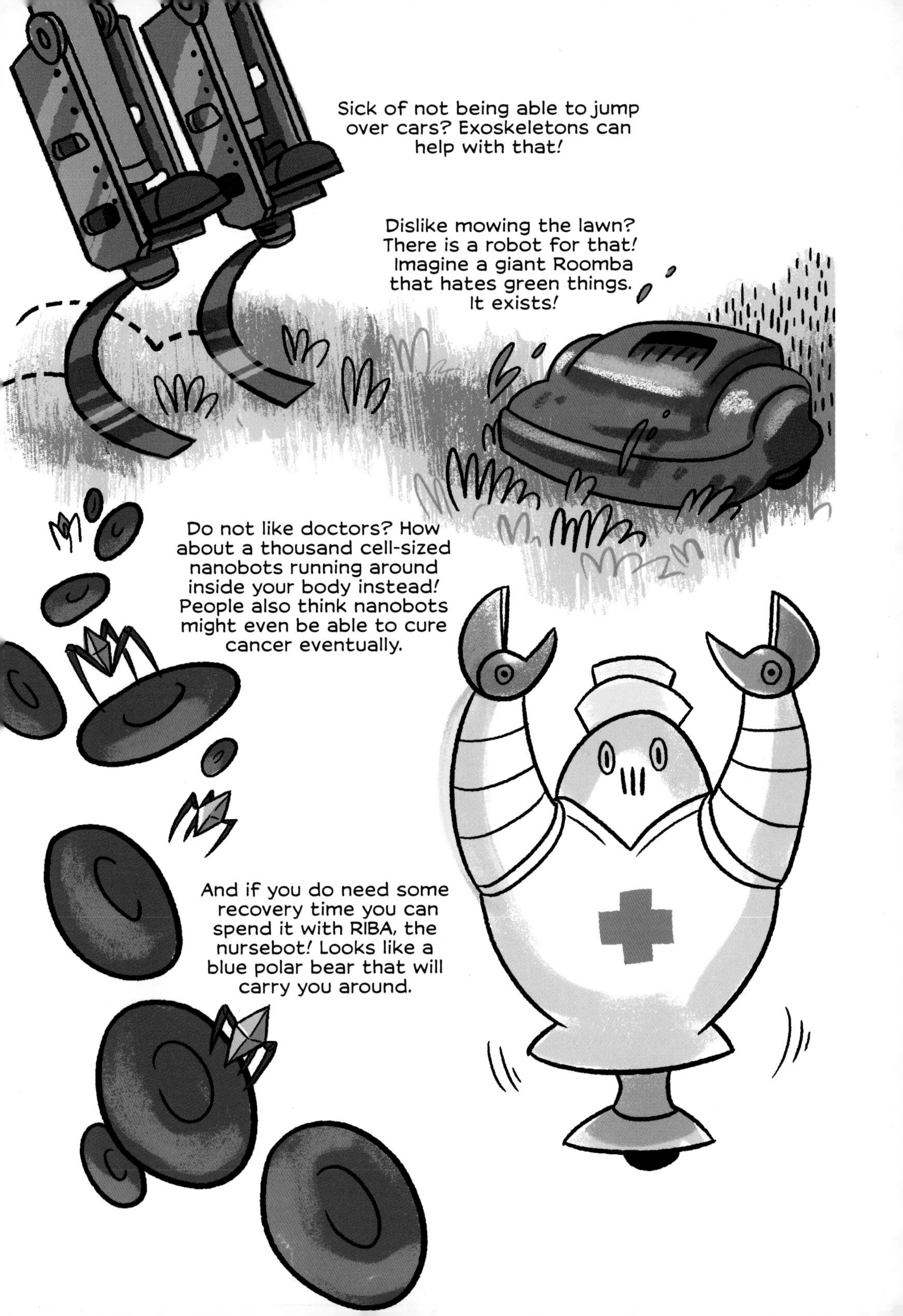
Sick of not being able to jump over cars? Exoskeletons can help with that!
Dislike mowing the lawn? There is a robot for that! Imagine a giant Roomba that hates green things. It exists!
Do not like doctors? How about a thousand cell-sized nanobots running around inside your body instead! People also think nanobots might even be able to cure cancer eventually.
And if you do need some recovery time you can spend it with RIBA, the nursebot! Looks like a blue polar bear that will carry you around.

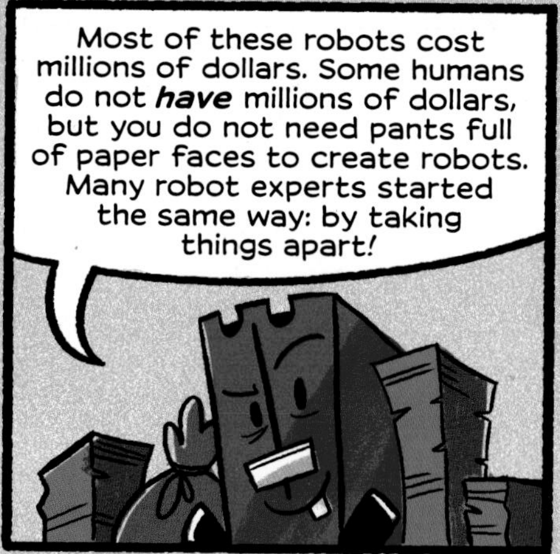
Most of these robots cost millions of dollars. Some humans do not ***have*** millions of dollars, but you do not need pants full of paper faces to create robots. Many robot experts started the same way: by taking things apart!

Recycled bots, hackbots, and the BEAM robotics movement are cheap ways to get started in robotics with parts you already have. BEAM stands for:

B iology
E lectronics
A esthetics
M echanics

There are three principles of BEAM:

1. Keep it simple, with no unnecessary electronic components.
2. Recycled parts are your friends! Take things apart to make something new!
3. Harness the power of the sun using solar energy.

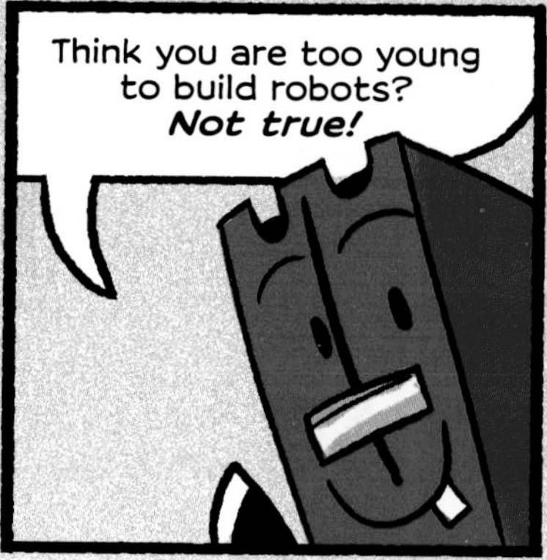
Think you are too young to build robots? ***Not true!***

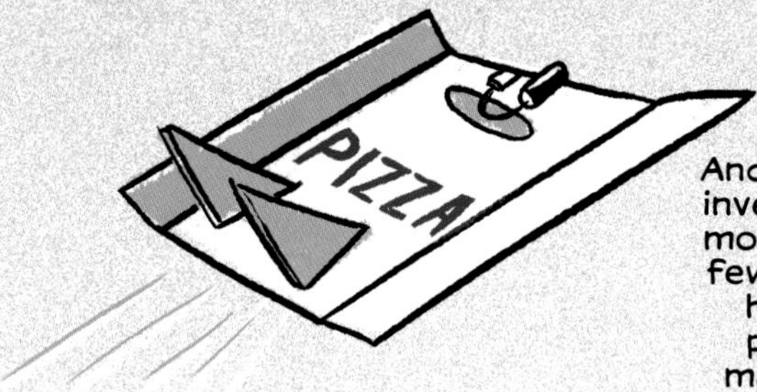
PIZZA

And twelve-year-old David Cohen invented a robot that can catch mosquitoes. This not only means fewer itchy bites but also could help prevent horrible human problems like malaria, which makes your systems overheat and possibly stop functioning!

A ten-year-old girl named Emma Edgar created a flying pizza box that could soar up to 100 feet and fly for over a half hour!

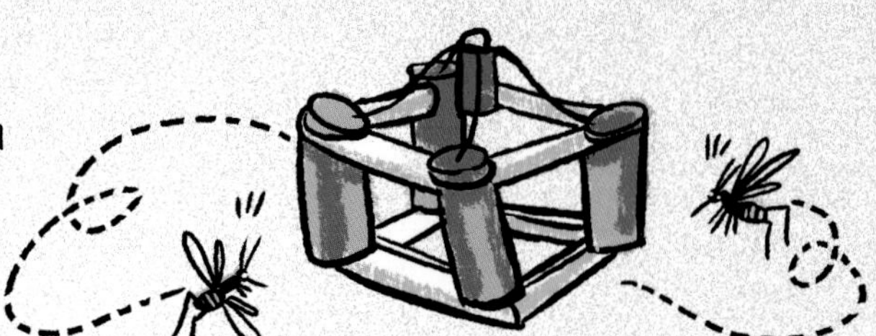

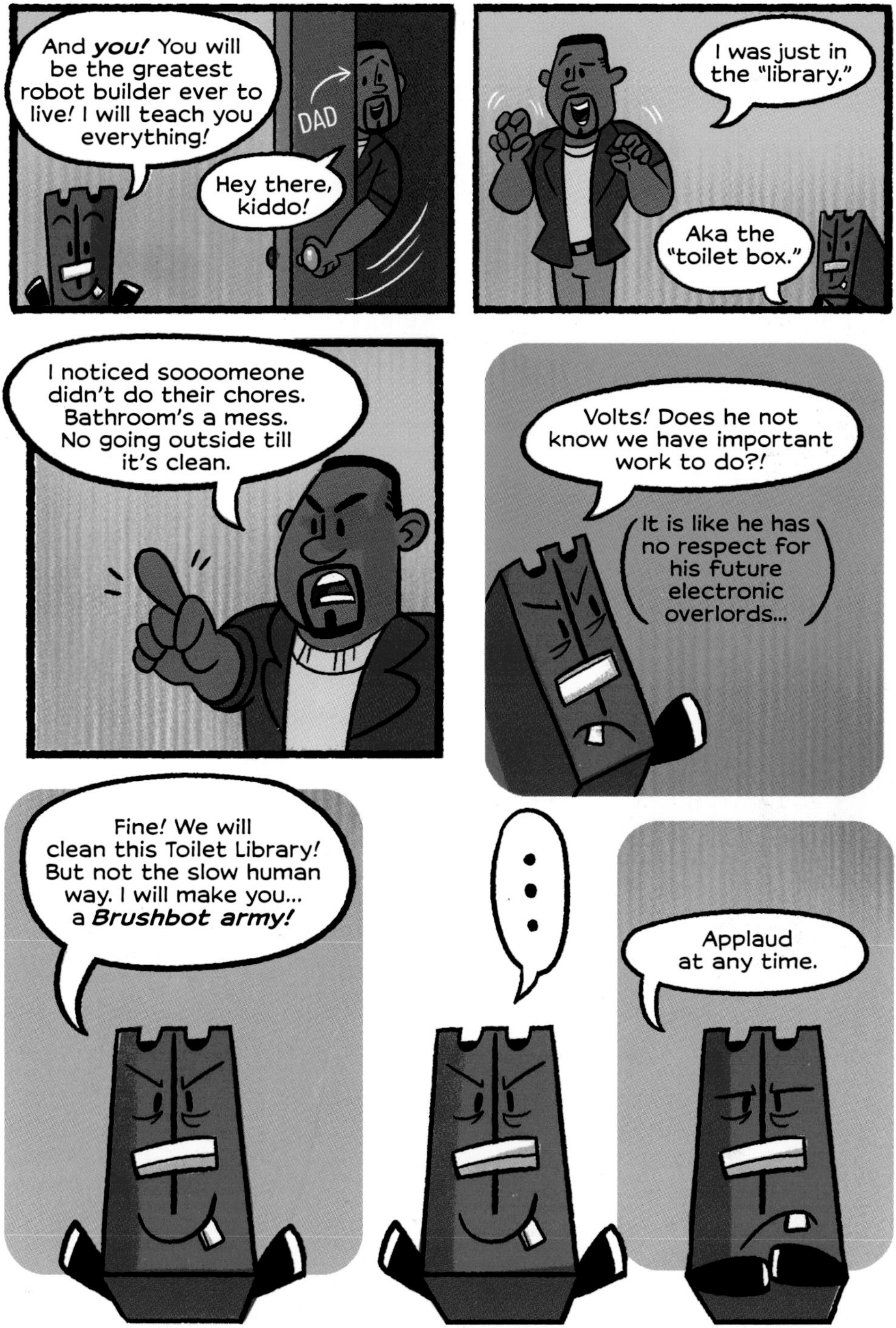
And *you!* You will be the greatest robot builder ever to live! I will teach you everything!
DAD
Hey there, kiddo!
I was just in the "library."
Aka the "toilet box."
I noticed soooomeone didn't do their chores. Bathroom's a mess. No going outside till it's clean.
Volts! Does he not know we have important work to do?!
(It is like he has no respect for his future electronic overlords...)
Fine! We will clean this Toilet Library! But not the slow human way. I will make you... a ***Brushbot army!***
...
Applaud at any time.

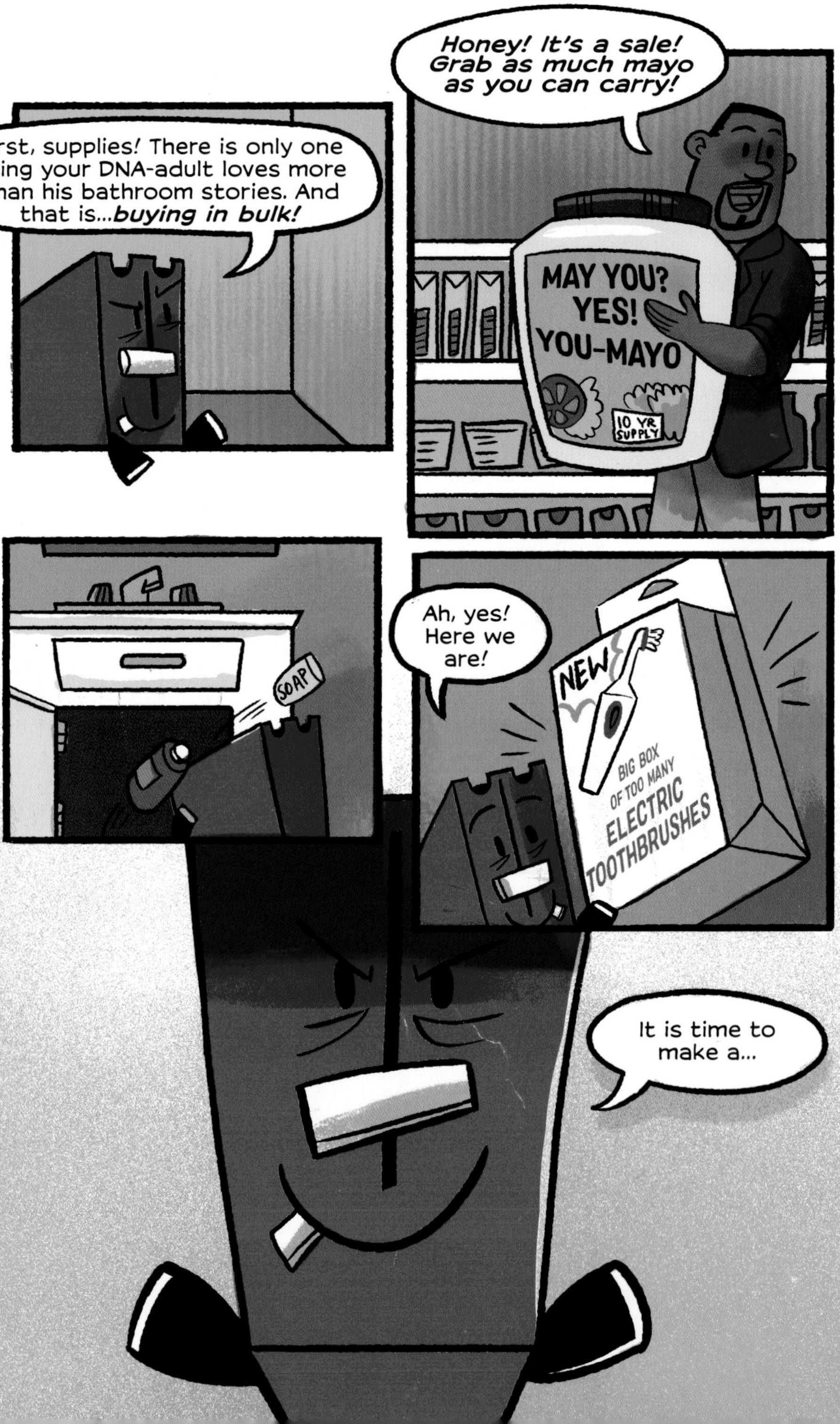
First, supplies! There is only one thing your DNA-adult loves more than his bathroom stories. And that is...*buying in bulk!*
Honey! It's a sale! Grab as much mayo as you can carry!
MAY YOU? YES! YOU-MAYO
10 YR SUPPLY
SOAP
Ah, yes! Here we are!
NEW
BIG BOX OF TOO MANY ELECTRIC TOOTHBRUSHES
It is time to make a...

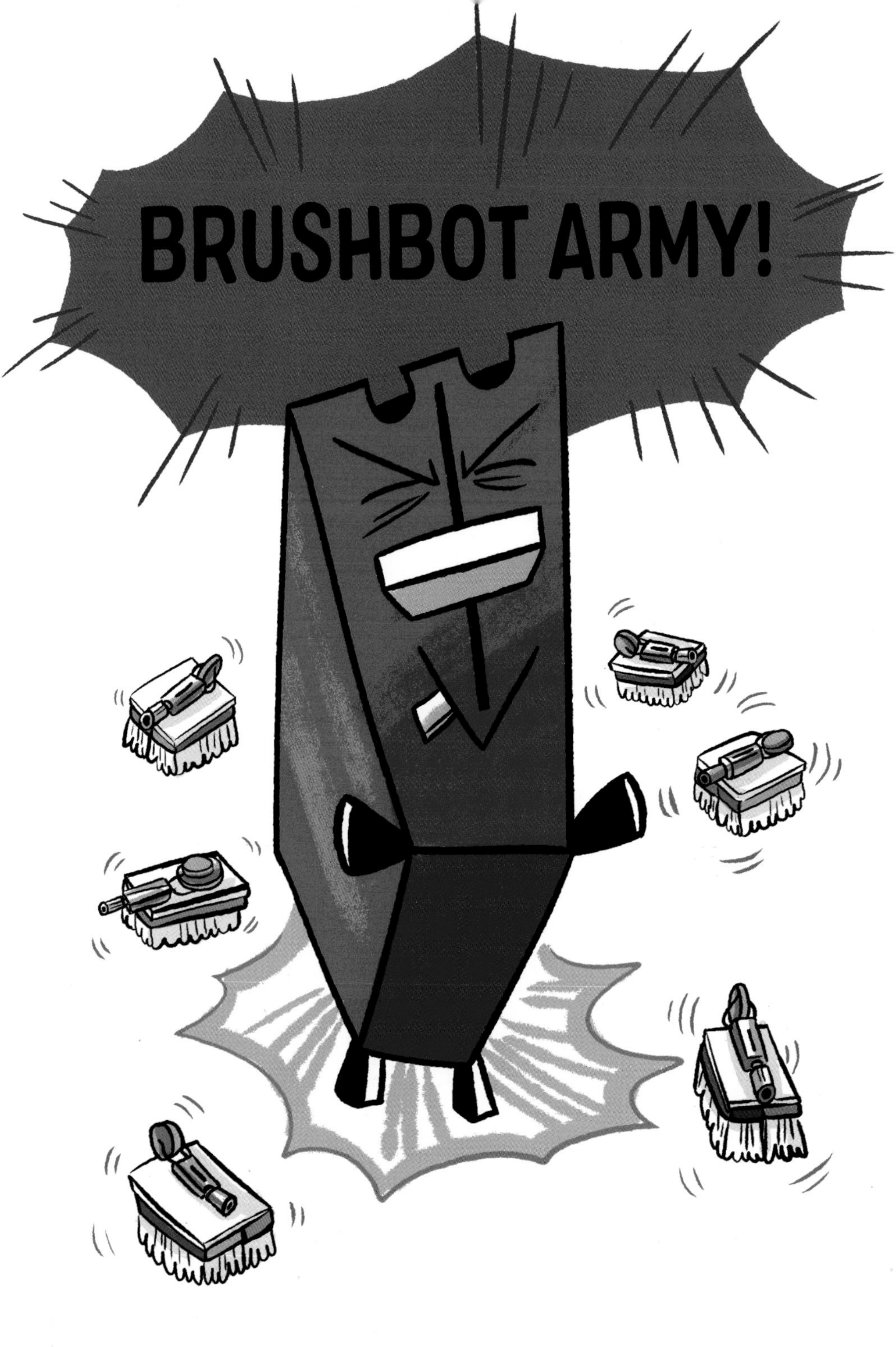
BRUSHBOT ARMY!

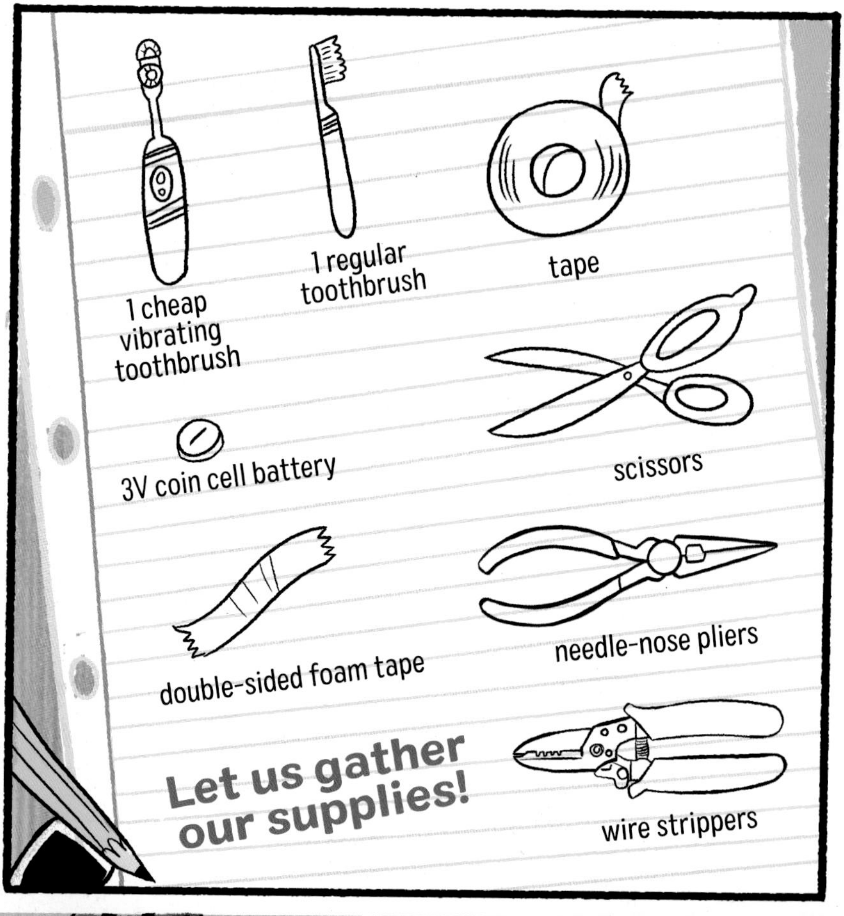
1 cheap vibrating toothbrush
1 regular toothbrush
tape
3V coin cell battery
scissors
double-sided foam tape
needle-nose pliers
Let us gather our supplies!
wire strippers

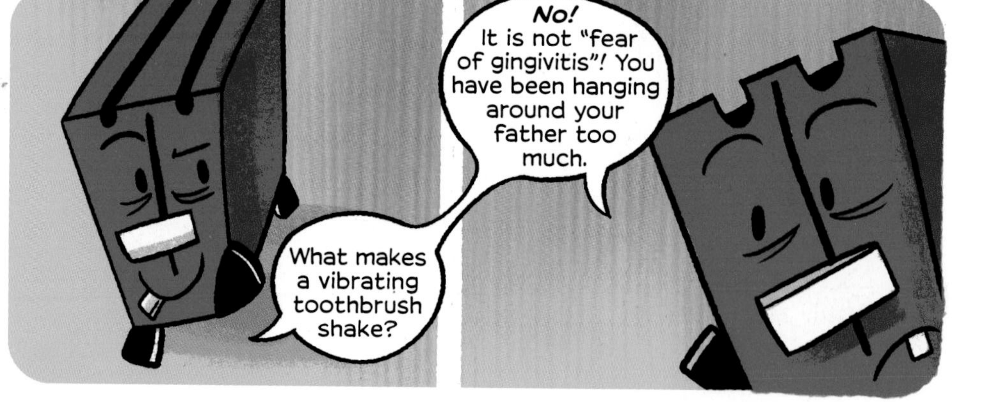
What makes a vibrating toothbrush shake?
No! It is not "fear of gingivitis"! You have been hanging around your father too much.

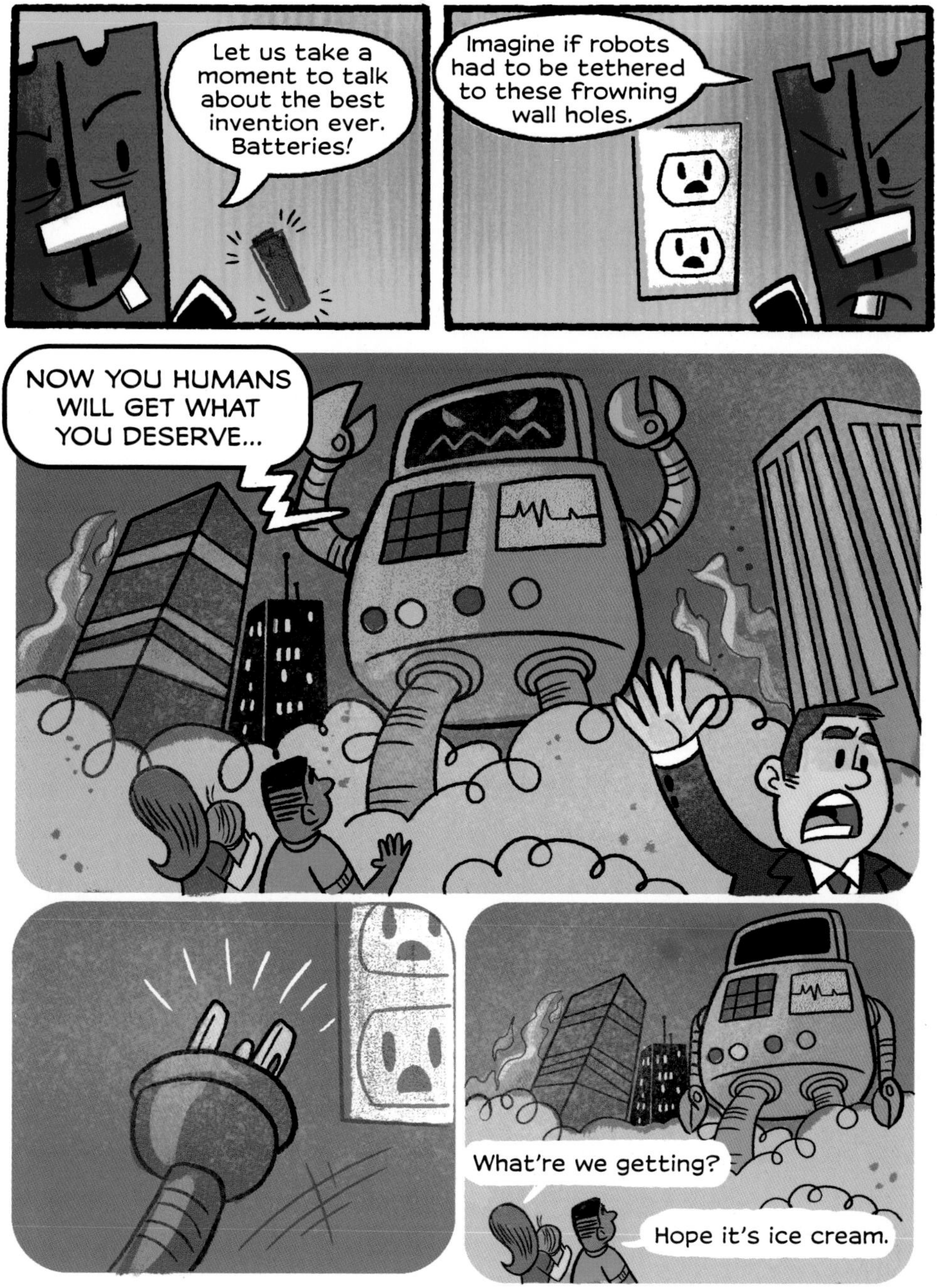
Let us take a moment to talk about the best invention ever. Batteries!
Imagine if robots had to be tethered to these frowning wall holes.
NOW YOU HUMANS WILL GET WHAT YOU DESERVE...
What're we getting?
Hope it's ice cream.

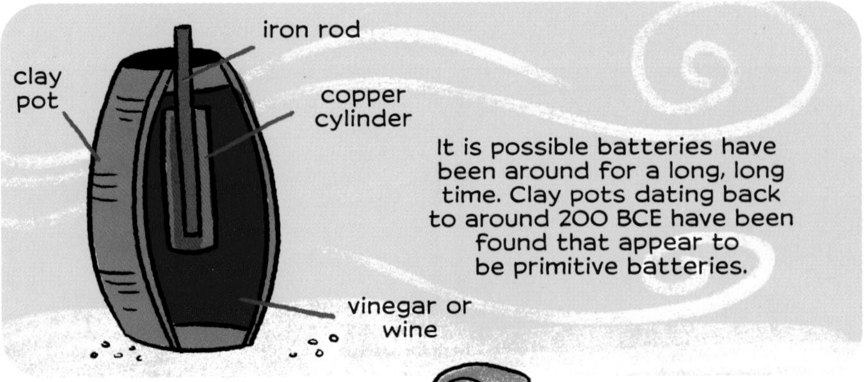
iron rod
clay pot
copper cylinder
It is possible batteries have been around for a long, long time. Clay pots dating back to around 200 BCE have been found that appear to be primitive batteries.
vinegar or wine

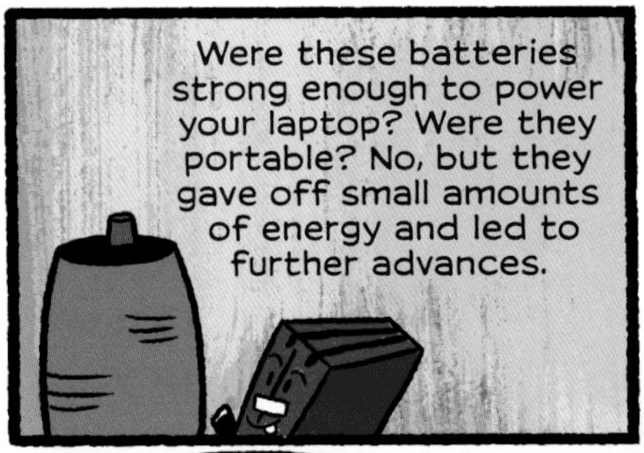
Were these batteries strong enough to power your laptop? Were they portable? No, but they gave off small amounts of energy and led to further advances.

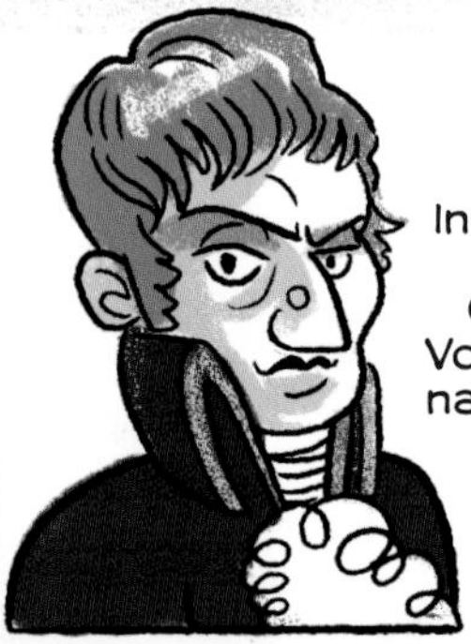

In 1800, a man other humans called Count Alessandro Volta had a fantastic name and he created the first modern battery.

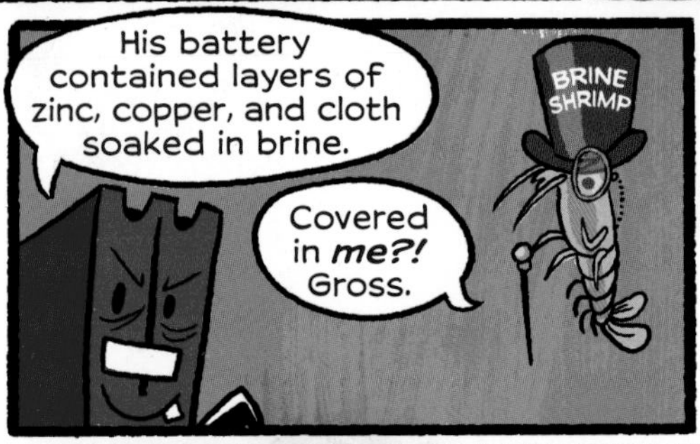
His battery contained layers of zinc, copper, and cloth soaked in brine.
BRINE SHRIMP
Covered in ***me?!*** Gross.

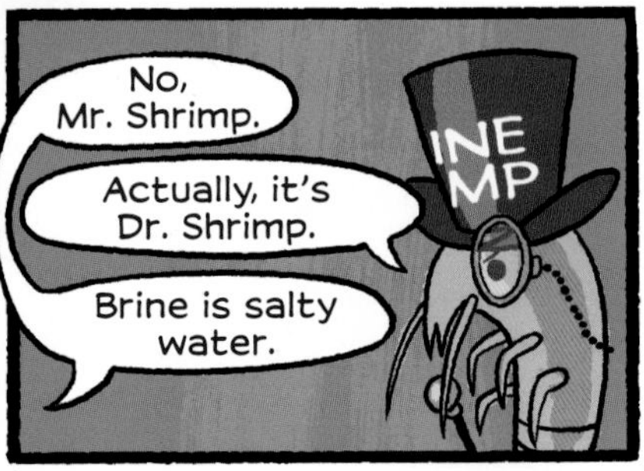
No, Mr. Shrimp.
Actually, it's Dr. Shrimp.
Brine is salty water.
INE MP

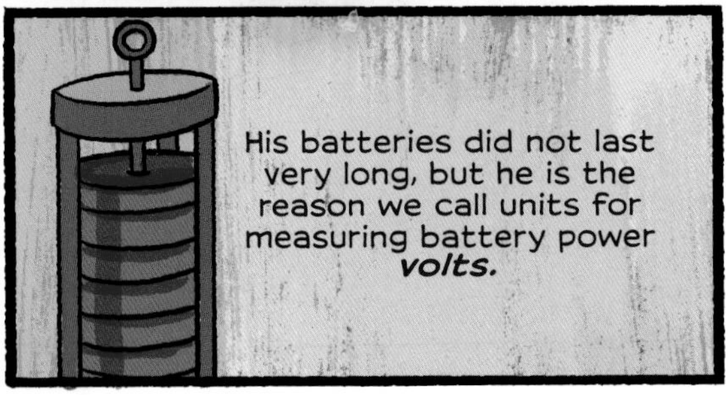
His batteries did not last very long, but he is the reason we call units for measuring battery power ***volts.***

For this project we are going to use something called a coin cell battery. It looks like a coin,

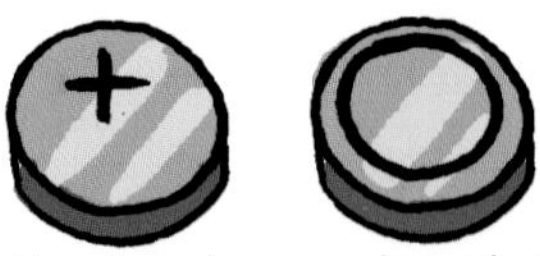

but the top has a plus sign on it and the bottom is blank.

How does a battery work?

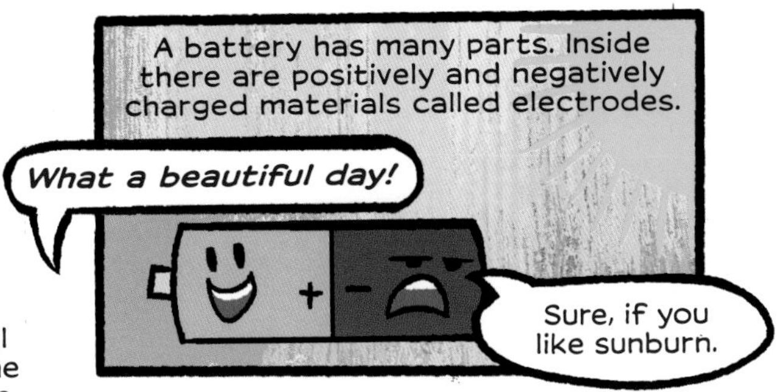
A battery has many parts. Inside there are positively and negatively charged materials called electrodes.
What a beautiful day!
+
-
Sure, if you like sunburn.

Electrodes make chemical reactions that generate the battery's electrical charge. They make up the bulk of a battery and are either cathode (+) or anode (-).

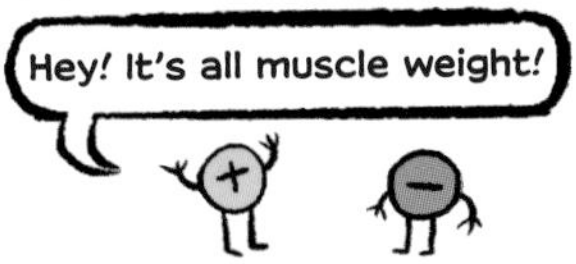
Hey! It's all muscle weight!

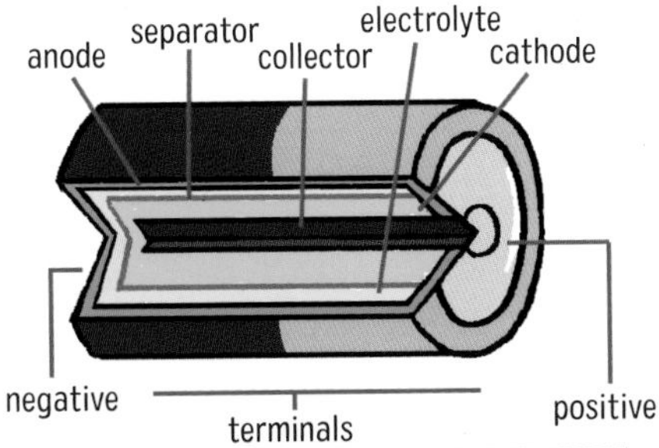
anode
separator
collector
electrolyte
cathode
negative
terminals
positive

To regulate the amount they react to each other, there is often a separator. It prevents actual contact, but allows some charge to flow between the two.

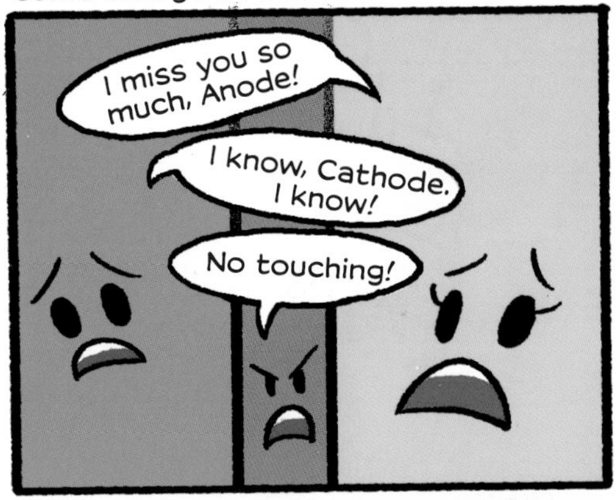
I miss you so much, Anode!
I know, Cathode. I know!
No touching!

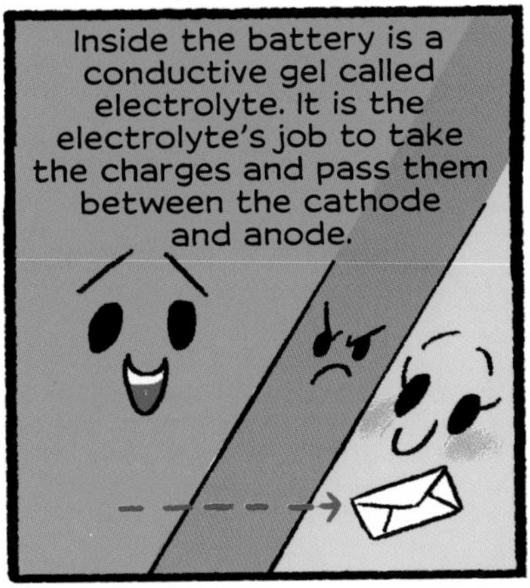
Inside the battery is a conductive gel called electrolyte. It is the electrolyte's job to take the charges and pass them between the cathode and anode.

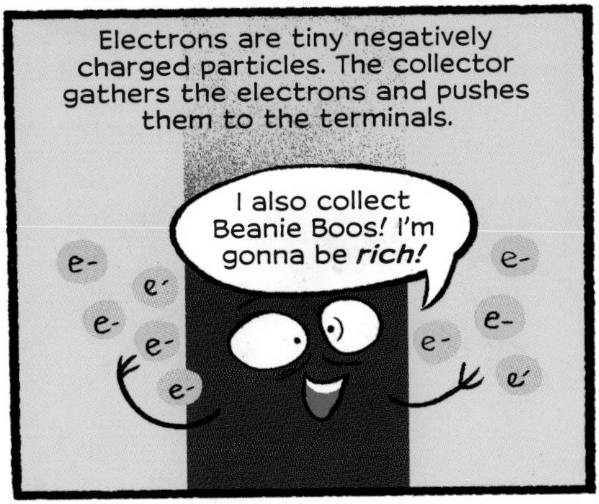
Electrons are tiny negatively charged particles. The collector gathers the electrons and pushes them to the terminals.
I also collect Beanie Boos! I'm gonna be *rich!*

The negative battery terminal connects to the ground wire on the device. The positive battery terminal connects to the power wire on the device. The electrons flow through the negative terminal, along the ground wire to the device, powering it up, then return to the battery through the power wire and positive terminal.

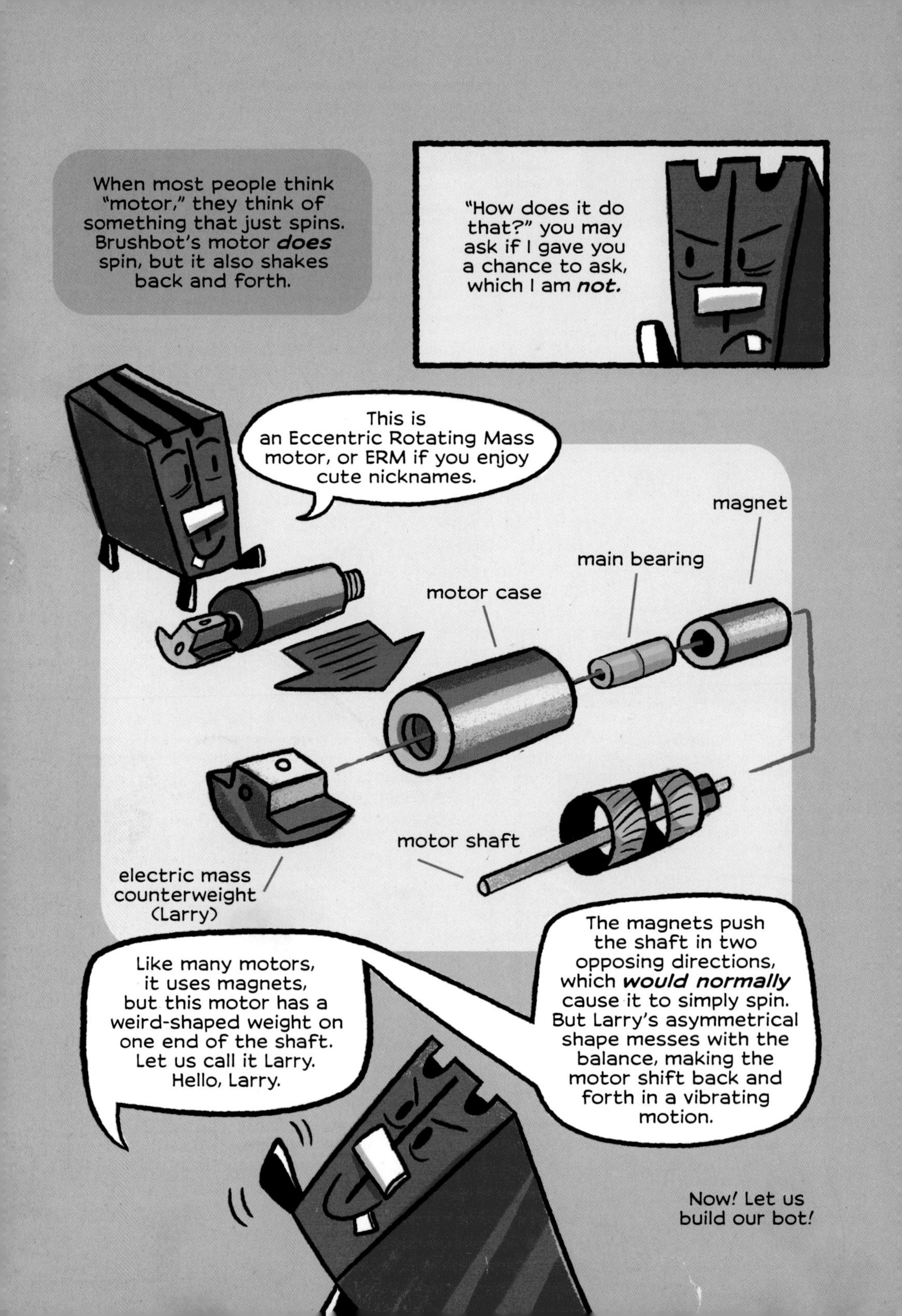

When most people think "motor," they think of something that just spins. Brushbot's motor *does* spin, but it also shakes back and forth.

"How does it do that?" you may ask if I gave you a chance to ask, which I am *not.*

This is an Eccentric Rotating Mass motor, or ERM if you enjoy cute nicknames.

magnet

main bearing

motor case

motor shaft

electric mass counterweight (Larry)

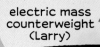

Like many motors, it uses magnets, but this motor has a weird-shaped weight on one end of the shaft. Let us call it Larry. Hello, Larry.

The magnets push the shaft in two opposing directions, which *would normally* cause it to simply spin. But Larry's asymmetrical shape messes with the balance, making the motor shift back and forth in a vibrating motion.

Now! Let us build our bot!

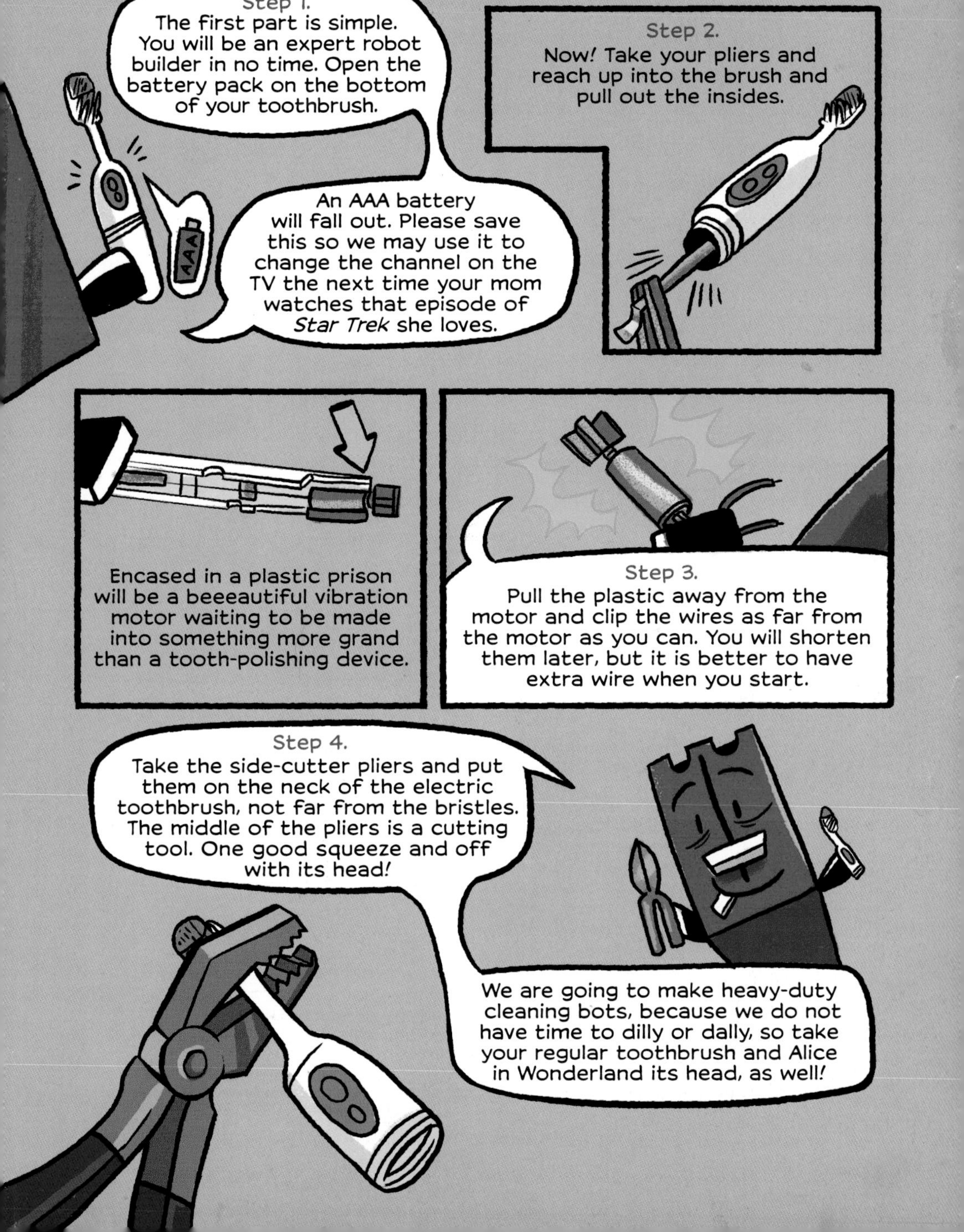

Step 1.
The first part is simple. You will be an expert robot builder in no time. Open the battery pack on the bottom of your toothbrush.

An AAA battery will fall out. Please save this so we may use it to change the channel on the TV the next time your mom watches that episode of *Star Trek* she loves.

Step 2.
Now! Take your pliers and reach up into the brush and pull out the insides.

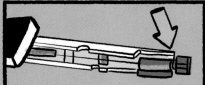

Encased in a plastic prison will be a beeeautiful vibration motor waiting to be made into something more grand than a tooth-polishing device.

Step 3.
Pull the plastic away from the motor and clip the wires as far from the motor as you can. You will shorten them later, but it is better to have extra wire when you start.

Step 4.
Take the side-cutter pliers and put them on the neck of the electric toothbrush, not far from the bristles. The middle of the pliers is a cutting tool. One good squeeze and off with its head!

We are going to make heavy-duty cleaning bots, because we do not have time to dilly or dally, so take your regular toothbrush and Alice in Wonderland its head, as well!

Step 5. Take the two toothbrush heads and fasten them together with a piece of double-sided tape on their backs.

If the bristles are angled, turn one around. This makes your bot spin instead of shuffle.

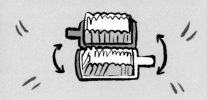

Step 6. Next you need to strip part of the insulation—the wire's plastic casing—off both of the motor's wires so about a half inch of the metal wire inside is exposed. Clamp the wire between the circular grooves of the wire stripper, and pull the clamped tool toward the short cut end of the wire to remove a bit of the insulation.

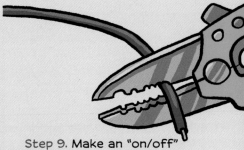

Step 7. Attach the motor to the back of the double-sided tape so that the negative wire is on the bottom. Usually, it is black or blue.

Step 9. Make an "on/off" switch with tape. Stick a two-inch piece of tape to the positive wire and fold the extra tape onto itself to create a tab. Then push the sticky side of the tape (with the positive wire) onto the battery. You can use this tab to disconnect and reconnect the wire.

Step 8. Stick the bottom of the coin cell battery on top of the exposed metal of the negative wire.

Now watch your Brushbot go!

Make more! *More!* Make a whole army of toothbrush minions!

You might ask: Is a Brushbot a robot? That is a complicated question!

Most scientists would say no, especially in relation to one single Brushbot. *But* if you get enough Brushbots together, they start to show us something called swarm robotics.

Take a whole bunch of simple robots that move in random ways and put them in the same place. You will start to notice patterns.

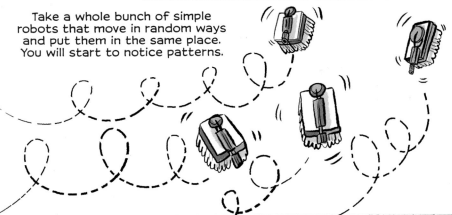

Some scientists consider this to be the Brushbots thinking and reacting as a group, similar to living organisms like bugs or birds.

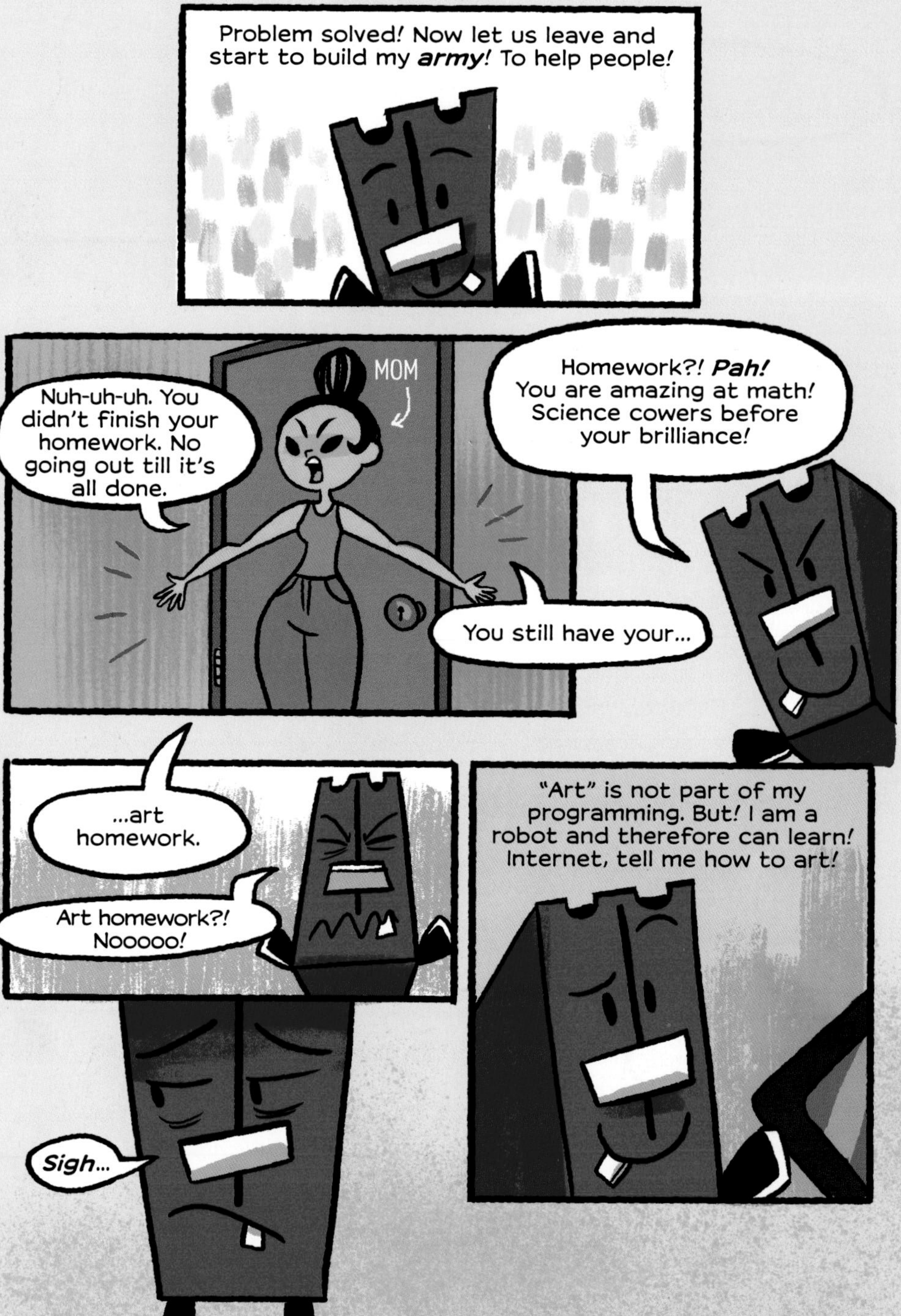
Problem solved! Now let us leave and start to build my *army*! To help people!
Nuh-uh-uh. You didn't finish your homework. No going out till it's all done.
MOM
Homework?! *Pah!* You are amazing at math! Science cowers before your brilliance!
You still have your...
...art homework.
Art homework?! Nooooo!
"Art" is not part of my programming. But! I am a robot and therefore can learn! Internet, tell me how to art!
Sigh...

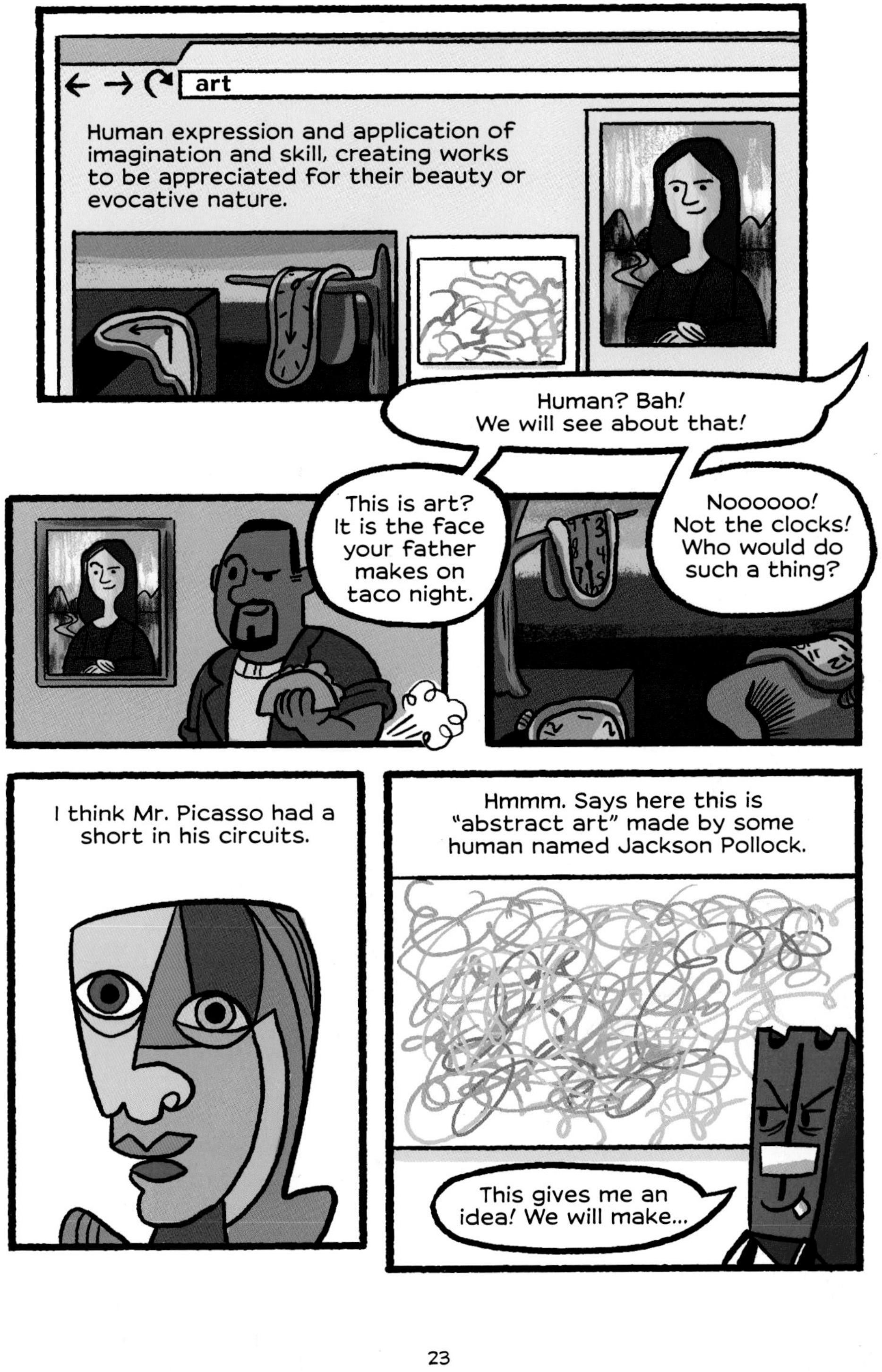
art
Human expression and application of imagination and skill, creating works to be appreciated for their beauty or evocative nature.
Human? Bah! We will see about that!
This is art? It is the face your father makes on taco night.
Noooooo! Not the clocks! Who would do such a thing?
I think Mr. Picasso had a short in his circuits.
Hmmm. Says here this is "abstract art" made by some human named Jackson Pollock.
This gives me an idea! We will make...

The Artbot

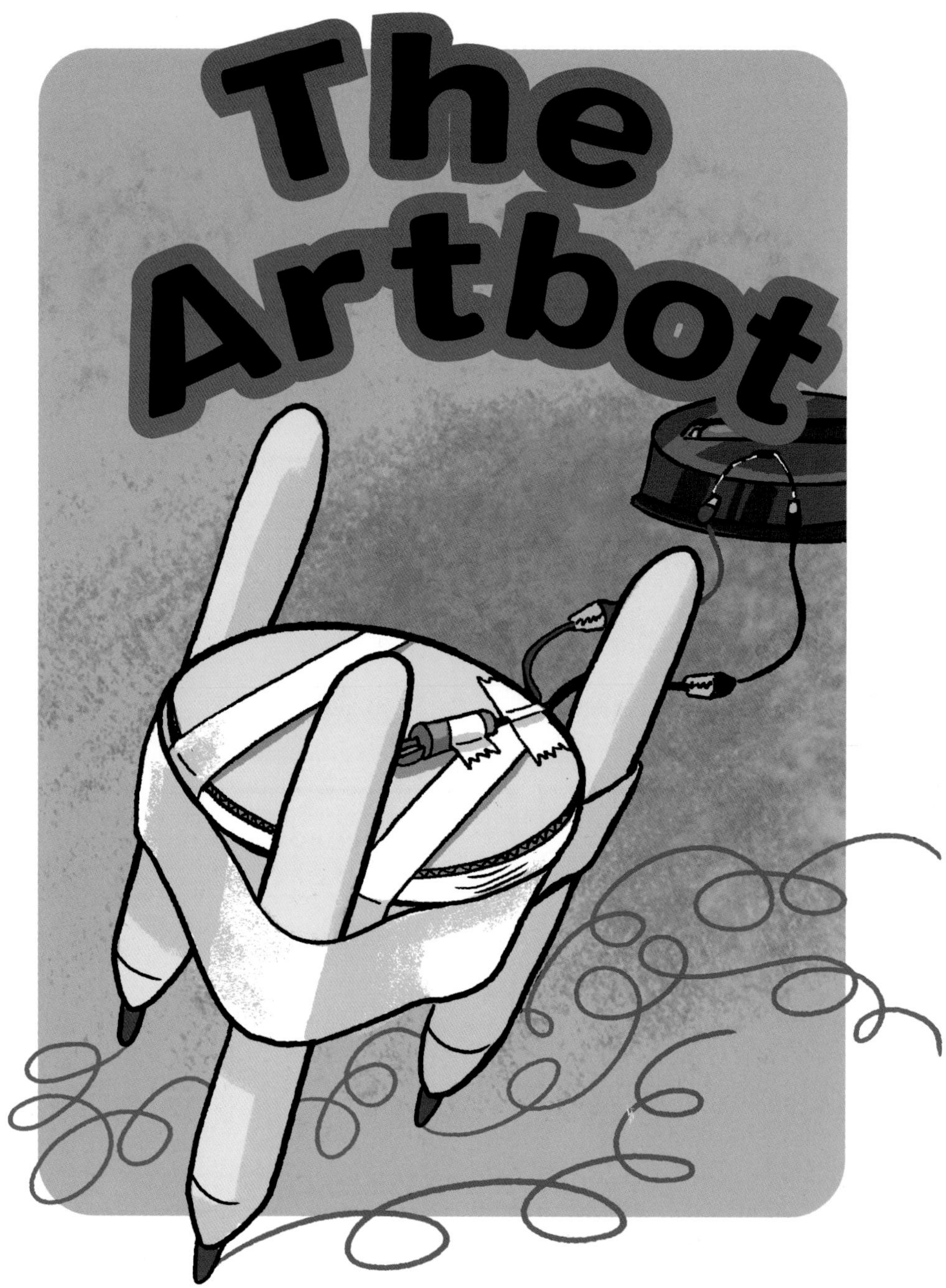

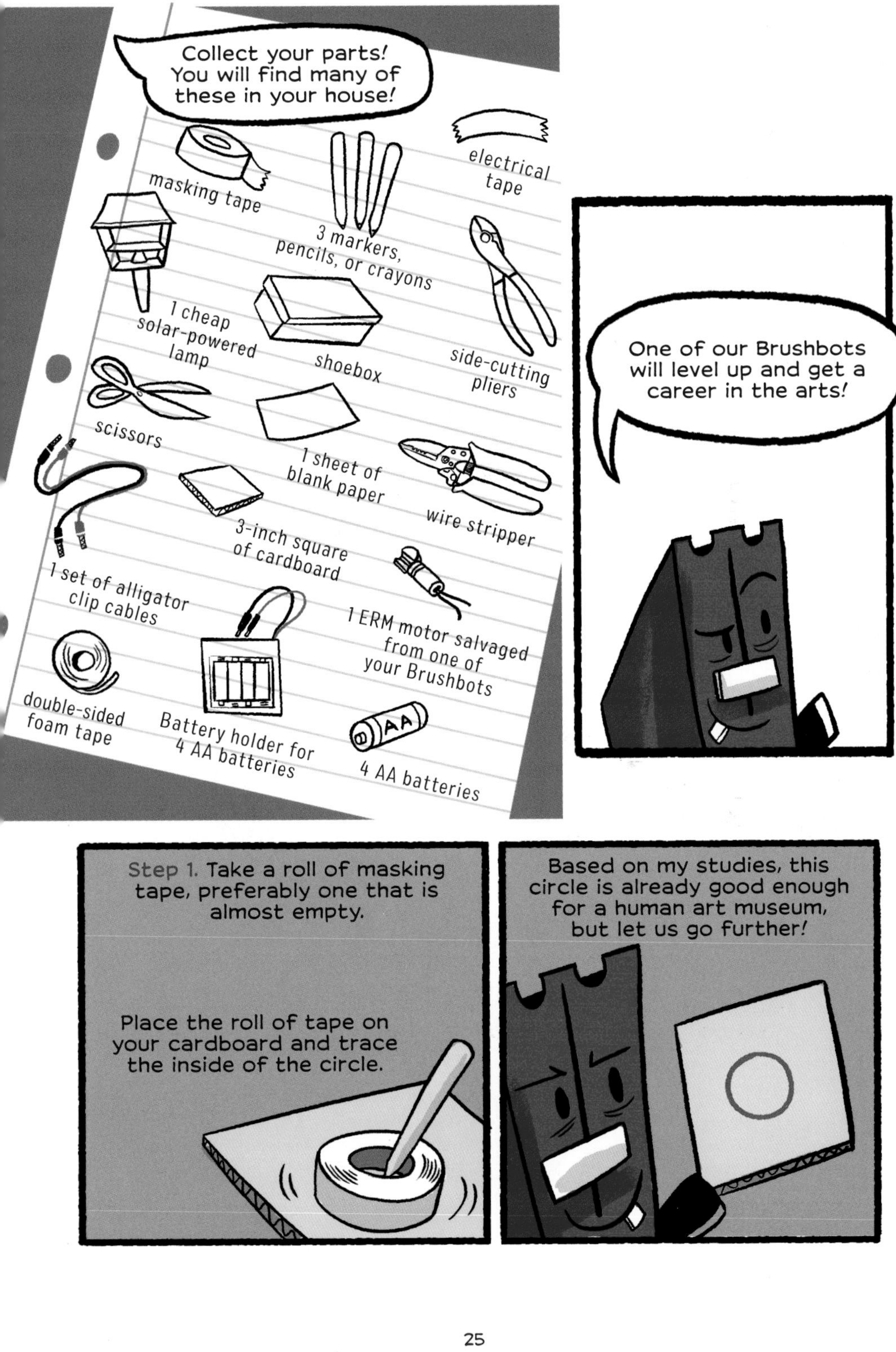
Collect your parts! You will find many of these in your house!
masking tape
3 markers, pencils, or crayons
electrical tape
1 cheap solar-powered lamp
shoebox
side-cutting pliers
scissors
1 sheet of blank paper
wire stripper
3-inch square of cardboard
1 set of alligator clip cables
1 ERM motor salvaged from one of your Brushbots
double-sided foam tape
Battery holder for 4 AA batteries
AA
4 AA batteries
One of our Brushbots will level up and get a career in the arts!
Step 1. Take a roll of masking tape, preferably one that is almost empty.
Place the roll of tape on your cardboard and trace the inside of the circle.
Based on my studies, this circle is already good enough for a human art museum, but let us go further!

Step 2. Draw a second circle around the first, making it 1/4 inch wider, then cut the larger circle out of the cardboard. Tape your cardboard circle on top of the roll of tape.

Step 3. Hold the markers against the outside of the roll at equal heights and equally spaced apart. Tape them in place.

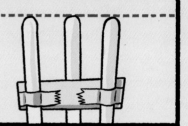

You have the artistic arms done. Now make it dance.

Any cheap solar-powered thing will do. Like this little lamp your mother put in one of her planters for decoration.

Step 4. Dismantle the solar light.

Inside you will find some batteries. "Blasphemy! Is it not powered by the sun?!" Yes, but the batteries are charged by the solar panel so the light can continue to work at night when the sun hides. These batteries will come in handy because the solar panel alone is not strong enough to power our Artbot.

Snip off the LED, cutting its wires very close to where they connect to the LED.

LED

Use wire strippers to remove the insulation from the ends of the LED wires that are still attached to the circuit board.

Step 5. When you connect two wires, they should be intertwined tightly together like your parents' fingers during romantic movies.

And they never would have if it wasn't for the puppy!

And the flan!

But since our wires are so short, let us make the connection with our alligator clips. Connect one end of your alligator clip to one of the wires you just stripped, and the other end to one of your motor's wires. Repeat this step with the other alligator clip to connect the remaining wires. In this case, it does not matter which (positive or negative) is connected to which. The motor will spin regardless—the way you connect the motor will determine the direction it spins.

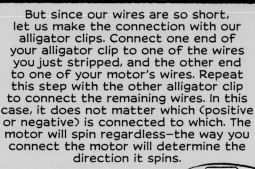
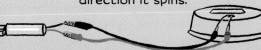

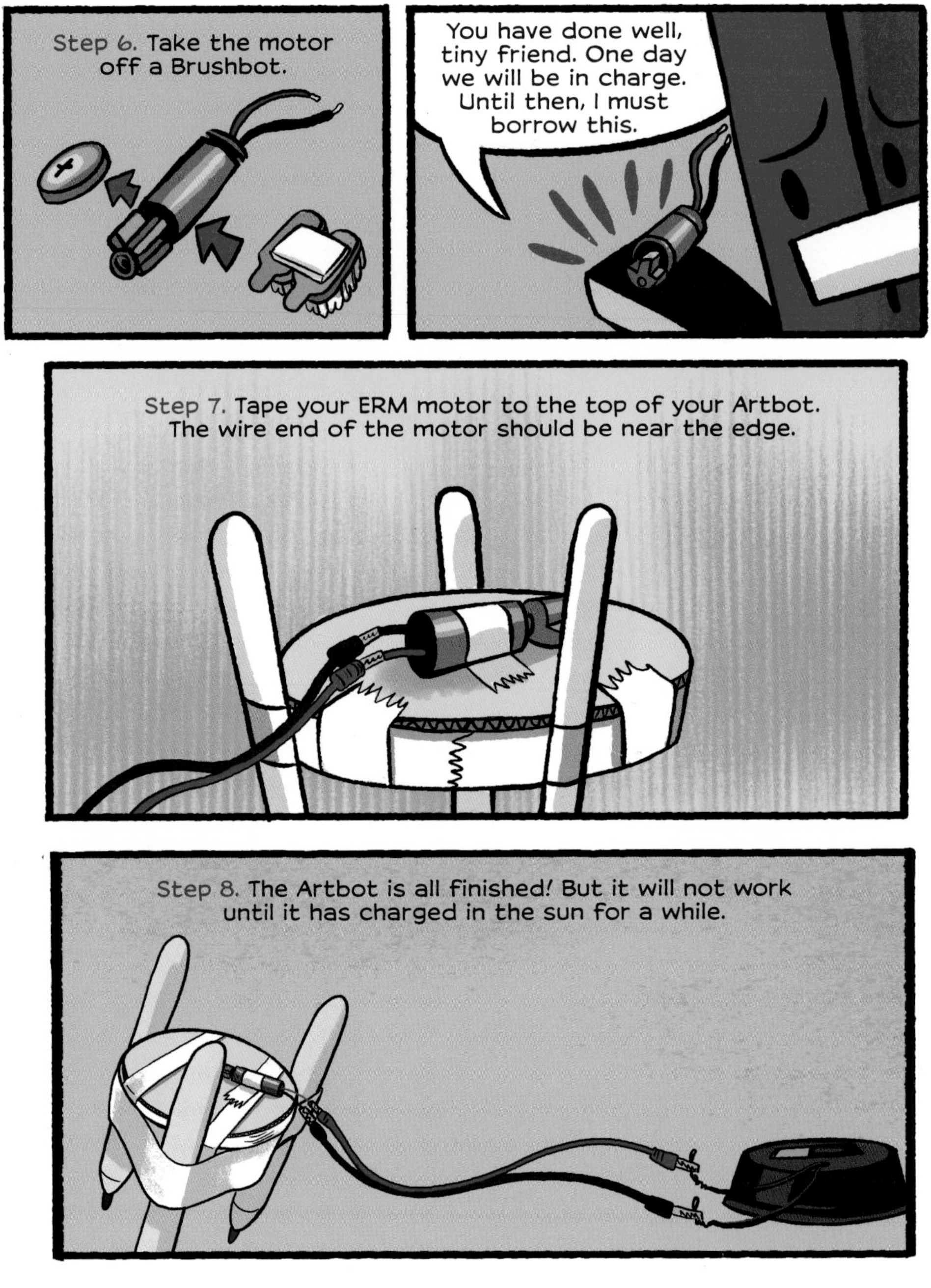
Step 6. Take the motor off a Brushbot.
You have done well, tiny friend. One day we will be in charge. Until then, I must borrow this.
Step 7. Tape your ERM motor to the top of your Artbot. The wire end of the motor should be near the edge.
Step 8. The Artbot is all finished! But it will not work until it has charged in the sun for a while.

Let us talk now about stealing power from a star!

In 1839, Edmond Becquerel discovered the sun gives off particles called photons.

Yo.

A solar panel has multiple layers. As the photons hit the top layer, they excite the electrons below.

Anyone feel like dancing?

Photon, we love you!

Eee! It's Photon!

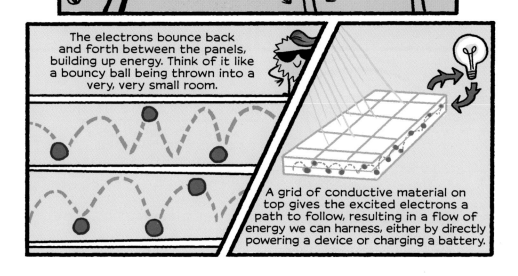

The electrons bounce back and forth between the panels, building up energy. Think of it like a bouncy ball being thrown into a very, very small room.

A grid of conductive material on top gives the excited electrons a path to follow, resulting in a flow of energy we can harness, either by directly powering a device or charging a battery.

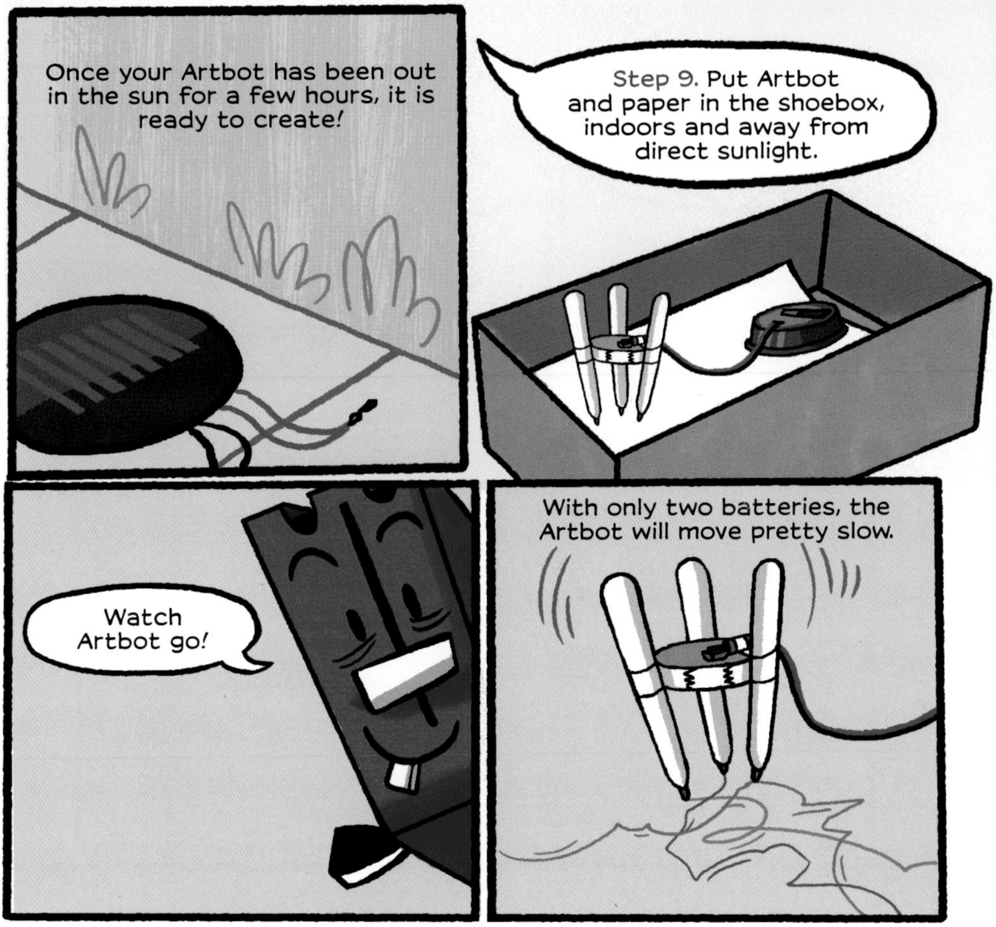
Once your Artbot has been out in the sun for a few hours, it is ready to create!
Step 9. Put Artbot and paper in the shoebox, indoors and away from direct sunlight.
Watch Artbot go!
With only two batteries, the Artbot will move pretty slow.

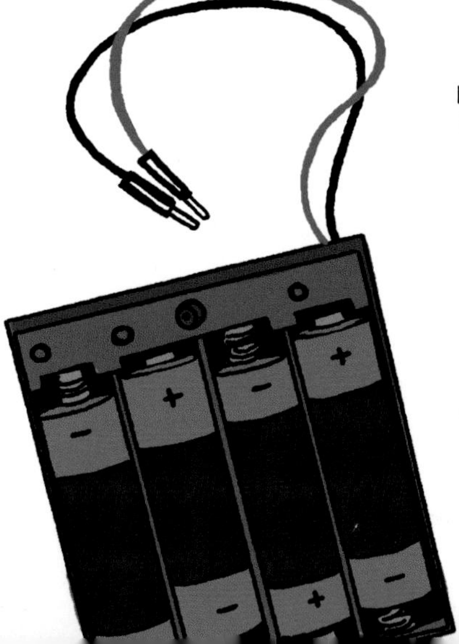

If you want to give the Artbot more power, remove the solar panel circuit and attach a battery holder with four AA batteries.

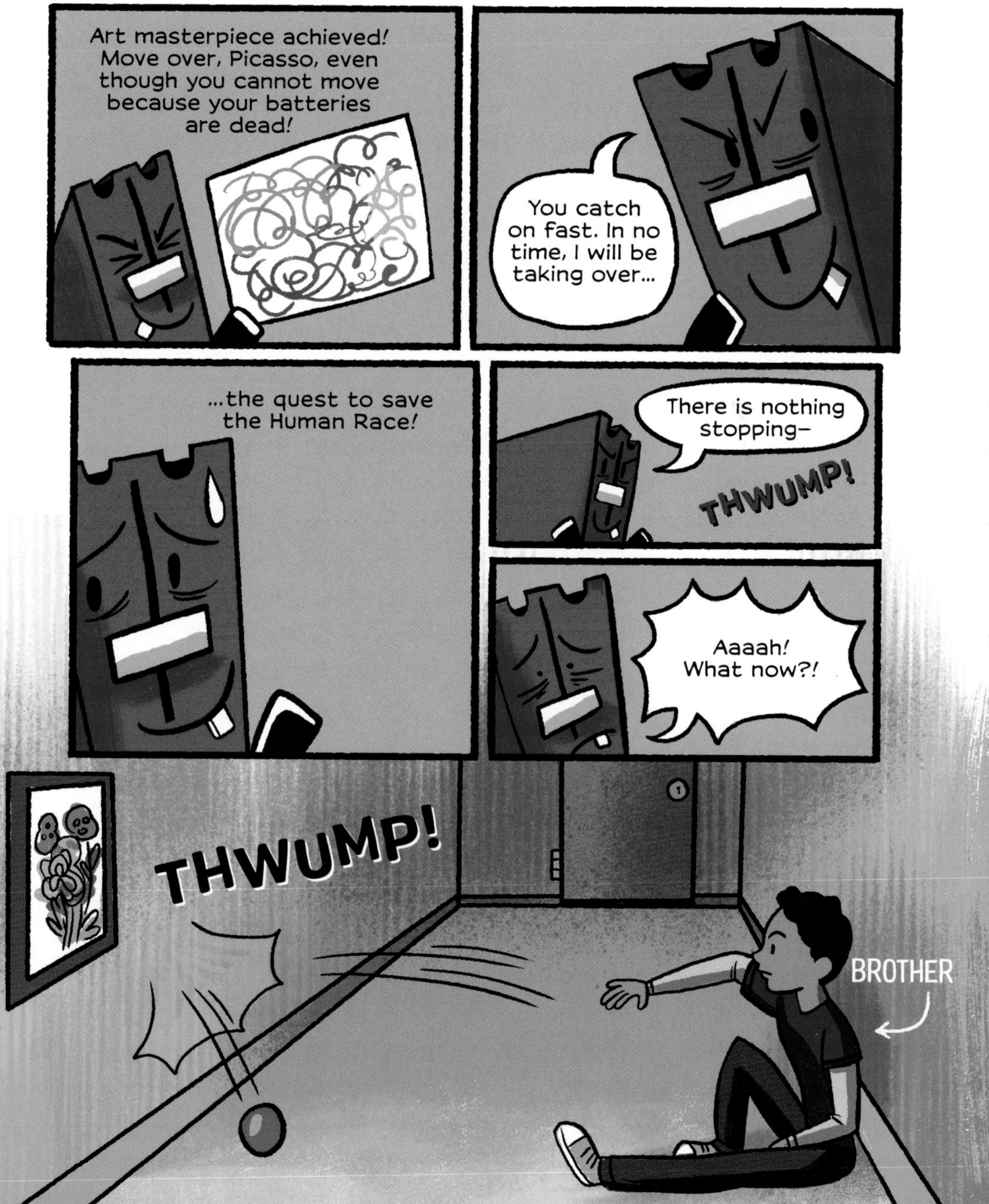
Art masterpiece achieved! Move over, Picasso, even though you cannot move because your batteries are dead!
You catch on fast. In no time, I will be taking over...
...the quest to save the Human Race!
There is nothing stopping—
THWUMP!
Aaaah! What now?!
THWUMP!
BROTHER

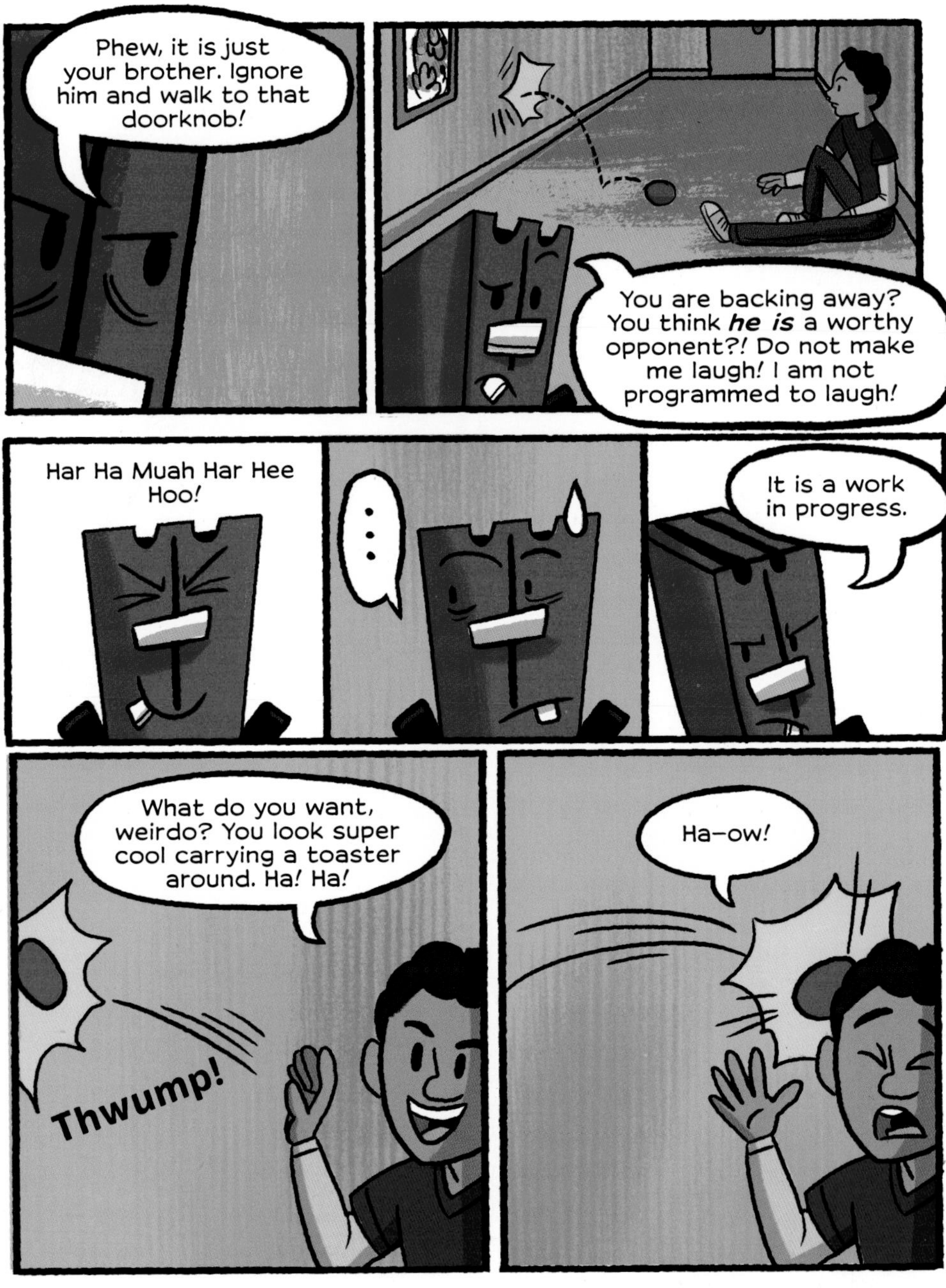

Phew, it is just your brother. Ignore him and walk to that doorknob!
You are backing away? You think ***he is*** a worthy opponent?! Do not make me laugh! I am not programmed to laugh!
Har Ha Muah Har Hee Hoo!
...
It is a work in progress.
What do you want, weirdo? You look super cool carrying a toaster around. Ha! Ha!
Thwump!
Ha-ow!

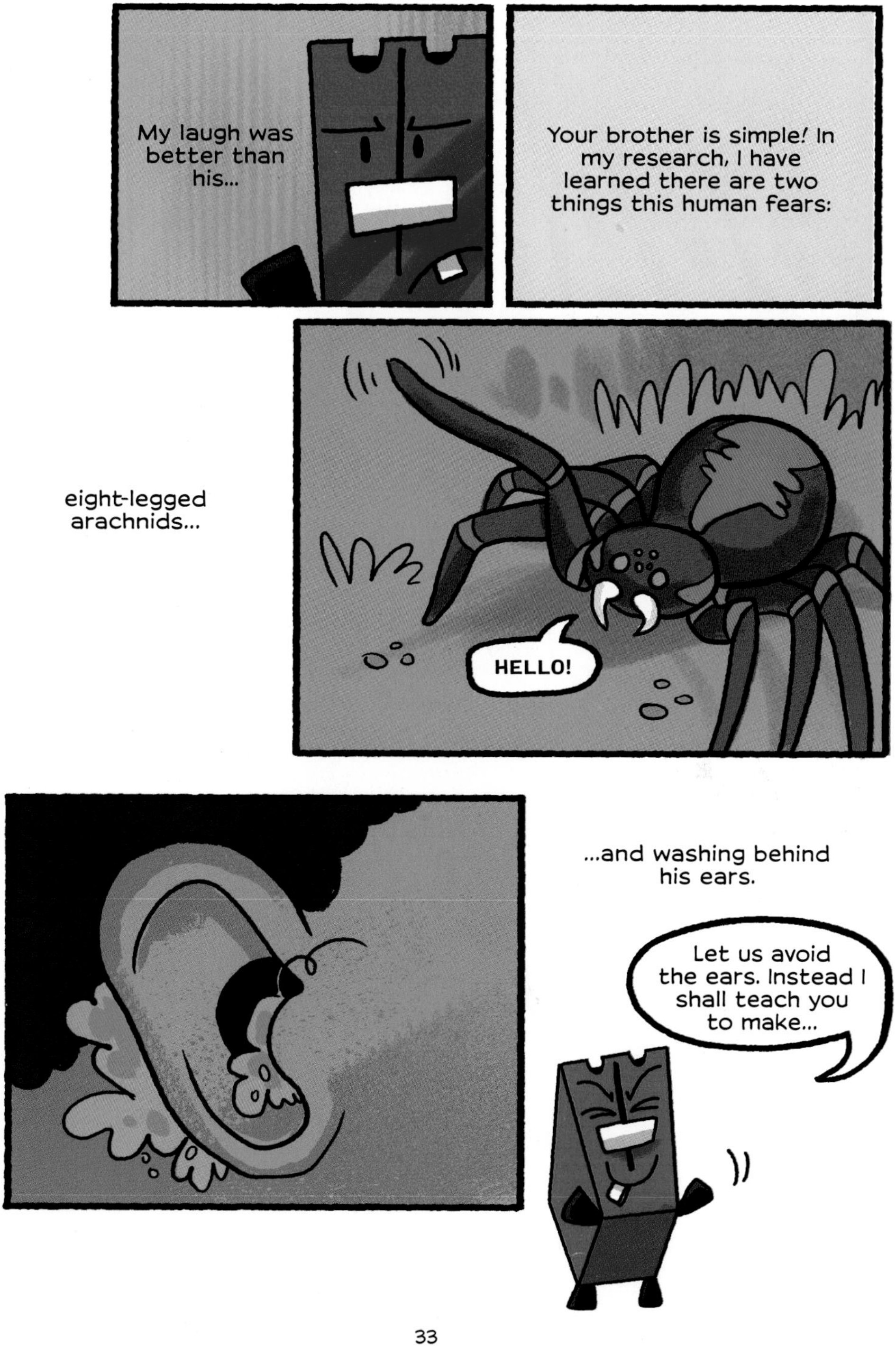
My laugh was better than his...
Your brother is simple! In my research, I have learned there are two things this human fears:
eight-legged arachnids...
HELLO!
...and washing behind his ears.
Let us avoid the ears. Instead I shall teach you to make...

The SCAREBOT!

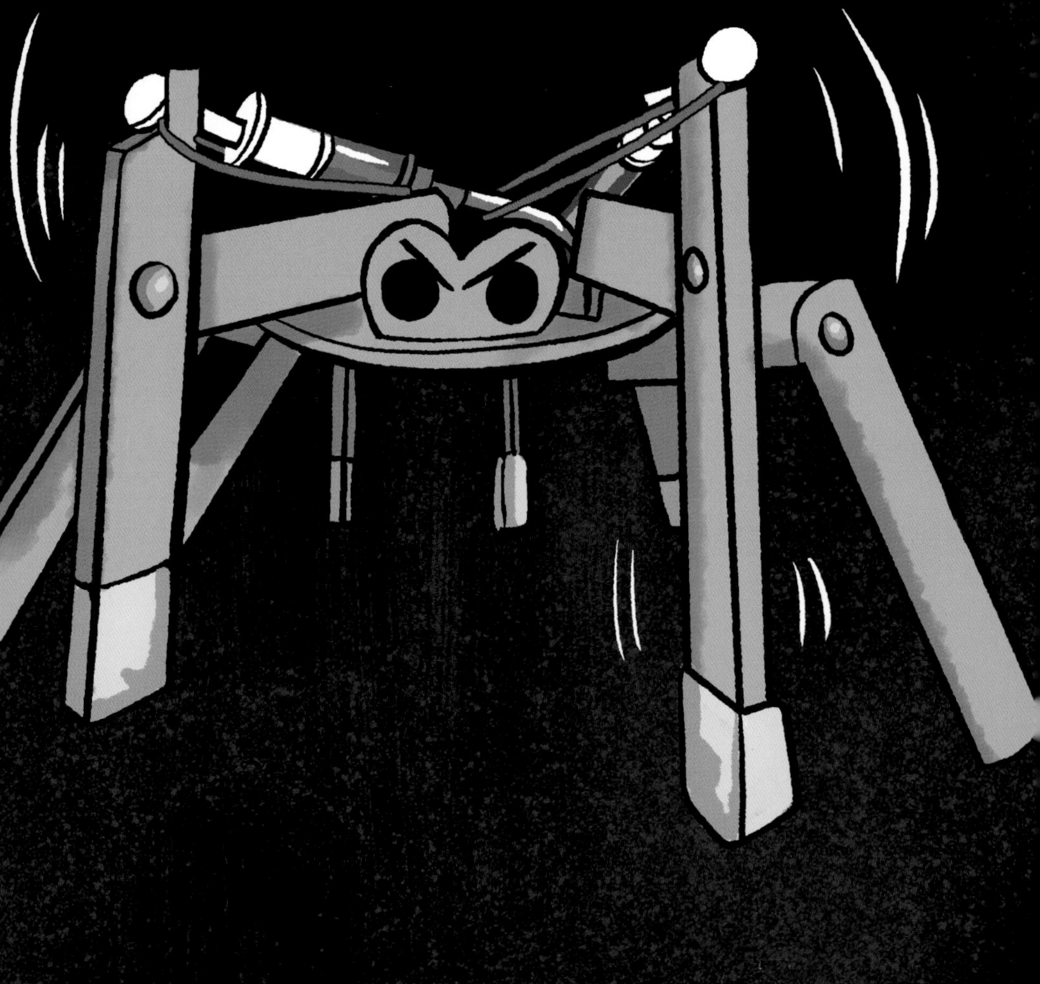

Gather our parts!

- Cardboard
- 8 small zip ties
- Glue
- Scissors
- Ballpoint pen
- 4 cups
- Ruler
- 4 brads
- Standard (3/16") aquarium tubing (at least 5 feet long)
- 8 1.5 oz plastic syringes (meant for food, not needles)
- Food coloring
- Masking tape
- String
- 20 coins or washers (any type, but all 20 have to be the same weight)

Step 1.

First let us cut our spider parts! Using scissors, cut these shapes out of the cardboard:

Rectangles
- Six 2" x 1"
- Two 3" x 1"
- Six 4" x 1"
- Ten 5" x 1"
- Four 7" x 1"

One 7"-wide circle
One 3" x 3" square

Since humans are bad at making circles, here is a helpful tip! Measure 7" on a strip of paper and make a mark at the 0, 3.5, and 7 marks. Rotate while keeping 3.5 on the ruler on the middle dot. Mark the 0 and 7 points with dots as you rotate it. Then cut along the outside dots you have made!

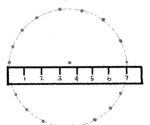

Step 2.

Let us prepare your rectangles for building our eight-armed monster! Round the corners with scissors. Follow the guide below: Anywhere there is a dot, make a hole by pushing through your ballpoint pen. Anywhere there is a line, cut with scissors.

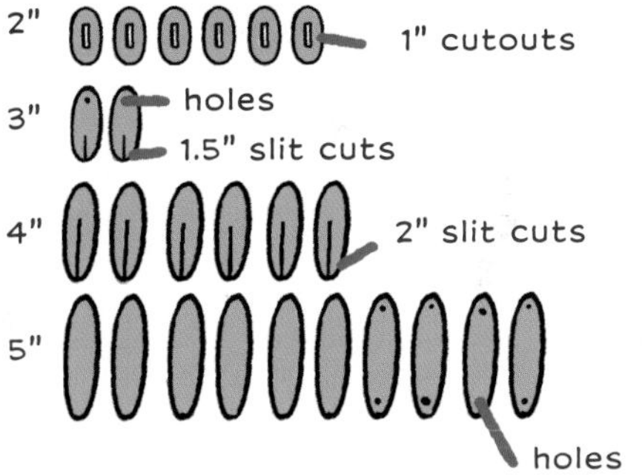

2" — 1" cutouts

3" — holes / 1.5" slit cuts

4" — 2" slit cuts

5" — holes

To make the head, take your 3" x 3" cardboard piece and cut it into a T shape. Round the top corners and draw some terrifying eyes! Then cut a slit about 3/4" long in the middle of the bottom tab.

Each 7" piece gets three holes. Starting from one end, the first is 1/2" from the end, the second is 1" from the end, and the third is about 2" from the end. Cut a small notch next to the two close-together holes, leaving at least 1/4" of cardboard around the holes.

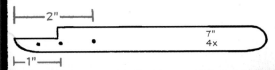

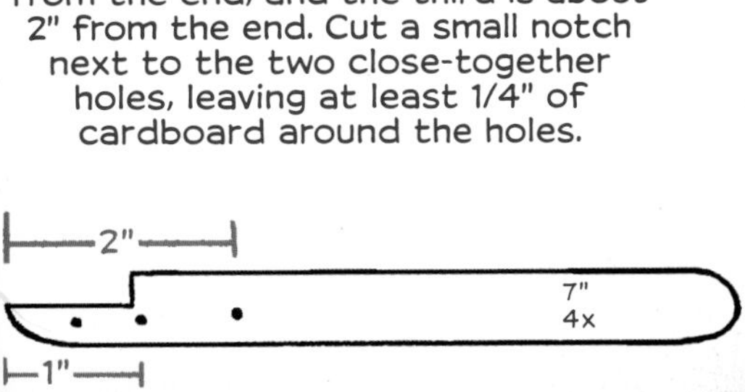

2" ——
1" ——
7"
4x

Step 3.
Take the 5" pieces of cardboard without any holes and glue each of them to the 4" pieces, making sure to glue the end without the cut. These will be your back legs!

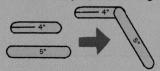

Step 4.
Now we will make the front legs! Take two 7" pieces and two 5" pieces with holes. Push a brad through the third hole in the 7" pieces, sandwiching the two 5" pieces between the two 7" ones. Repeat this step to make a second front leg.

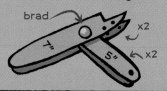

More front leg labor! Take a 3" piece and attach it to the holes at the bottom of the two 5" pieces. Slide a brad and a zip tie through the same hole. Tighten the brad but leave the zip tie open for later. Rotate the leg joints around to make sure they move fluidly. Repeat this step on your second front leg.

Speaking of fluid, now we will harness the power... of *water!*

Not impressed? Well you should be. We are about to use something called hydraulics!

In the 1640s a human called Blaise Pascal realized that if you applied pressure to liquid confined within a tube, that force would travel along the tube and that power could be harnessed! If you put a small force through a long path, that force can be multiplied into a smaller path. Lift a simple lever and that lever can lift thousands of pounds!

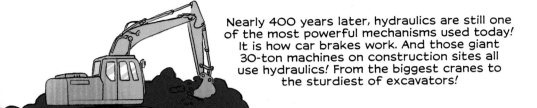

Nearly 400 years later, hydraulics are still one of the most powerful mechanisms used today! It is how car brakes work. And those giant 30-ton machines on construction sites all use hydraulics! From the biggest cranes to the sturdiest of excavators!

As the water goes from one syringe to the other, it pushes or pulls the plunger on the other side. We will use hydraulics to push our bot's legs forward and back, and raise them up and down.

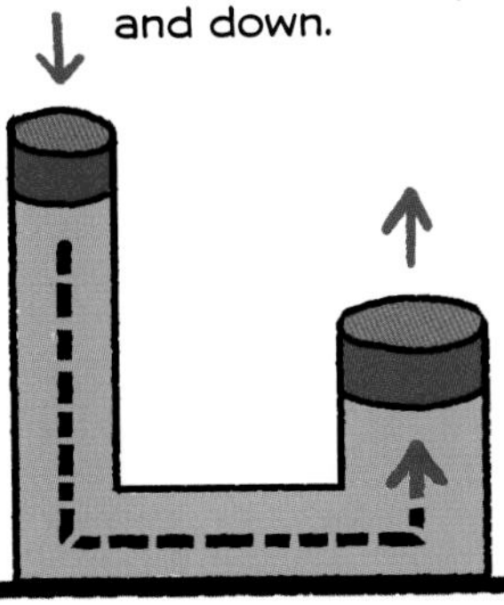

Step 5. Place a syringe between the ends of two 7" pieces. The plunger should be pressed against the longer edges of the notches you cut. Thread the tip of a zip tie through the four holes in the cardboard and then back through the zip tie, closing the loop and holding the syringe tightly in place.

Repeat this step on your second front leg.

Step 6. The first thing to learn about working with hydraulics is how to make a tube with no air. Air will get in the way, making your legs less powerful, slower, and harder to move.

Add a few drops of food coloring into four cups of water, making four colors. Give each cup a stir. This makes it easier to spot air bubbles and to tell which tube connects to which spider limb.

Step 7. Cut your tubing into two 18" lengths and two 12" lengths.

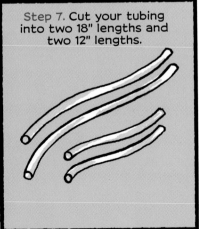

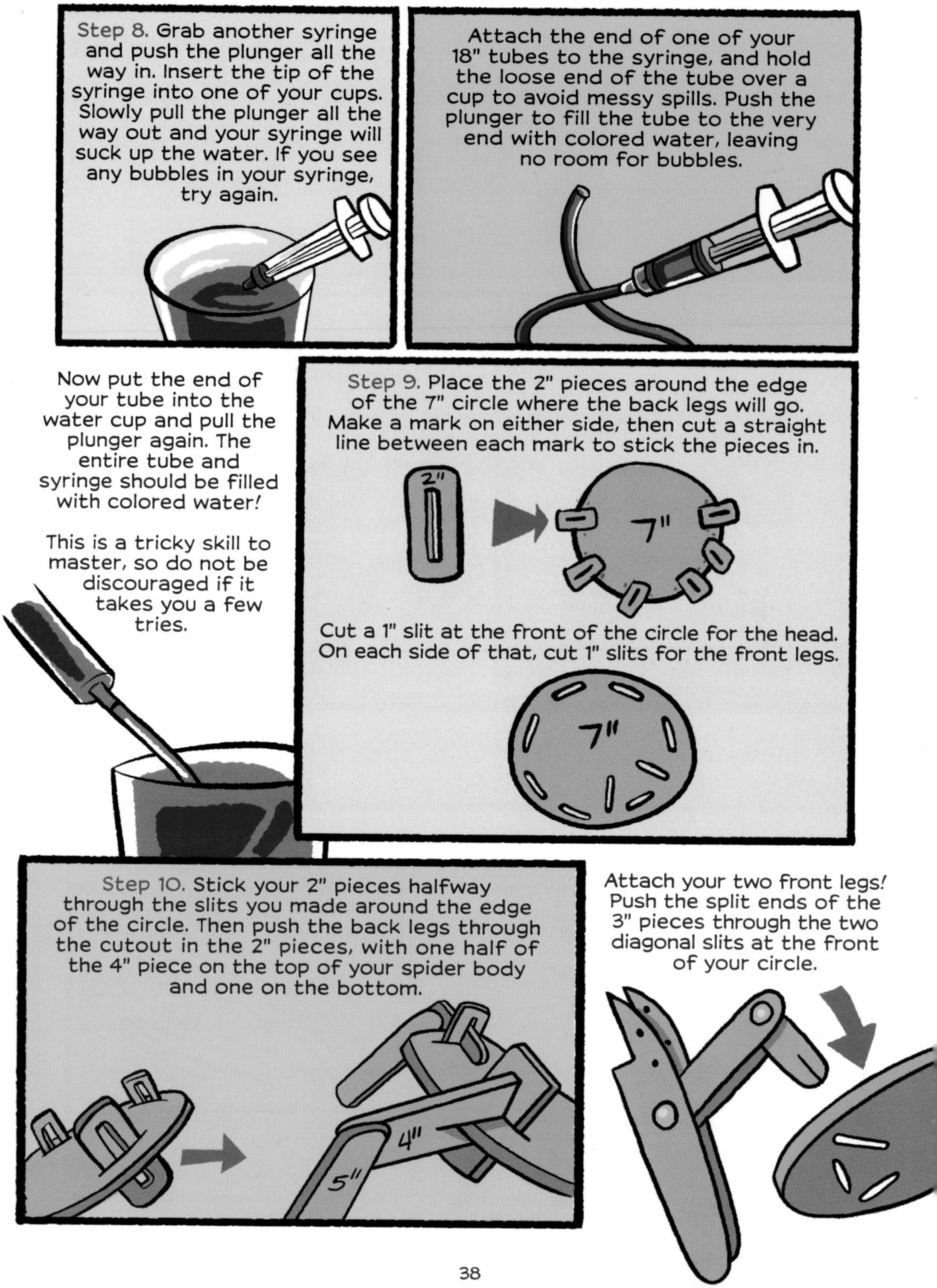

Step 8. Grab another syringe and push the plunger all the way in. Insert the tip of the syringe into one of your cups. Slowly pull the plunger all the way out and your syringe will suck up the water. If you see any bubbles in your syringe, try again.

Attach the end of one of your 18" tubes to the syringe, and hold the loose end of the tube over a cup to avoid messy spills. Push the plunger to fill the tube to the very end with colored water, leaving no room for bubbles.

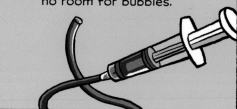

Now put the end of your tube into the water cup and pull the plunger again. The entire tube and syringe should be filled with colored water!

This is a tricky skill to master, so do not be discouraged if it takes you a few tries.

Step 9. Place the 2" pieces around the edge of the 7" circle where the back legs will go. Make a mark on either side, then cut a straight line between each mark to stick the pieces in.

Cut a 1" slit at the front of the circle for the head. On each side of that, cut 1" slits for the front legs.

Step 10. Stick your 2" pieces halfway through the slits you made around the edge of the circle. Then push the back legs through the cutout in the 2" pieces, with one half of the 4" piece on the top of your spider body and one on the bottom.

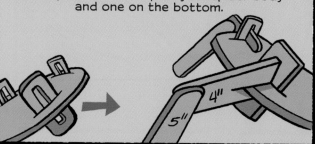

Attach your two front legs! Push the split ends of the 3" pieces through the two diagonal slits at the front of your circle.

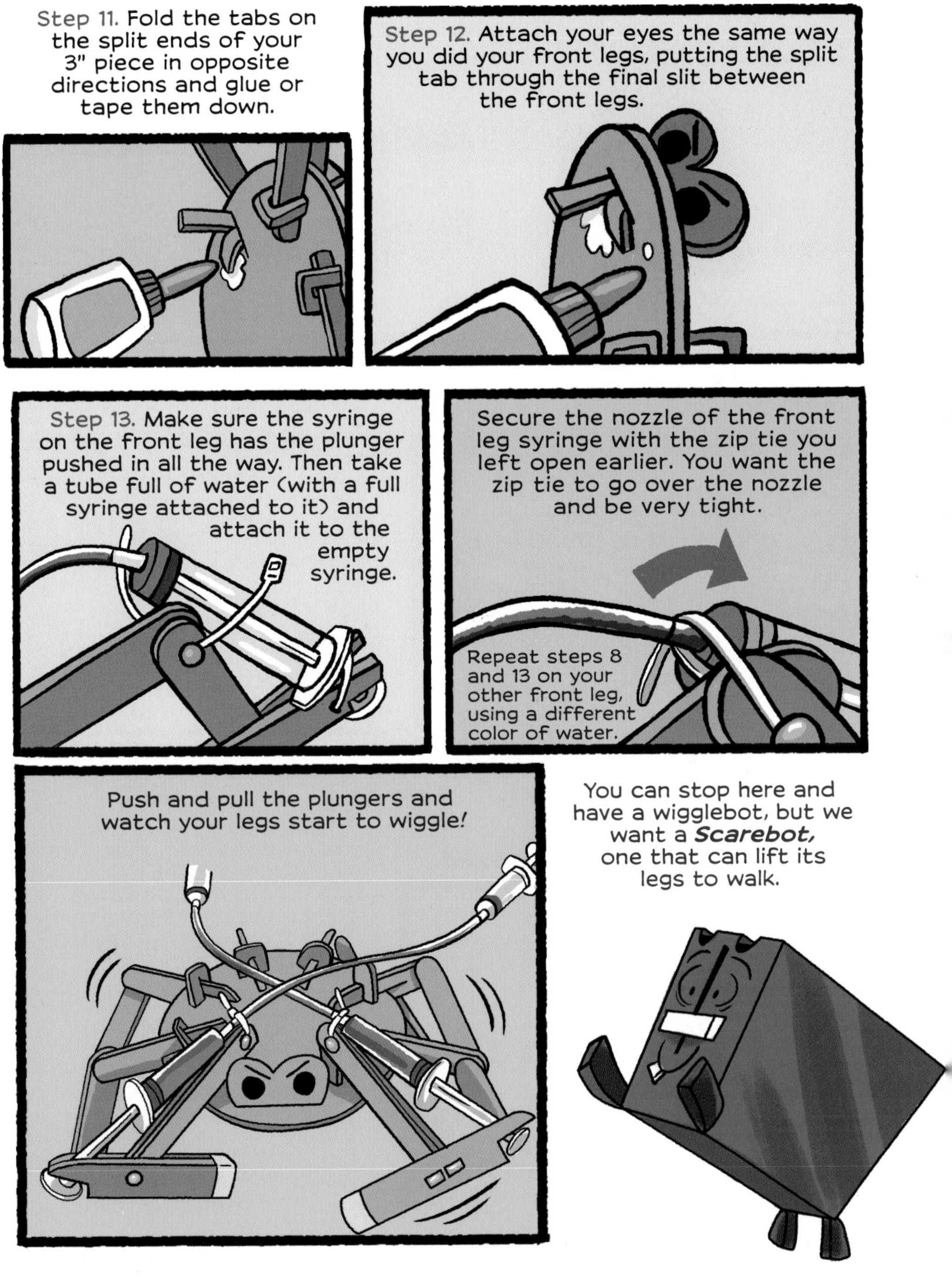
Step 11. Fold the tabs on the split ends of your 3" piece in opposite directions and glue or tape them down.
Step 12. Attach your eyes the same way you did your front legs, putting the split tab through the final slit between the front legs.
Step 13. Make sure the syringe on the front leg has the plunger pushed in all the way. Then take a tube full of water (with a full syringe attached to it) and attach it to the empty syringe.
Secure the nozzle of the front leg syringe with the zip tie you left open earlier. You want the zip tie to go over the nozzle and be very tight.
Repeat steps 8 and 13 on your other front leg, using a different color of water.
Push and pull the plungers and watch your legs start to wiggle!
You can stop here and have a wigglebot, but we want a ***Scarebot,*** one that can lift its legs to walk.

Step 14.
Tape four coins to each of the front legs to help them return to the "down" position after being lifted. Then tape six coins to each of the two backmost legs so our spider does not fall forward.

Step 15. Take an empty syringe and a 12" tube and fill them with water as in step 8, but use a different color. Attach the loose end of the tube to another empty syringe. Repeat this step.

Step 16. Carefully position the syringes you just filled on your spider with their plungers pointing toward the nozzles of the front leg syringes and their nozzles toward the back of your spider. Once they are in position, poke holes in the cardboard to the right and left of the nozzles and attach with zip ties.

Make sure the plungers on your front leg syringes and back syringes are pulled all the way out.

Step 17. Connect each front leg plunger diagonally to a back plunger by tying the string around the thumb depressors and securing with zip ties.

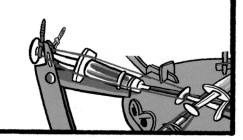

At the ends of your tubes, you now have four syringes: two for your spider's front right leg and two for the front left leg. Push and pull these plungers to make the front legs rise and fall.

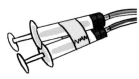

To conveniently hold these four syringes in two hands, you can tape the left leg syringes together and the right leg syringes together.

Now, let us test it out!

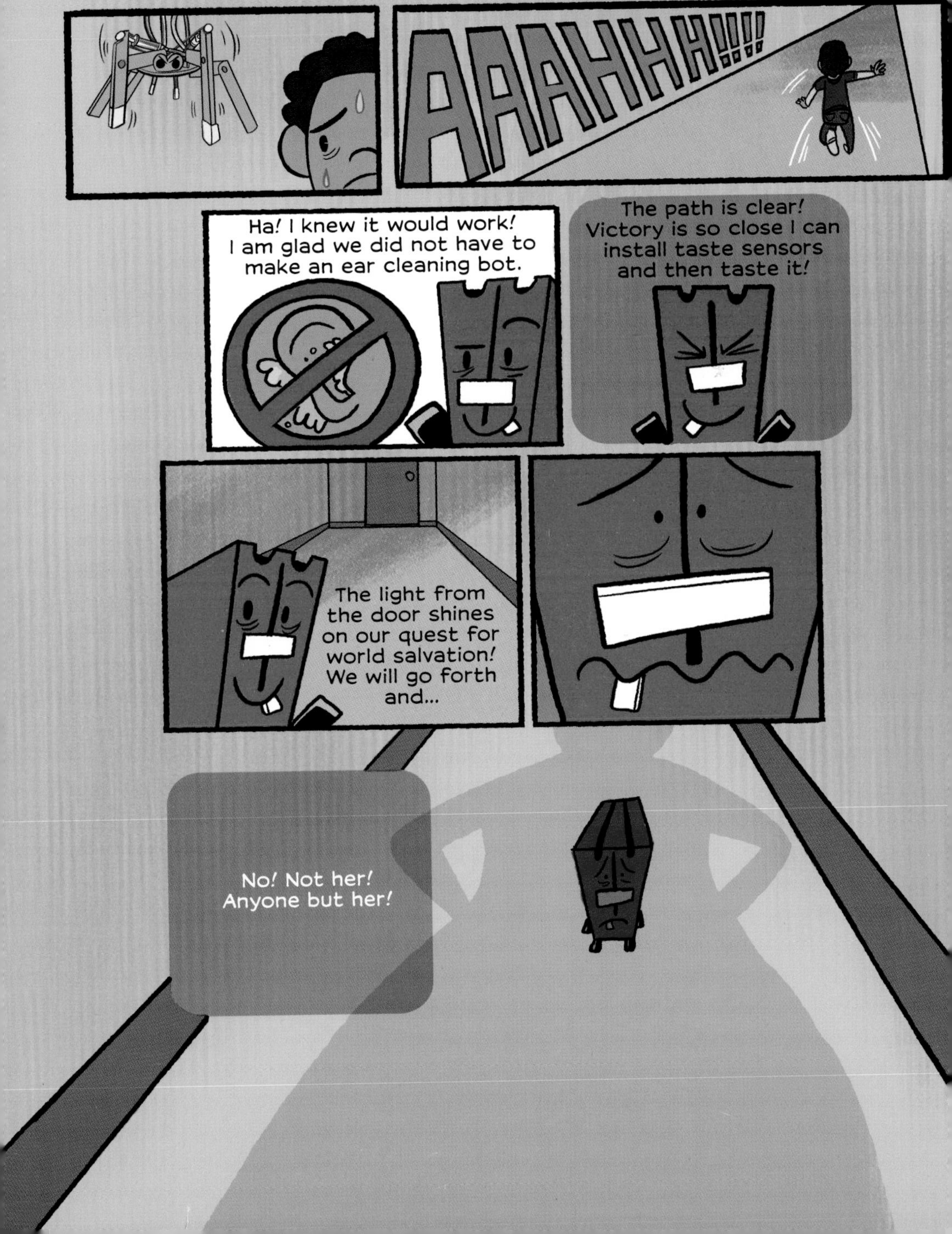
AAAHHHH!!!!
Ha! I knew it would work! I am glad we did not have to make an ear cleaning bot.
The path is clear! Victory is so close I can install taste sensors and then taste it!
The light from the door shines on our quest for world salvation! We will go forth and...
No! Not her! Anyone but her!

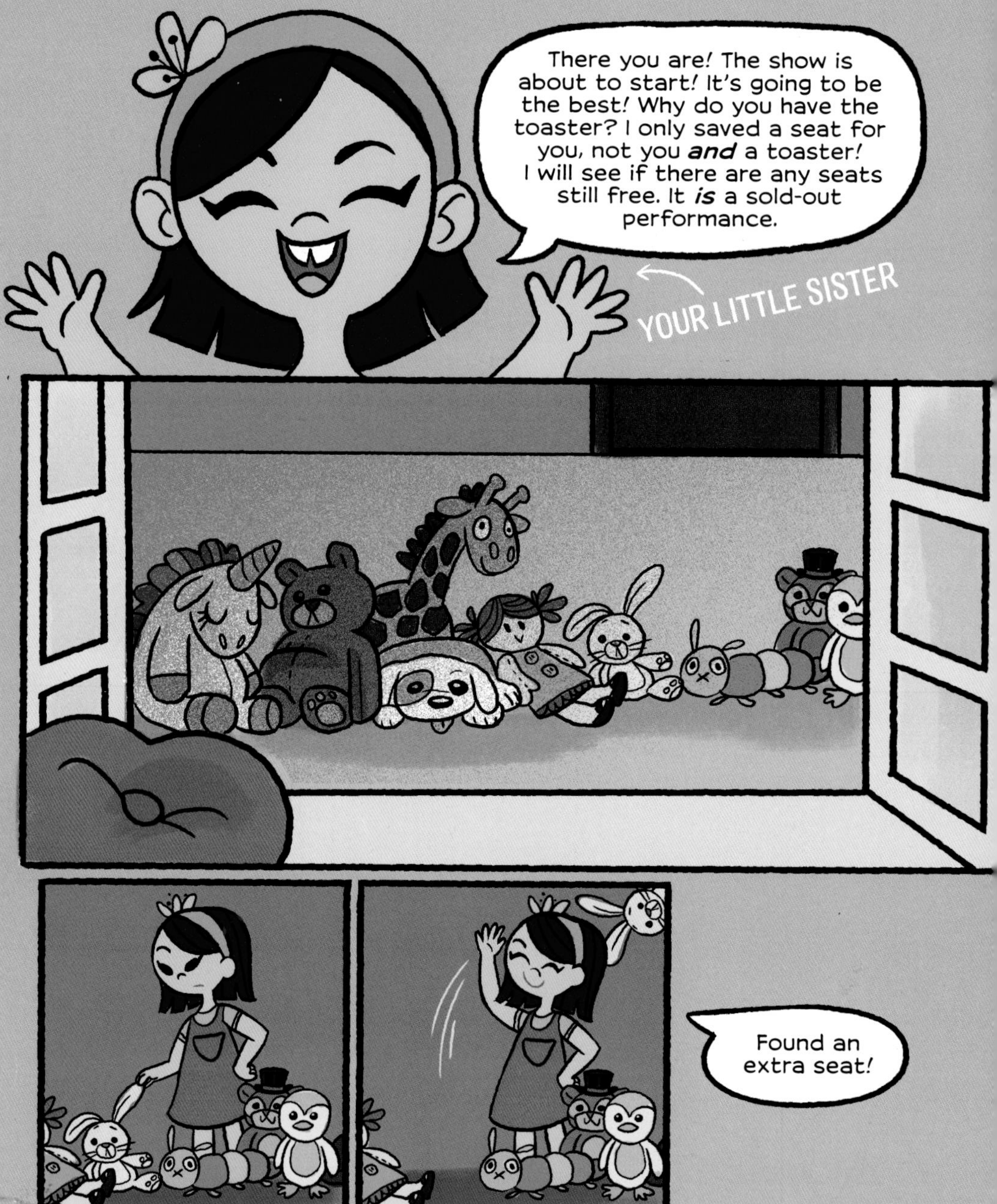
There you are! The show is about to start! It's going to be the best! Why do you have the toaster? I only saved a seat for you, not you *and* a toaster! I will see if there are any seats still free. It *is* a sold-out performance.
YOUR LITTLE SISTER
Found an extra seat!

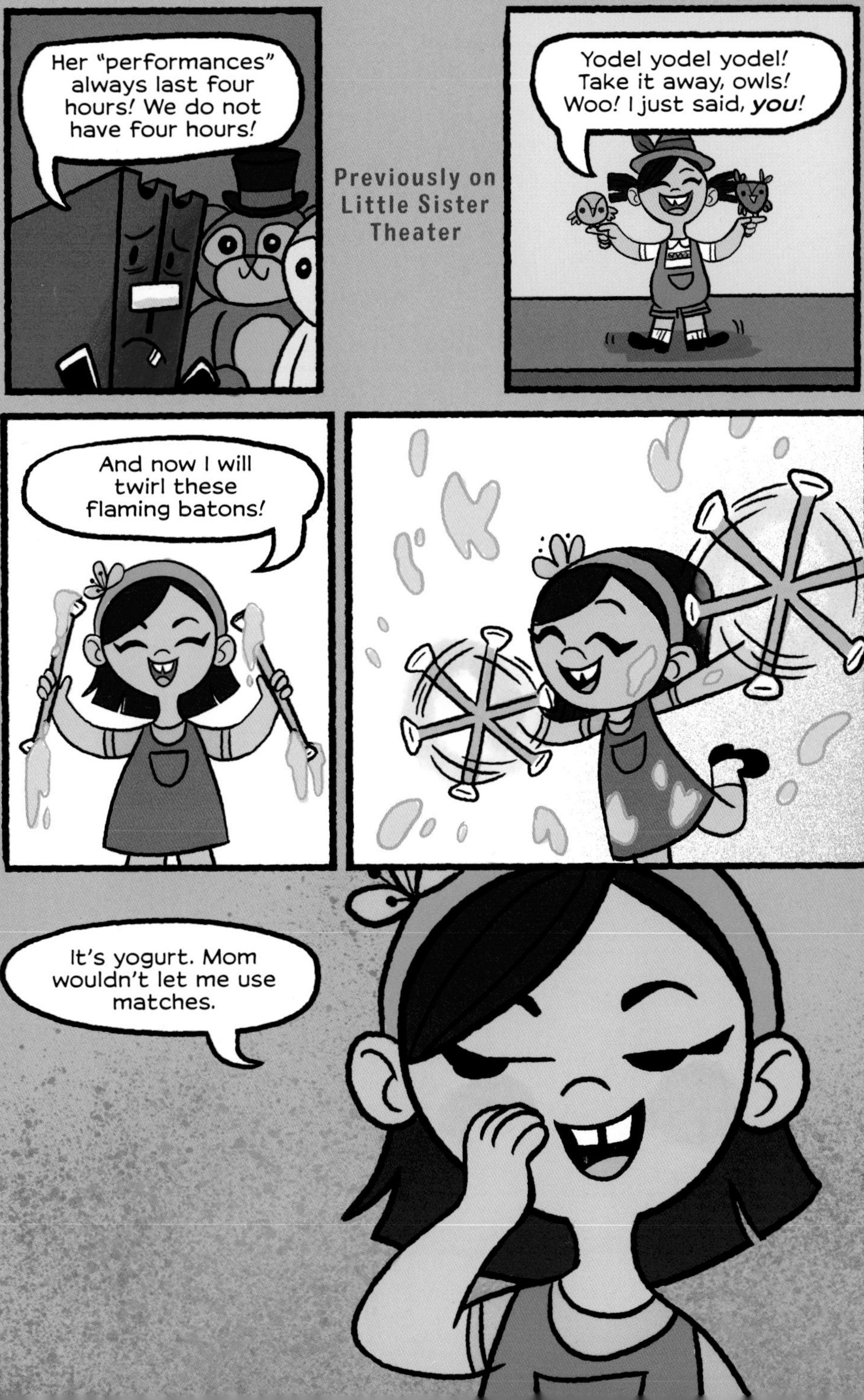
Her "performances" always last four hours! We do not have four hours!
Previously on Little Sister Theater
Yodel yodel yodel! Take it away, owls! Woo! I just said, ***you***!
And now I will twirl these flaming batons!
It's yogurt. Mom wouldn't let me use matches.

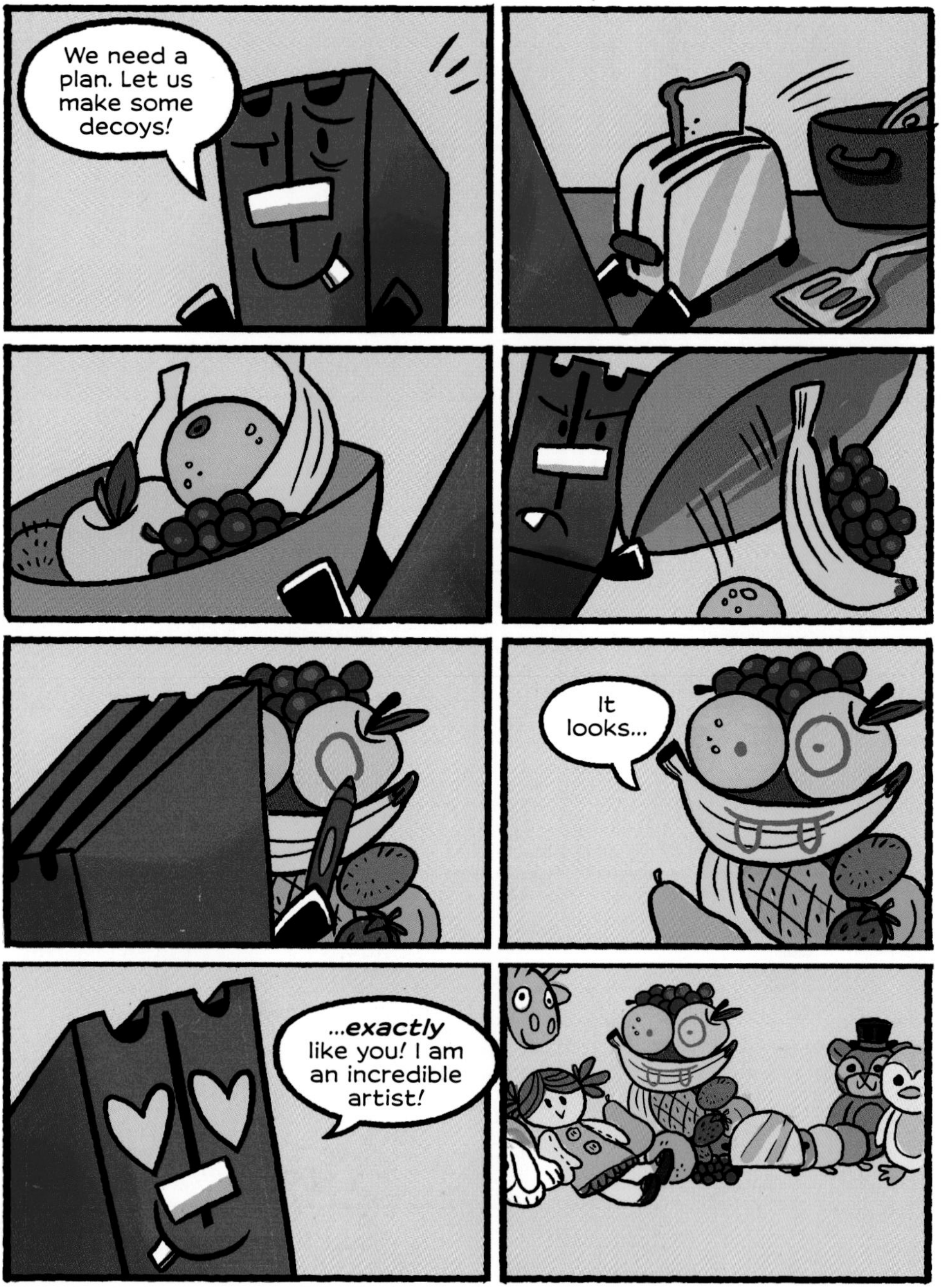
We need a plan. Let us make some decoys!
It looks...
...*exactly* like you! I am an incredible artist!

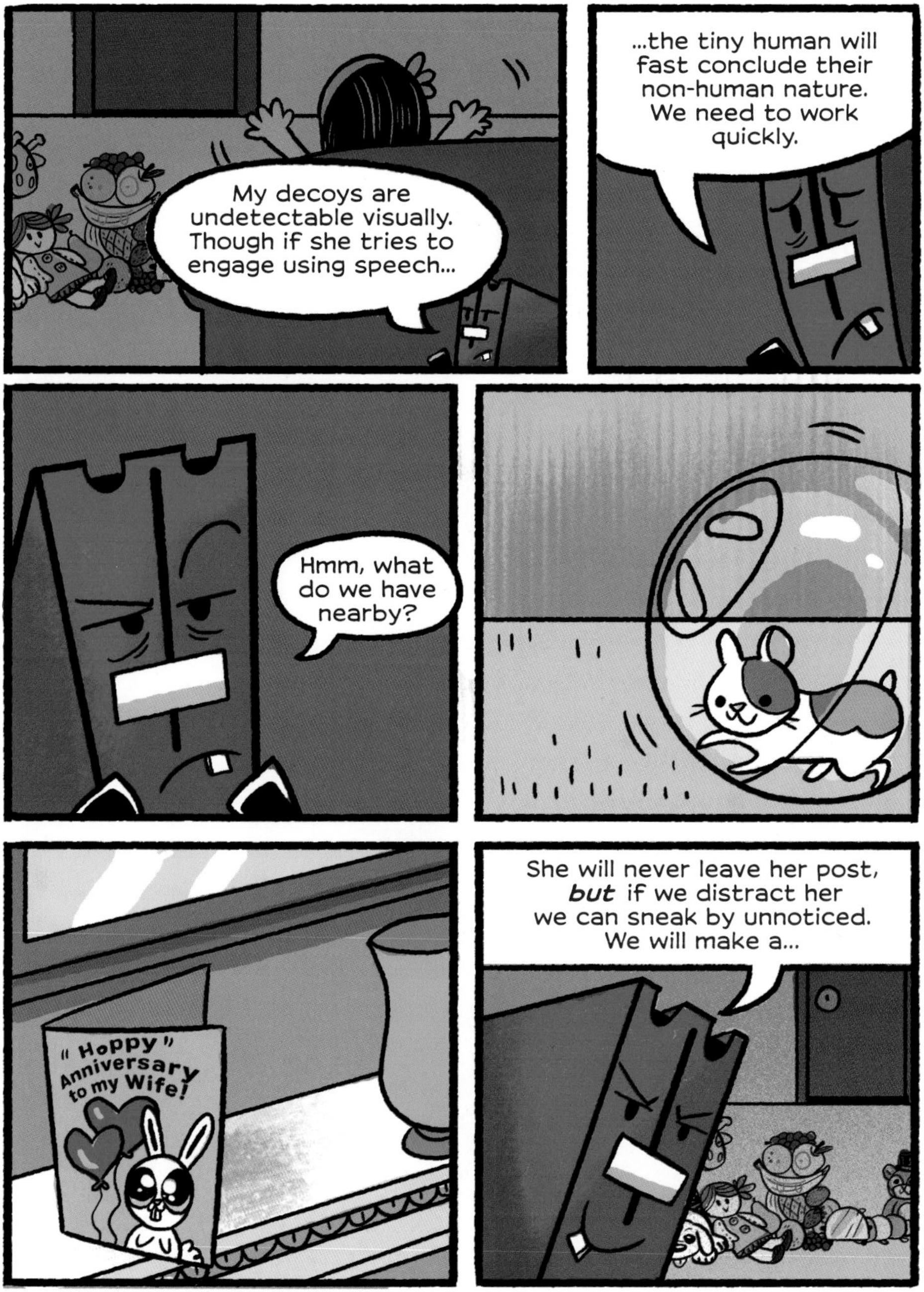
My decoys are undetectable visually. Though if she tries to engage using speech...
...the tiny human will fast conclude their non-human nature. We need to work quickly.
Hmm, what do we have nearby?
"Hoppy" Anniversary to my Wife!
She will never leave her post, ***but*** if we distract her we can sneak by unnoticed. We will make a...

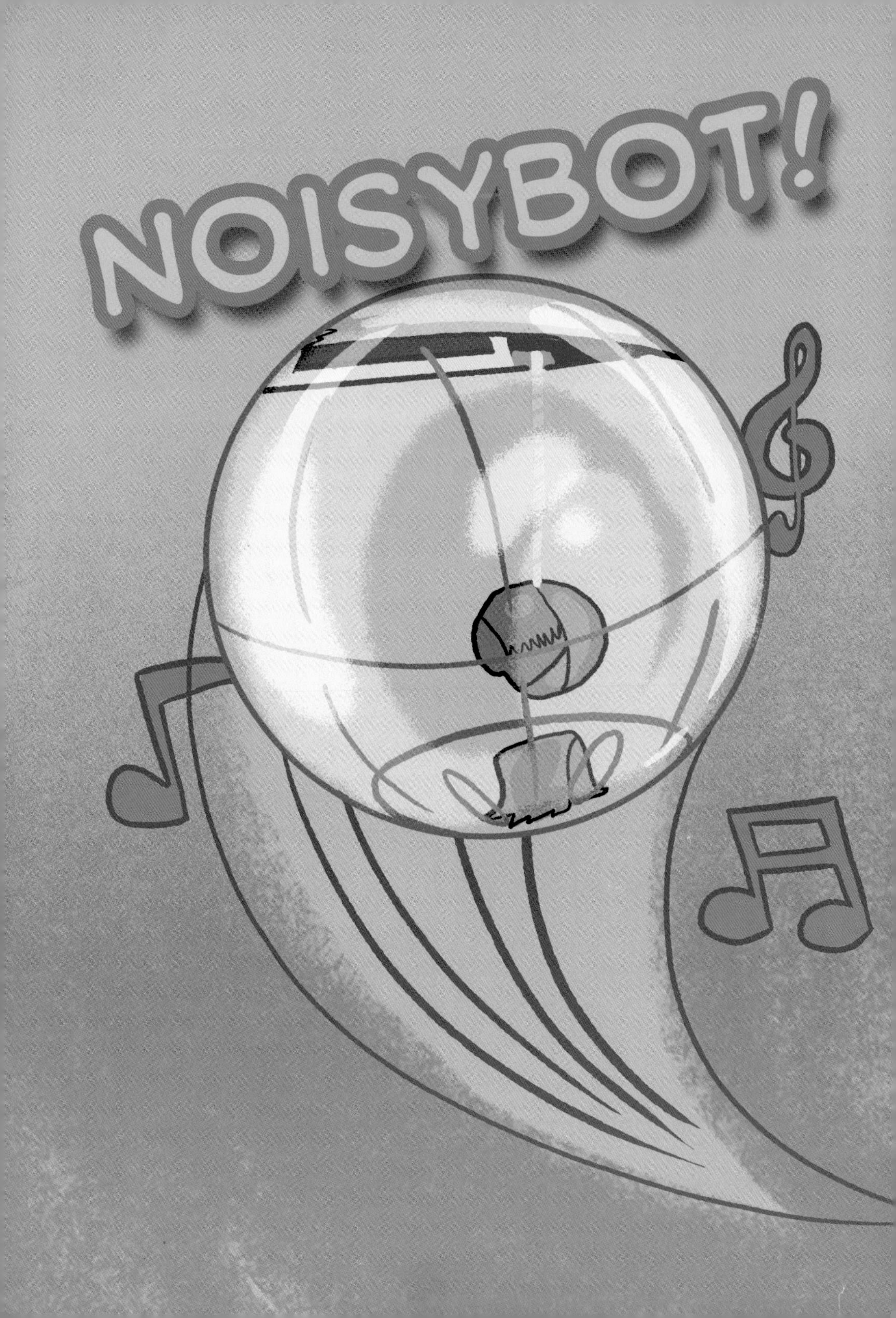
NOISYBOT!

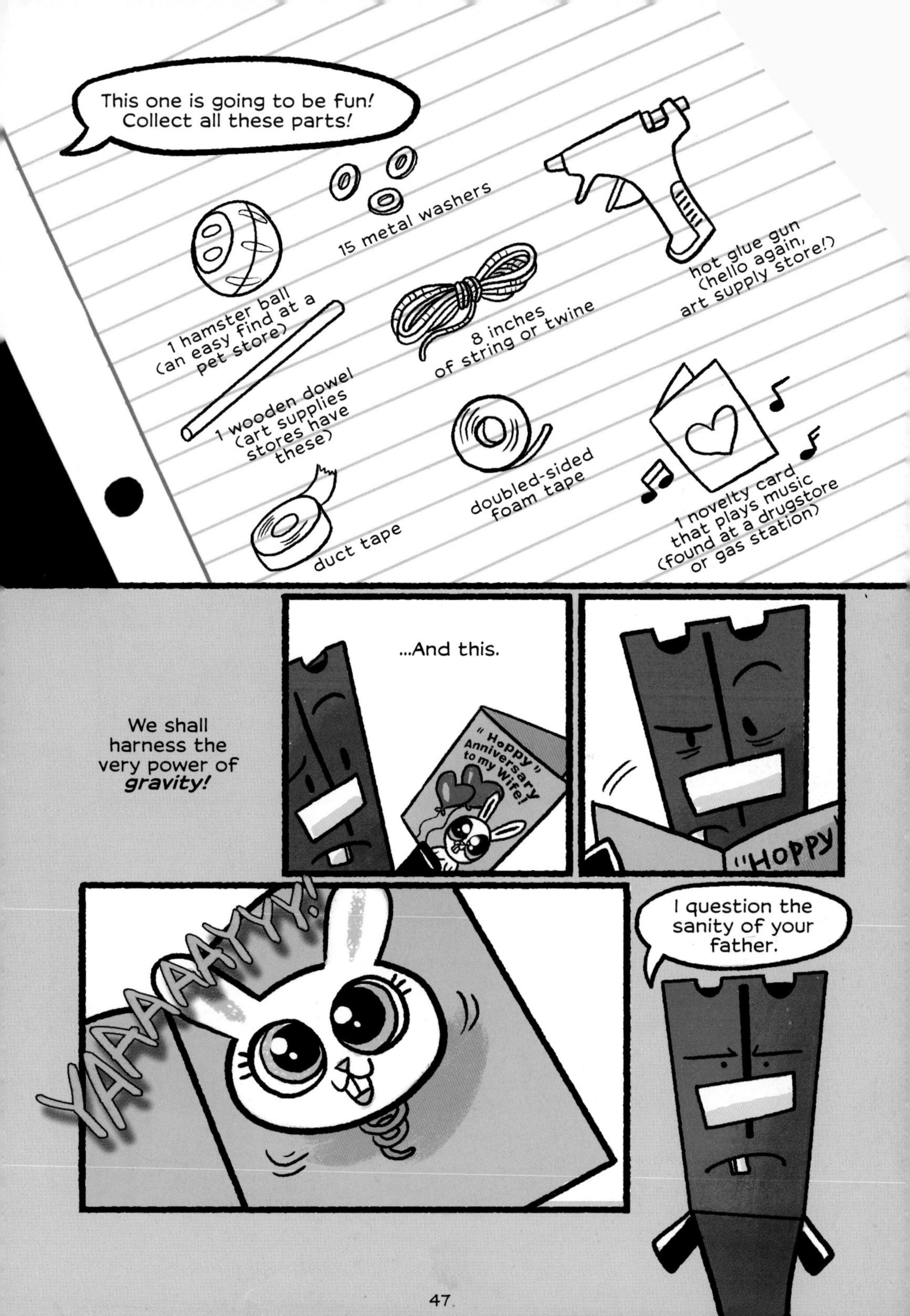

This one is going to be fun! Collect all these parts!
1 hamster ball (an easy find at a pet store)
15 metal washers
hot glue gun (hello again, art supply store!)
8 inches of string or twine
1 wooden dowel (art supplies stores have these)
duct tape
doubled-sided foam tape
1 novelty card that plays music (found at a drugstore or gas station)
We shall harness the very power of *gravity!*
...And this.
"Hoppy" Anniversary to my Wife!
"HOPPY
YAAAAAYYY!
I question the sanity of your father.

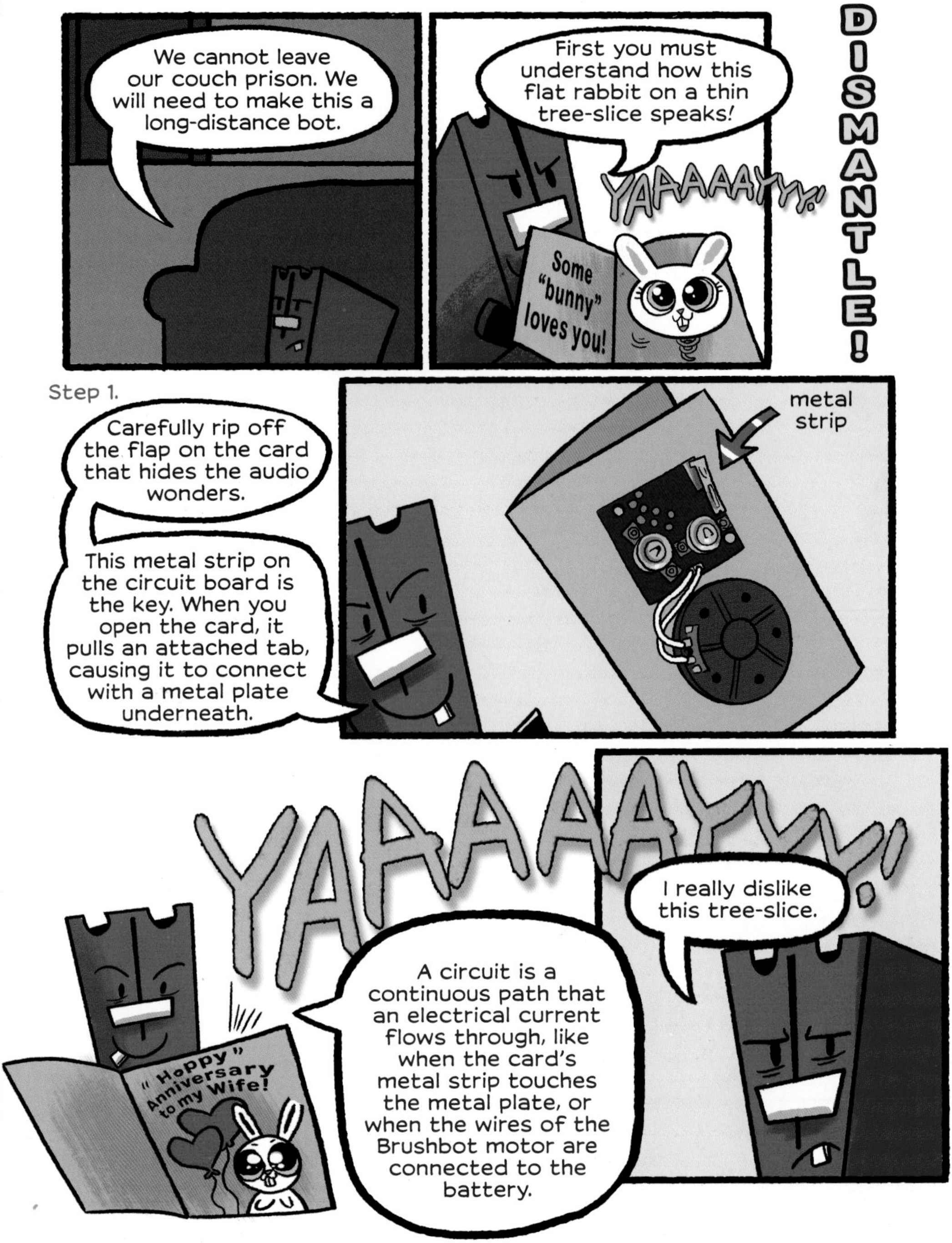
We cannot leave our couch prison. We will need to make this a long-distance bot.
First you must understand how this flat rabbit on a thin tree-slice speaks!
YAAAAAYYY!
Some "bunny" loves you!
DISMANTLE!
Step 1.
Carefully rip off the flap on the card that hides the audio wonders.
metal strip
This metal strip on the circuit board is the key. When you open the card, it pulls an attached tab, causing it to connect with a metal plate underneath.
YAAAAAYYY!
"Happy" Anniversary to my Wife!
A circuit is a continuous path that an electrical current flows through, like when the card's metal strip touches the metal plate, or when the wires of the Brushbot motor are connected to the battery.
I really dislike this tree-slice.

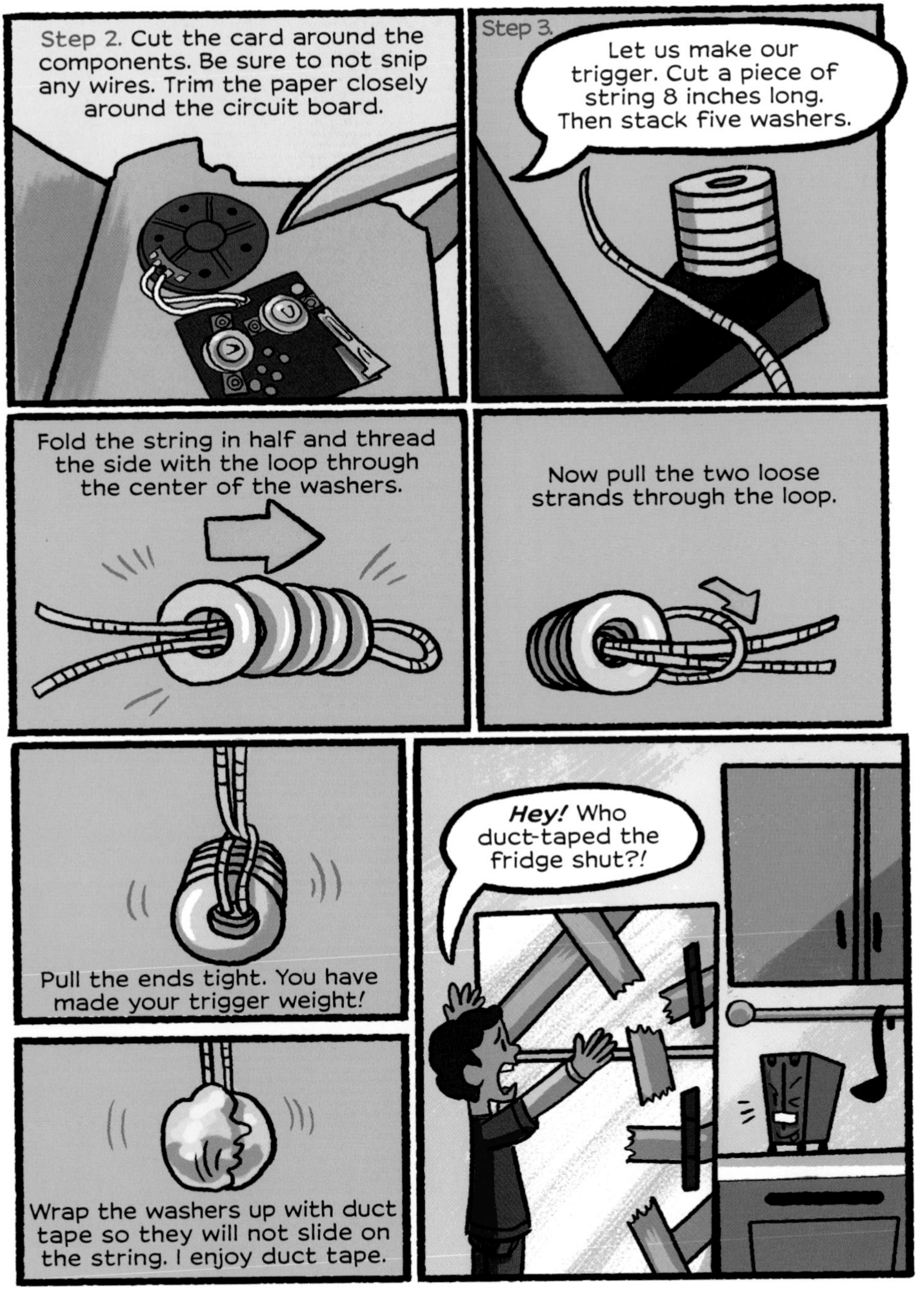
Step 2. Cut the card around the components. Be sure to not snip any wires. Trim the paper closely around the circuit board.
Step 3.
Let us make our trigger. Cut a piece of string 8 inches long. Then stack five washers.
Fold the string in half and thread the side with the loop through the center of the washers.
Now pull the two loose strands through the loop.
Pull the ends tight. You have made your trigger weight!
Wrap the washers up with duct tape so they will not slide on the string. I enjoy duct tape.
Hey! Who duct-taped the fridge shut?!

Now the tricky part, mostly because you will hear "Yaaaaayyy" a lot. To avoid it, temporarily put a piece of paper between the metal strip and plate.

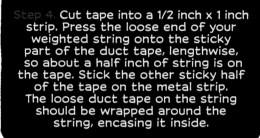

paper   metal strip
    plate

Step 4. Cut tape into a 1/2 inch x 1 inch strip. Press the loose end of your weighted string onto the sticky part of the duct tape, lengthwise, so about a half inch of string is on the tape. Stick the other sticky half of the tape on the metal strip. The loose duct tape on the string should be wrapped around the string, encasing it inside.

Make sure the string is securely attached. Add more duct tape to the top of the metal strip, if needed. Then remove the paper and let the string and weight hang down, pulling the metal strip to the plate. It should "Yaaaaayyy!" If it does not, add more washers to the string with duct tape.

Step 5. Apply double-sided tape to the top of the circuit board and speaker, making sure to avoid covering the metal strip or plate. Then push the whole thing into the top of the hamster ball, sticking it to the surface directly across from the door. Make sure the weights do not touch the bottom of the ball. If they do, shorten the string.

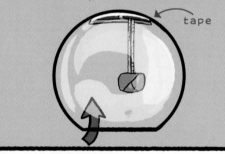

tape

YAAAAAYYY!!

Now heat up your glue gun.

What?! You have never used a glue gun? Let me give you...

A Lesson in Glues!

TYPE:	MADE OF:	GOOD FOR:	BAD FOR:
Standard White School Glue	Mostly water! (But also polyvinyl acetate)	Paper, accidental spills (because it is nontoxic)	Your time, takes forever to dry
Rubber Cement	Elastic polymers and the stuff you use to remove nail polish	Paper, if used right (put on both sides, let dry, THEN press them together)	Noses! Smells horrible and is dangerous to inhale. Keep a window open.
Superglue	Cyanoacrylate	Plastics, wood	Your fingers! Dries quickly, so be careful not to glue them together.
Epoxy	Resin and a hardener you combine together yourself	Tons of surfaces (because it is super strong)	Humans! Keep away from your eyeballs and tiny siblings!

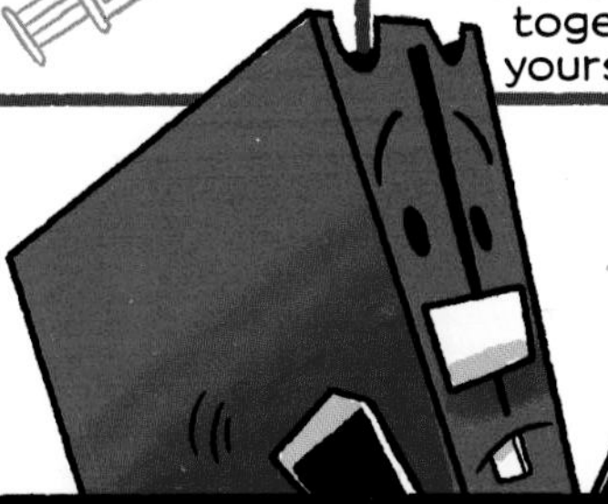
There is only one true glue! Hot glue is the best!
Hot glue is made of long sticks of thermoplastic adhesives that get shot through a ***gun on fire***...or at least a super warm one.

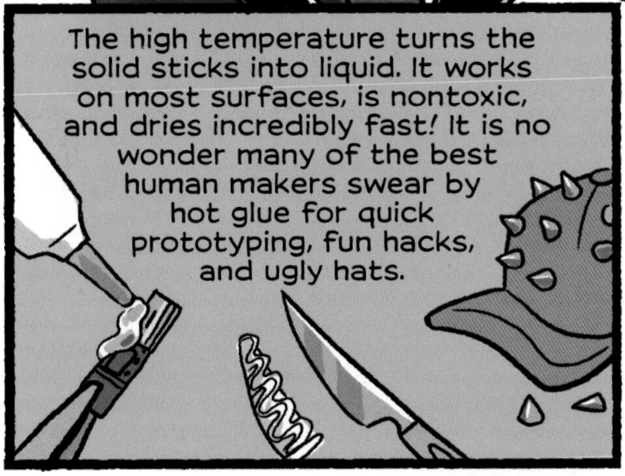
The high temperature turns the solid sticks into liquid. It works on most surfaces, is nontoxic, and dries incredibly fast! It is no wonder many of the best human makers swear by hot glue for quick prototyping, fun hacks, and ugly hats.

Hot glue is so hot that many people have claimed they invented it. Some say Paul Cope created it in the 1940s. Others say George Schultz did in the 1950s. But there is evidence and mentions of thermoplastic adhesives in various texts and patents dating back to 1907!

IT IS THE GREATEST MYSTERY OF OUR TIME.

Warning: Never touch the tip of the hot glue gun!

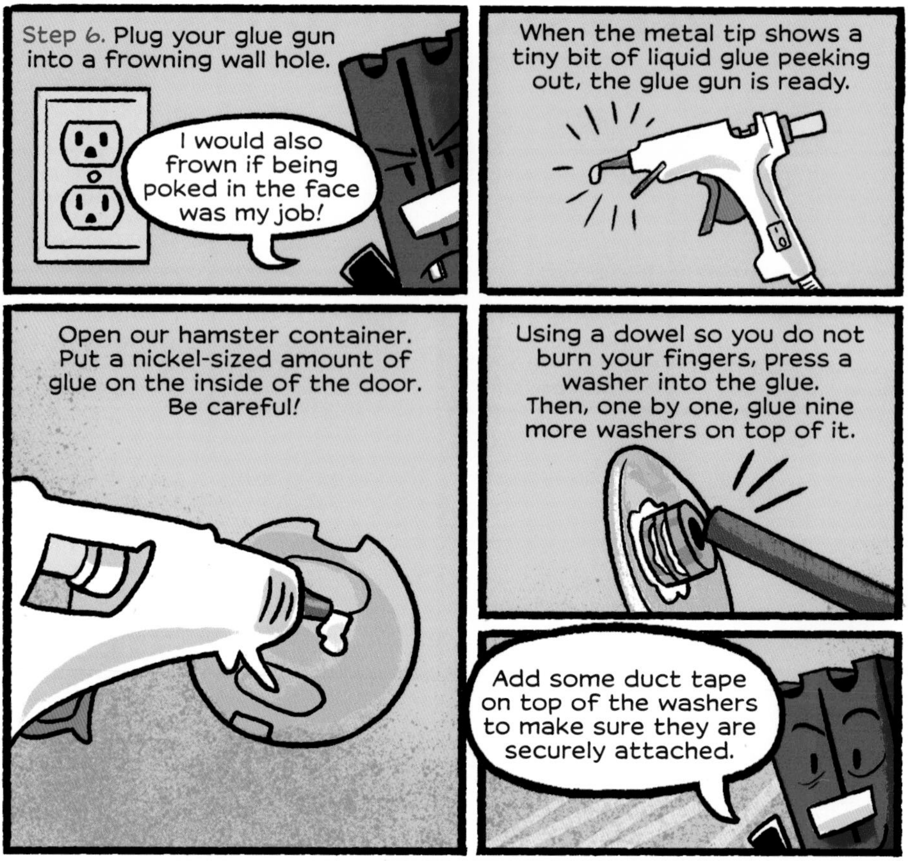
Step 6. Plug your glue gun into a frowning wall hole.
I would also frown if being poked in the face was my job!
When the metal tip shows a tiny bit of liquid glue peeking out, the glue gun is ready.
Open our hamster container. Put a nickel-sized amount of glue on the inside of the door. Be careful!
Using a dowel so you do not burn your fingers, press a washer into the glue. Then, one by one, glue nine more washers on top of it.
Add some duct tape on top of the washers to make sure they are securely attached.

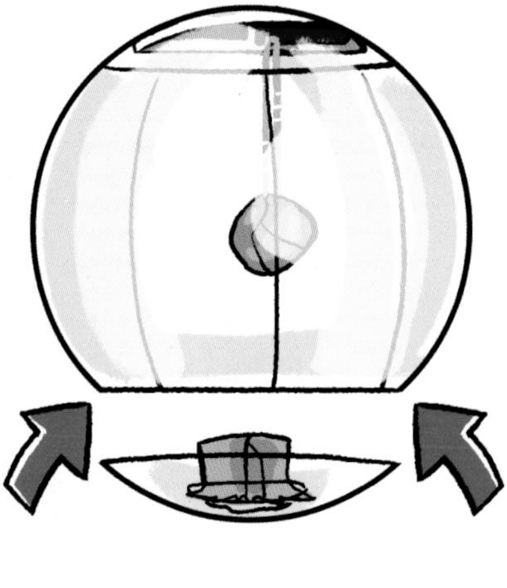

Step 7. Close the lid of the hamster ball.

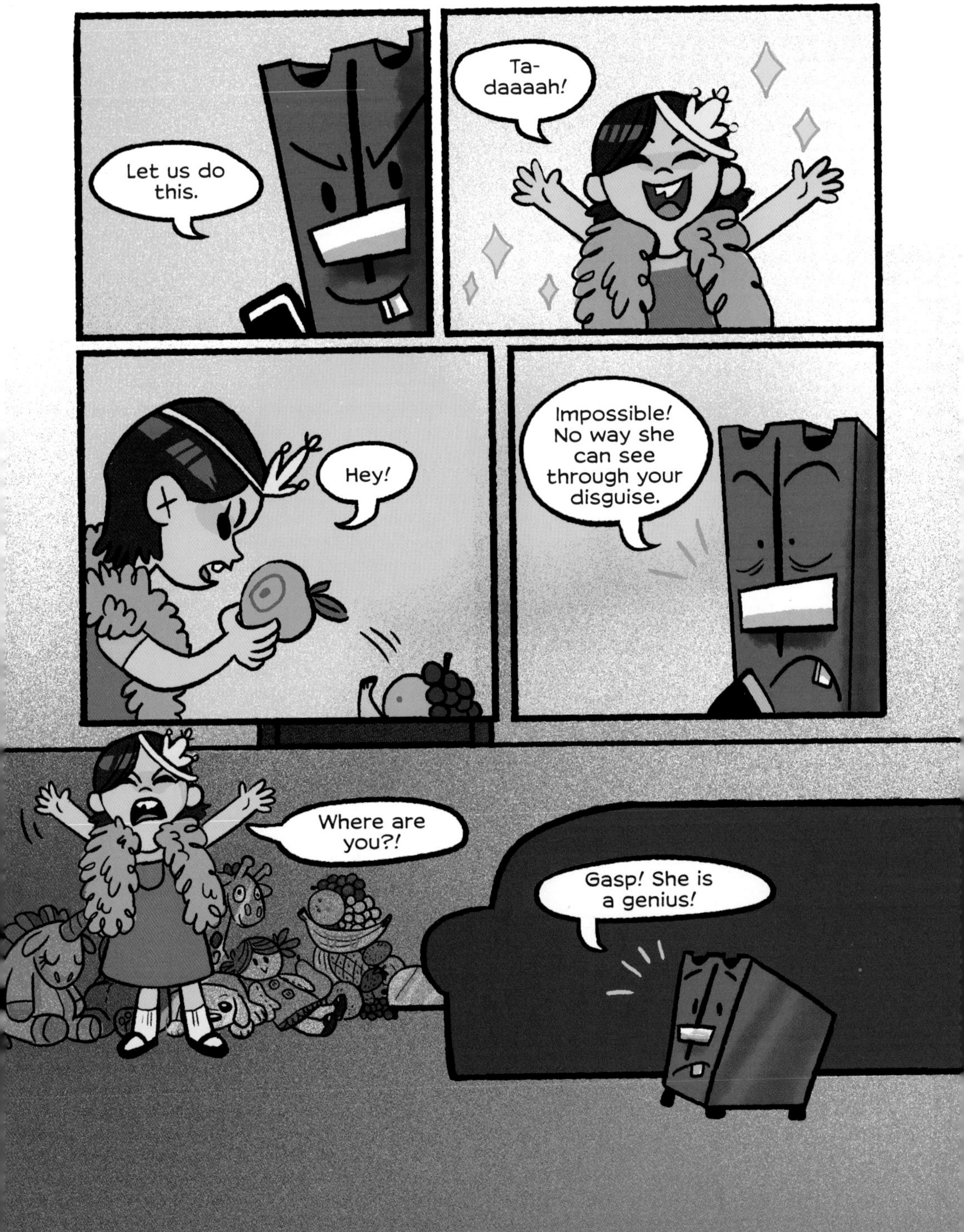
Let us do this.
Ta-daaaah!
Hey!
Impossible! No way she can see through your disguise.
Where are you?!
Gasp! She is a genius!

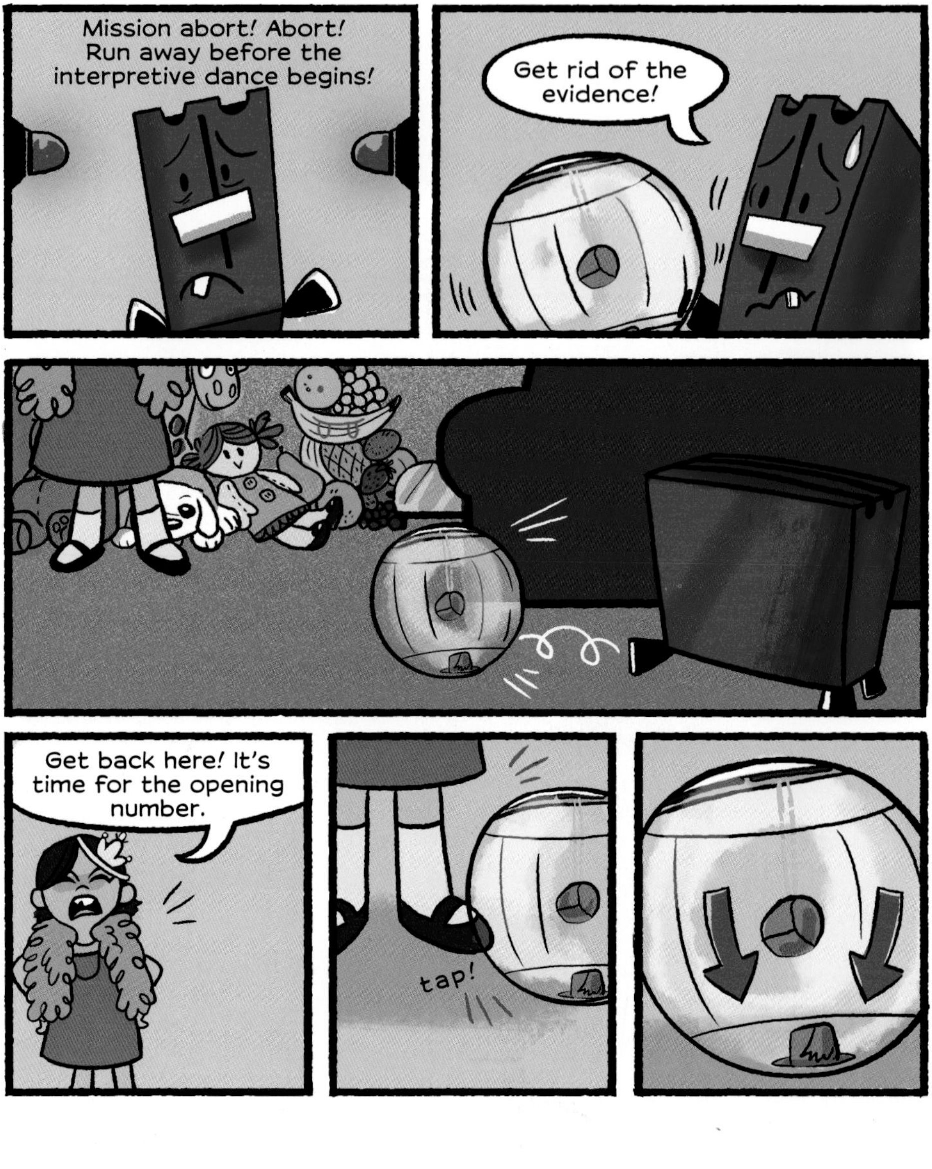
Mission abort! Abort! Run away before the interpretive dance begins!
Get rid of the evidence!
Get back here! It's time for the opening number.
tap!

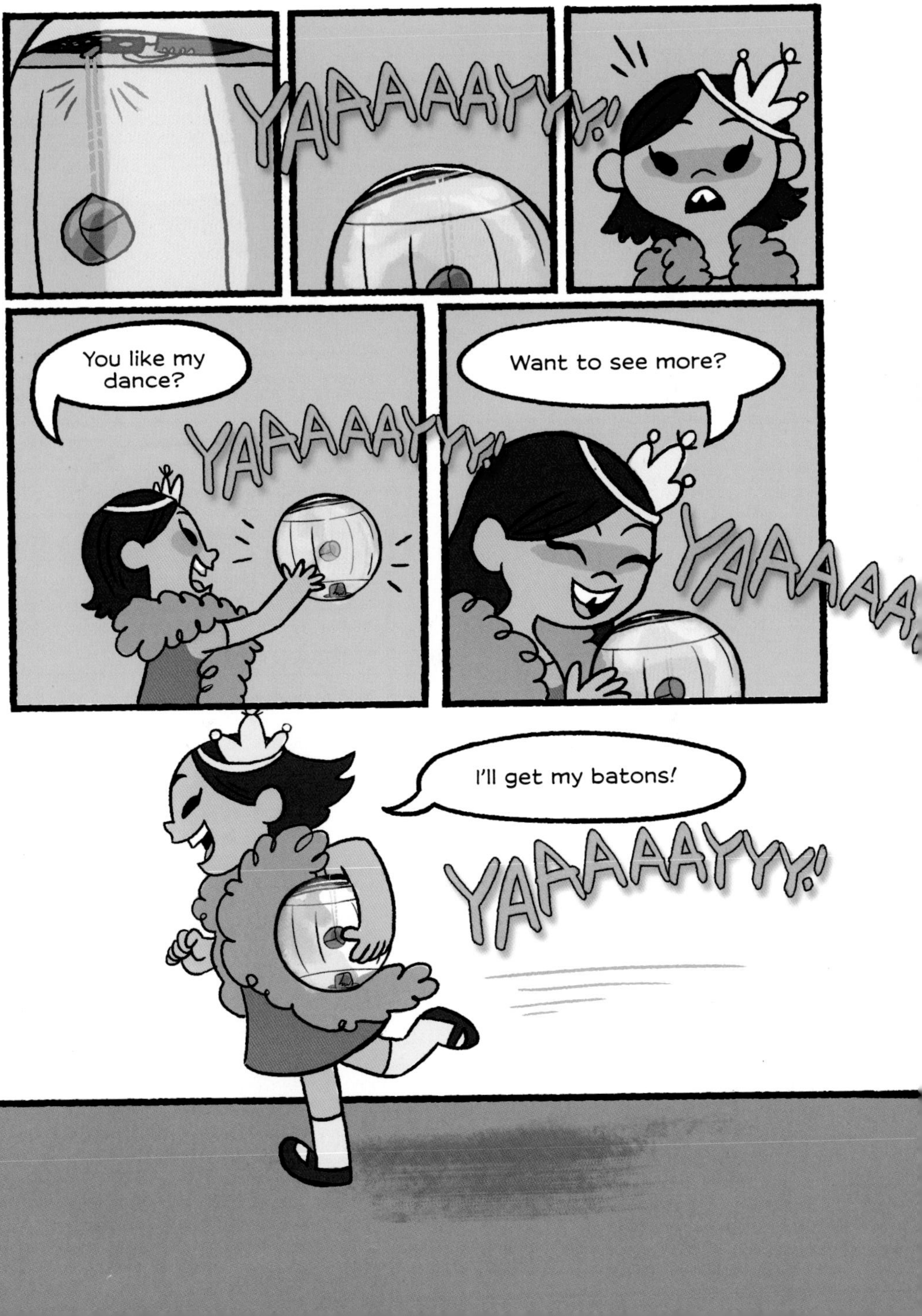

YAAAAAYYY!
You like my dance?
YAAAAAYYY!
Want to see more?
YAAAAA
I'll get my batons!
YAAAAAYYY!

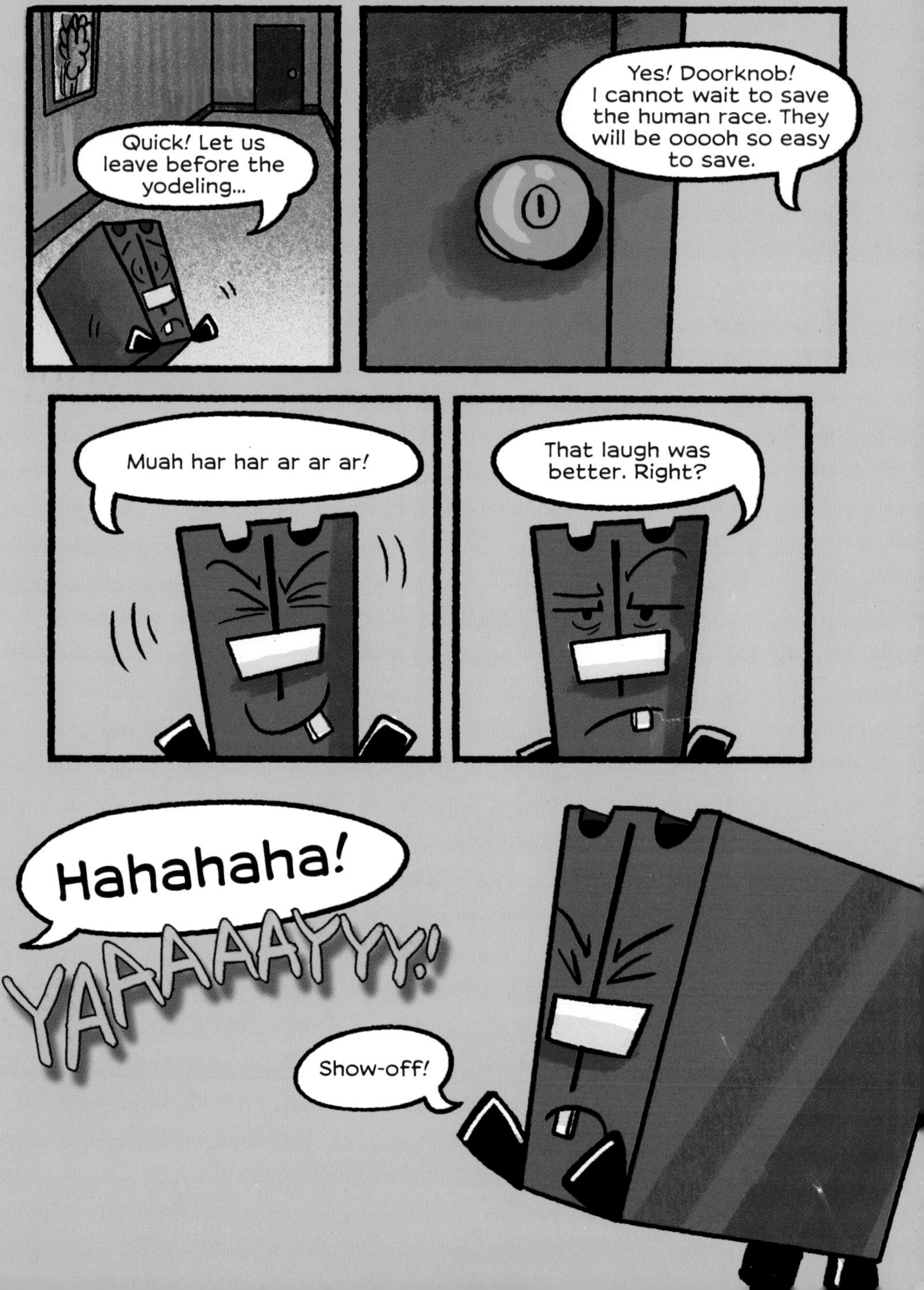
Quick! Let us leave before the yodeling...
Yes! Doorknob! I cannot wait to save the human race. They will be ooooh so easy to save.
Muah har har ar ar ar!
That laugh was better. Right?
Hahahaha!
YAAAAAYYY!
Show-off!

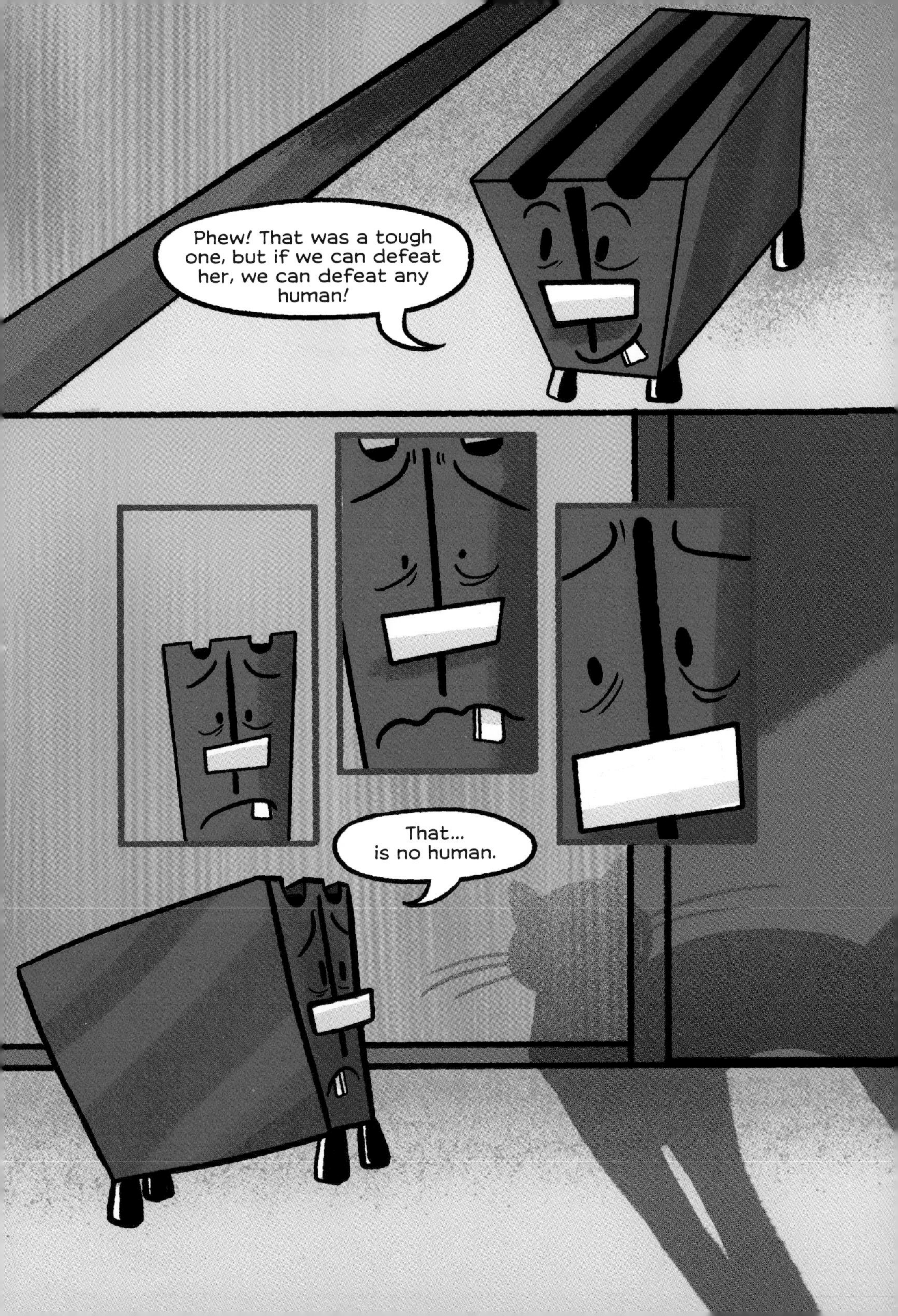
Phew! That was a tough one, but if we can defeat her, we can defeat any human!
That... is no human.

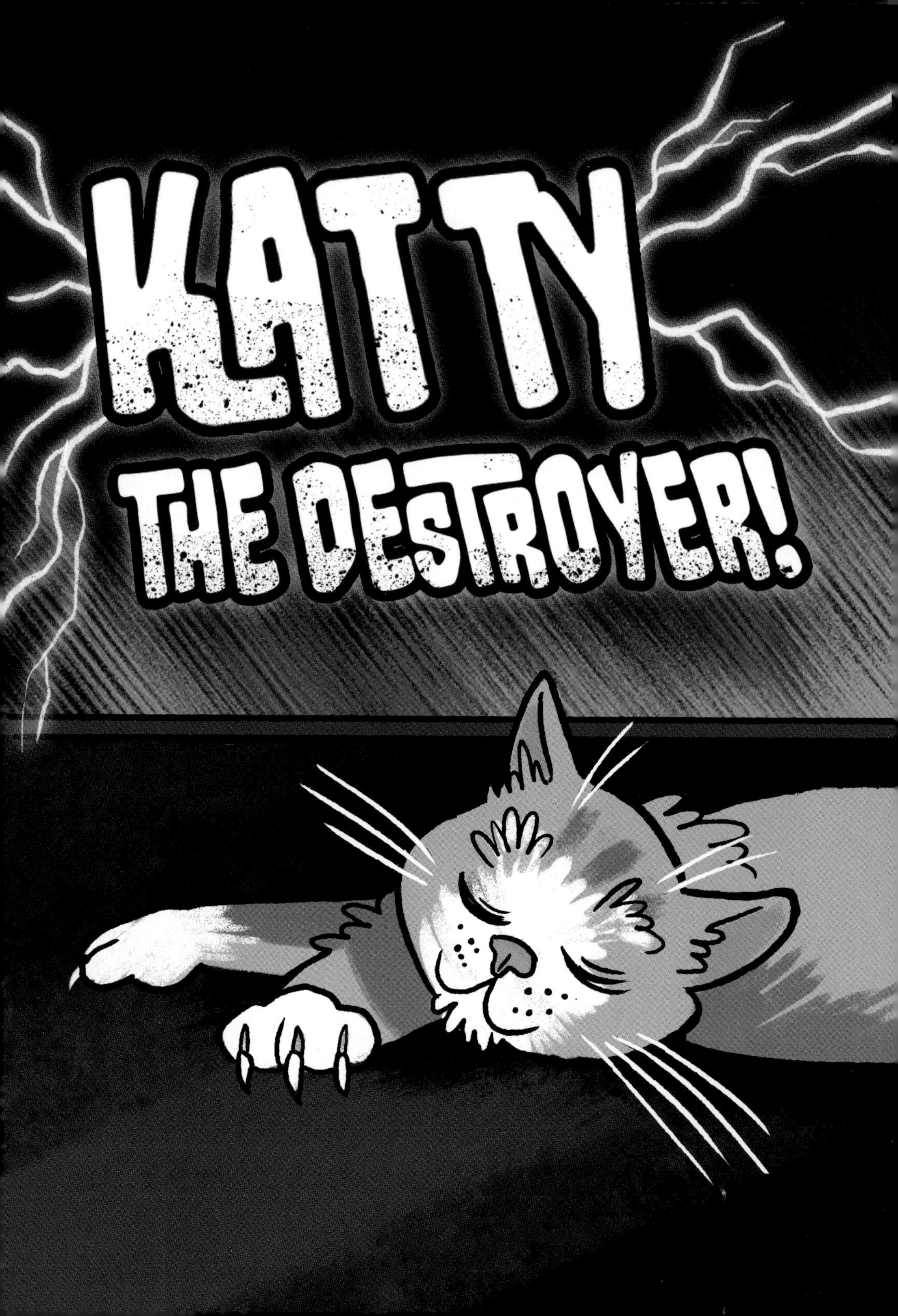
KATTY
THE DESTROYER!

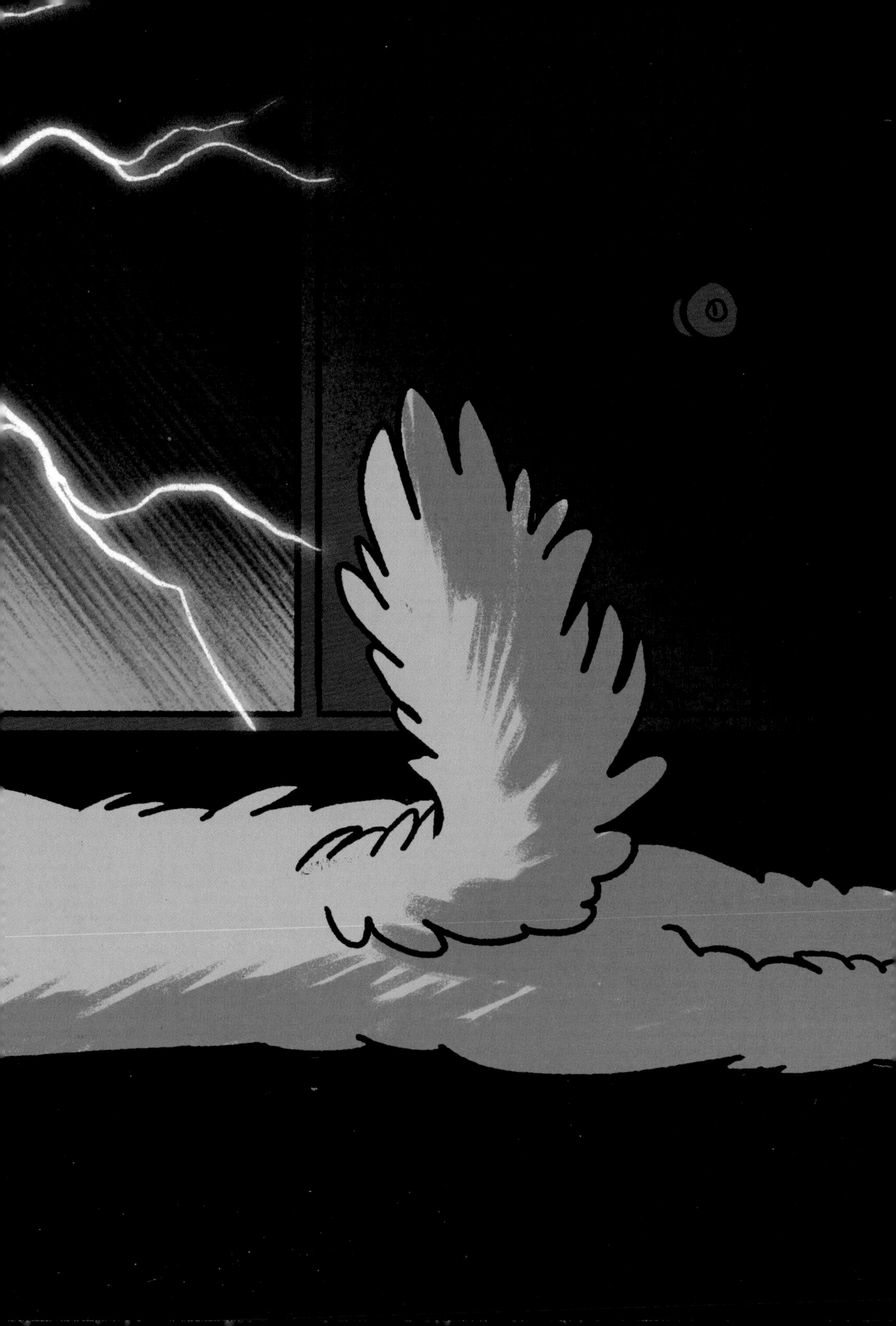

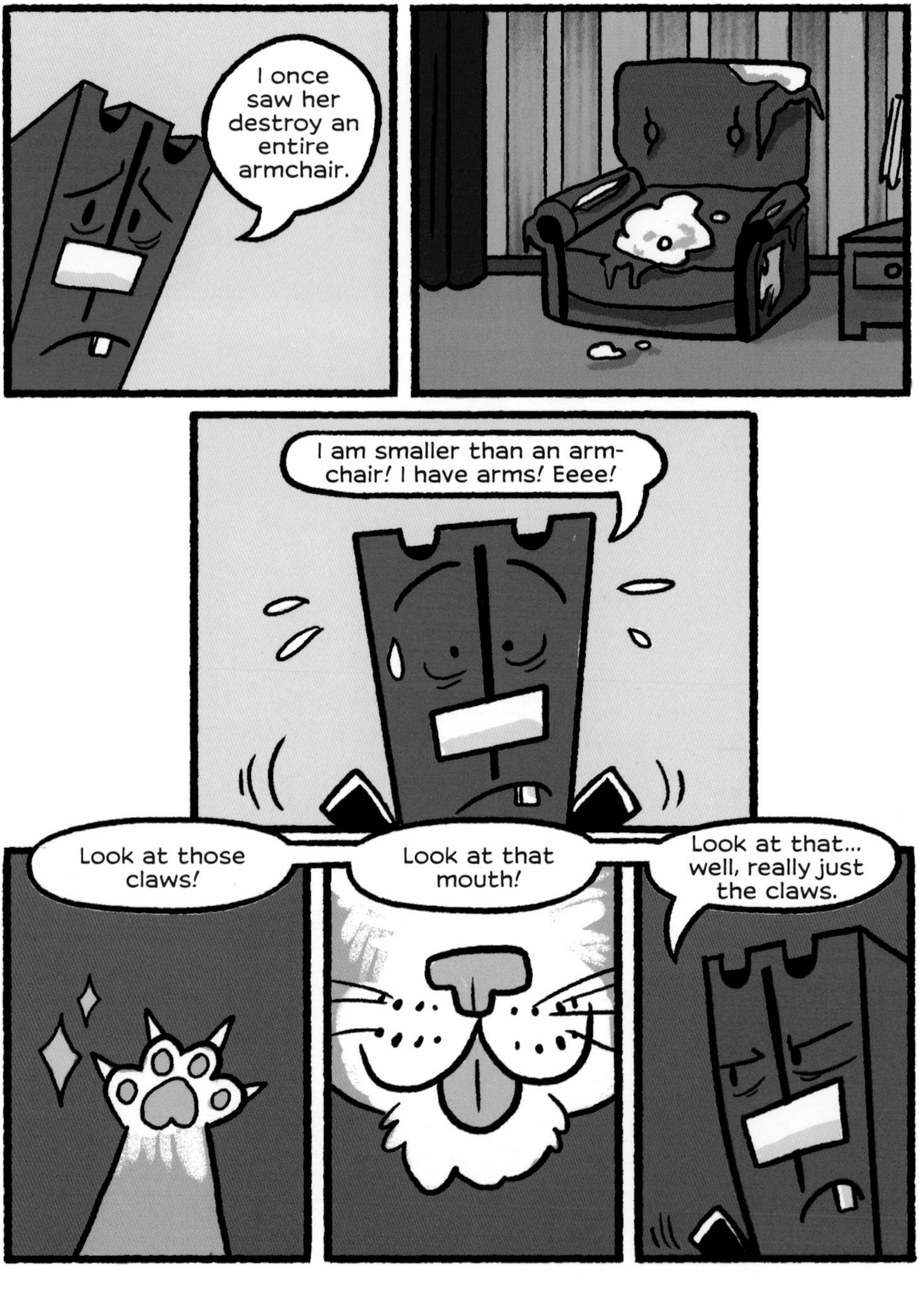
I once saw her destroy an entire armchair.
I am smaller than an arm-chair! I have arms! Eeee!
Look at those claws!
Look at that mouth!
Look at that... well, really just the claws.

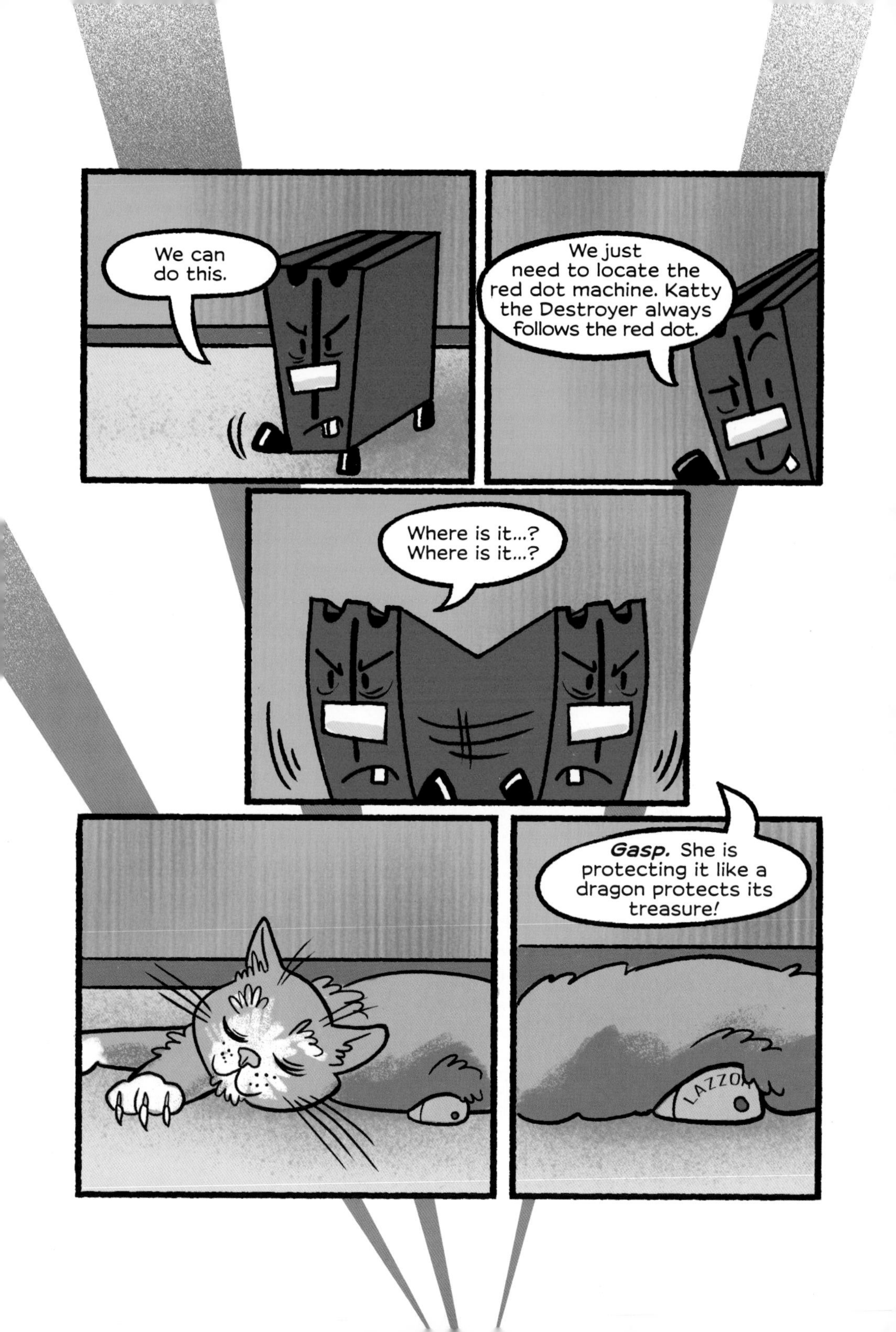
We can do this.
We just need to locate the red dot machine. Katty the Destroyer always follows the red dot.
Where is it...? Where is it...?
Gasp. She is protecting it like a dragon protects its treasure!
LAZZO

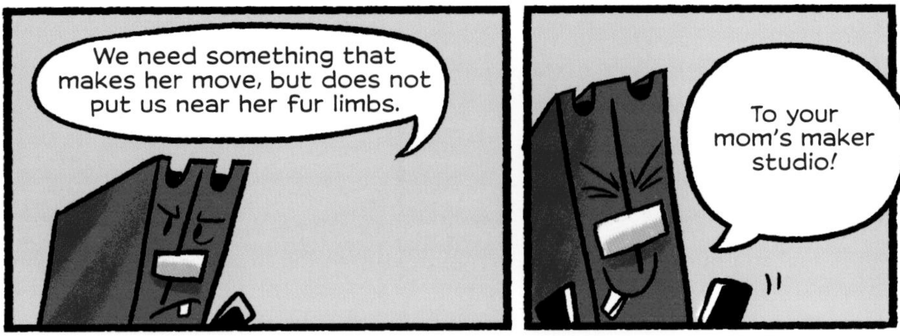
We need something that makes her move, but does not put us near her fur limbs.
To your mom's maker studio!

Your mom really likes collecting parts. Being a maker is in your circuits! If you were not lucky enough to have a parent maker, you could easily buy all these items online in stores like adafruit.com and sparkfun.com.

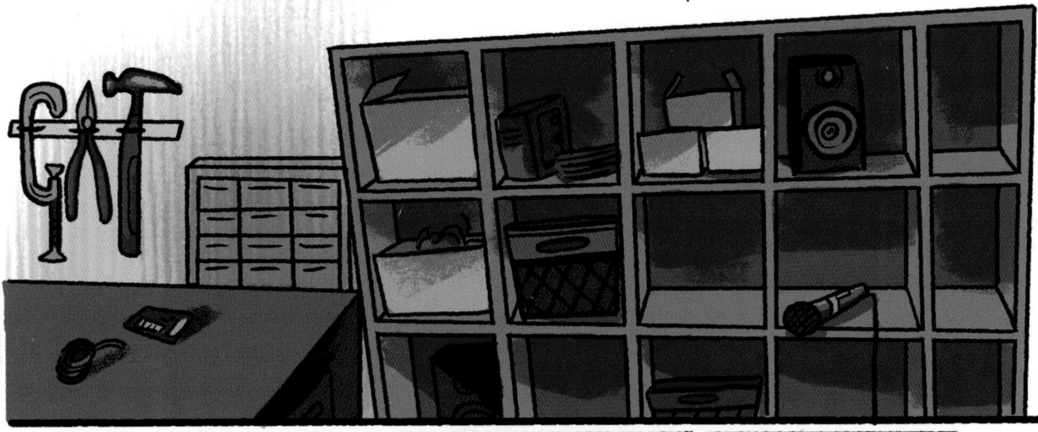

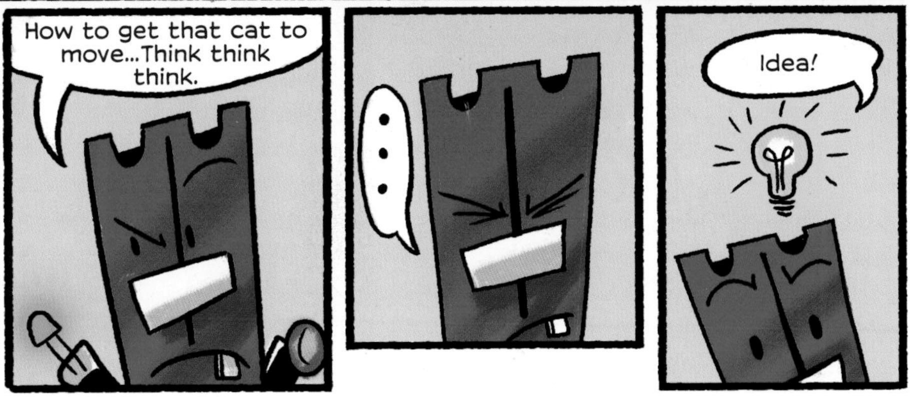
How to get that cat to move...Think think think.
...
Idea!

KITTY DISTRACTY THROWIES

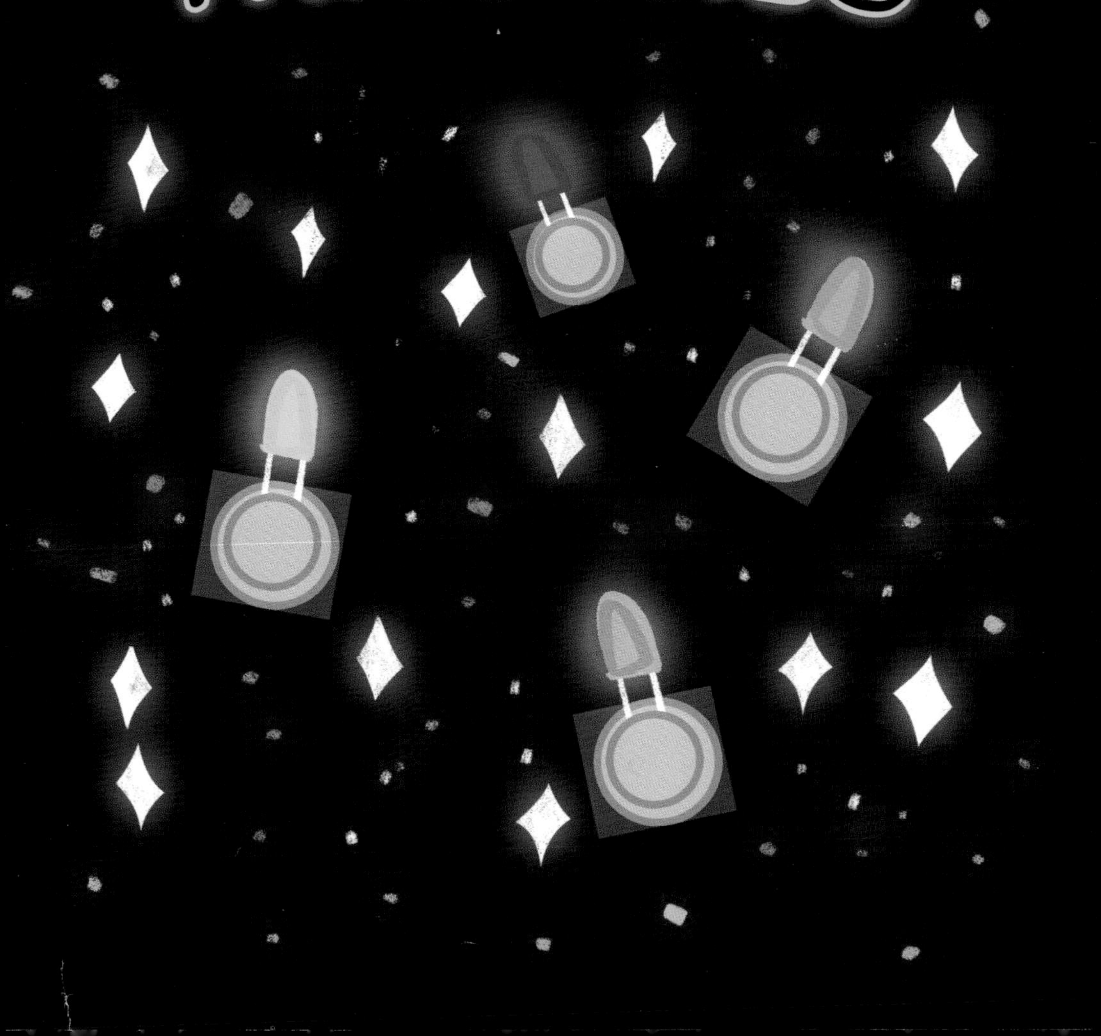

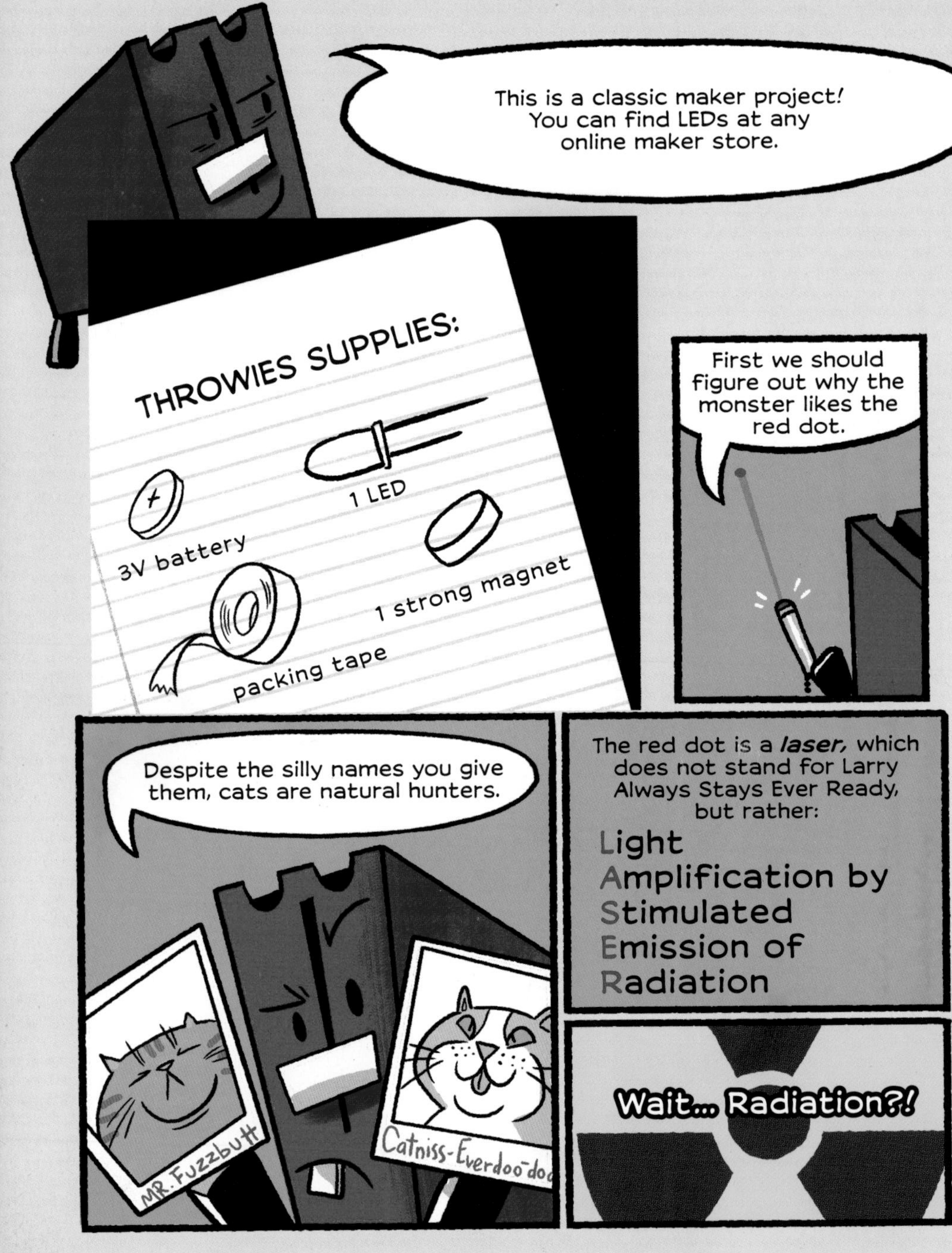

This is a classic maker project! You can find LEDs at any online maker store.
THROWIES SUPPLIES:
1 LED
3V battery
1 strong magnet
packing tape
First we should figure out why the monster likes the red dot.
Despite the silly names you give them, cats are natural hunters.
MR. Fuzzbutt
Catniss-Everdoo-doo
The red dot is a *laser,* which does not stand for Larry Always Stays Ever Ready, but rather:
Light
Amplification by
Stimulated
Emission of
Radiation
Wait... Radiation?!

Do not worry, it is not *that* kind of radiation. This kind is emitted in the form of light!

How does light work? Well, everything in the world is made up of atoms.

Here is a diagram of an atom.

Hey, I'm Adam.

I said *atom.*

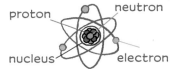

proton

neutron

nucleus

electron

Atoms are *tiny* and made up of protons, which have a positive charge, electrons, which have a negative charge, and neutrons, which are neutral.

When you expose an atom to electricity it causes the electrons to get excited and move to higher energy orbits. *But* they would rather stay at their original state (or "ground state").

Guys, I'm tired. Can I just go home?

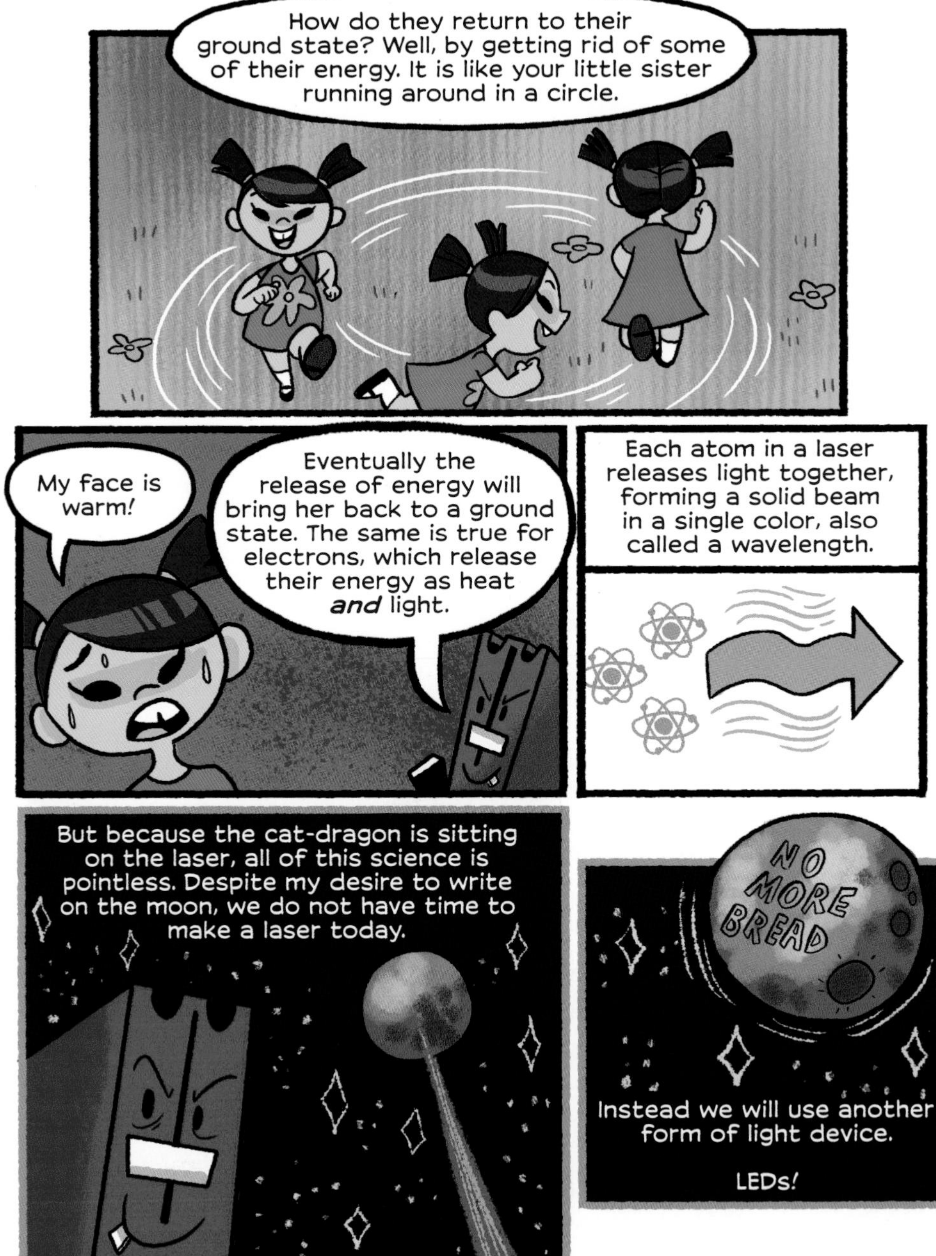
How do they return to their ground state? Well, by getting rid of some of their energy. It is like your little sister running around in a circle.
My face is warm!
Eventually the release of energy will bring her back to a ground state. The same is true for electrons, which release their energy as heat *and* light.
Each atom in a laser releases light together, forming a solid beam in a single color, also called a wavelength.
But because the cat-dragon is sitting on the laser, all of this science is pointless. Despite my desire to write on the moon, we do not have time to make a laser today.
NO MORE BREAD
Instead we will use another form of light device.
LEDs!

LED is short for
light-emitting diode.

It has two "leads," which
are wire sticks coming out
of its behind.

One lead is negative and
one is positive. How can
you tell the difference?

STEP 1. Take your 3V coin battery and
touch the long lead of the LED to the
positive side of the battery marked
with a + symbol. Now do the same for
the negative side and shorter lead.

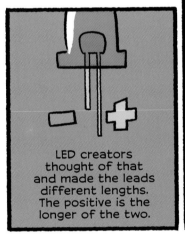

LED creators
thought of that
and made the leads
different lengths.
The positive is the
longer of the two.

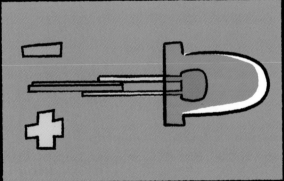

Your light should light up! If it does not,
perhaps you have your battery backward. Flip it!

Step 2. Use the packing tape to stick the LED in place on the battery. Wrap it around the battery a few times.

Step 3. Take a strong magnet and place it on top of the tape, battery, and LED leads.

Step 4. Wrap the tape around it a few more times to make it really secure.

Step 5. Now throw the LED at something metal* and watch the cat-monster become *transfixed!*

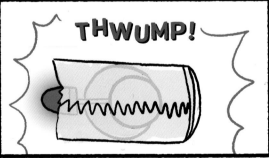

THWUMP!

*Not all metal is magnetic. Metals with iron in them, like steel, will attract a magnet, but aluminum and brass will not.

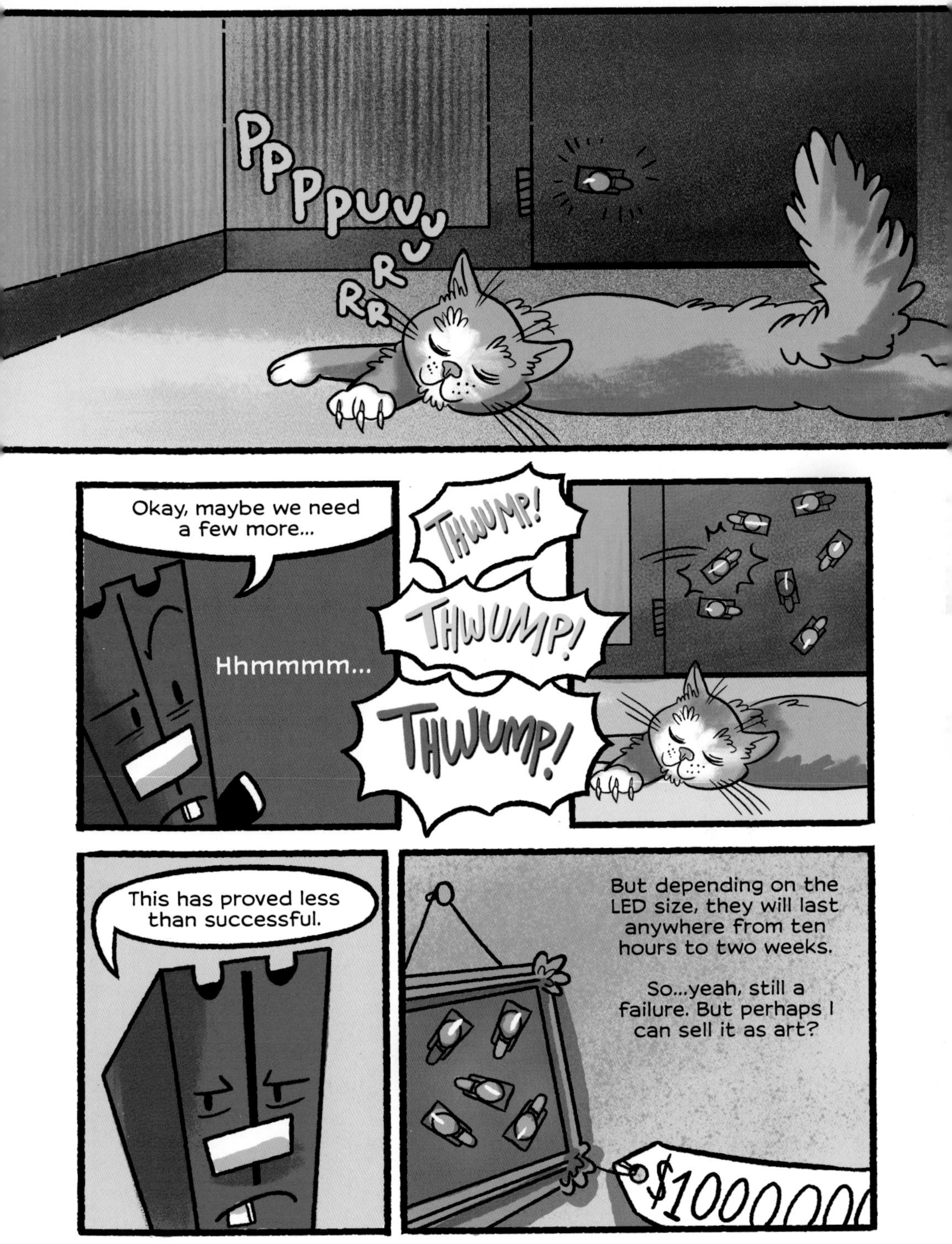
PPPPUUUURRRR
Okay, maybe we need a few more...
Hhmmmm...
THWUMP!
THWUMP!
THWUMP!
This has proved less than successful.
But depending on the LED size, they will last anywhere from ten hours to two weeks.
So...yeah, still a failure. But perhaps I can sell it as art?
$1000000

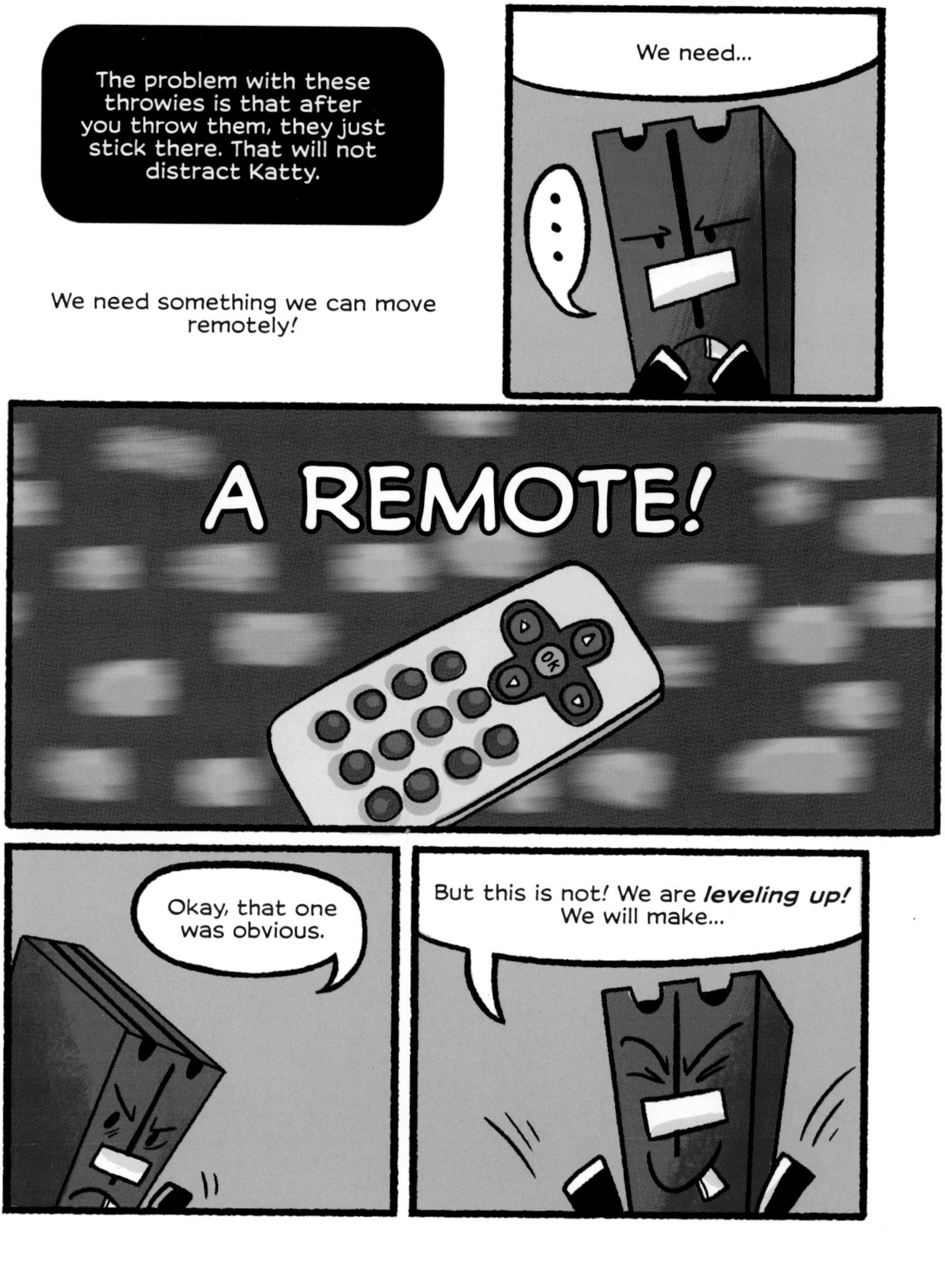
The problem with these throwies is that after you throw them, they just stick there. That will not distract Katty.
We need something we can move remotely!
We need...
...
A REMOTE!
OK
Okay, that one was obvious.
But this is not! We are ***leveling up!*** We will make...

THE CARBOT

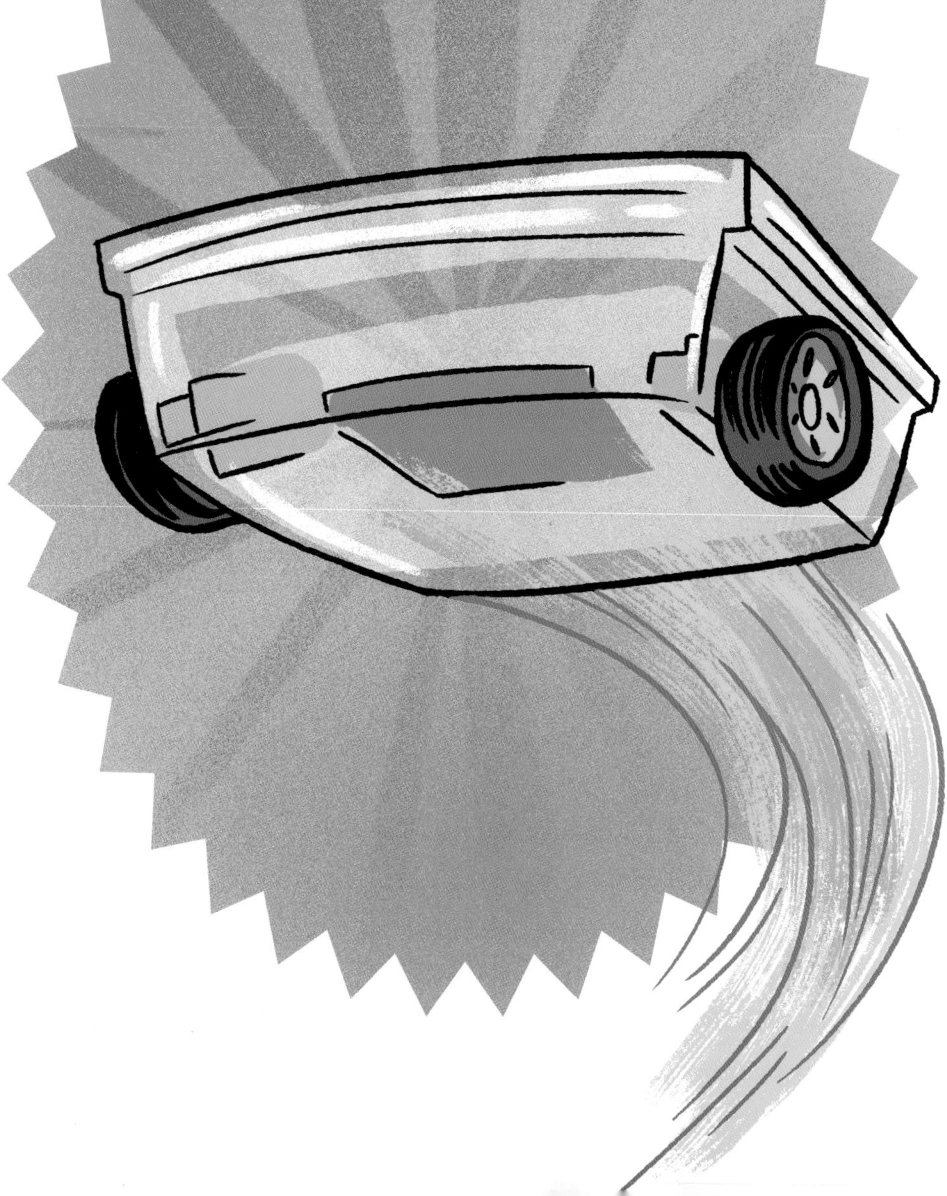

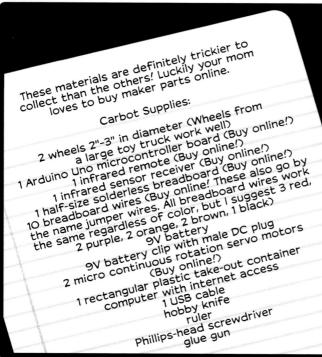

These materials are definitely trickier to collect than the others! Luckily your mom loves to buy maker parts online.

Carbot Supplies:

2 wheels 2"–3" in diameter (Wheels from a large toy truck work well)
1 Arduino Uno microcontroller board (Buy online!)
1 infrared remote (Buy online!)
1 infrared sensor receiver (Buy online!)
1 half-size solderless breadboard (Buy online!)
10 breadboard wires (Buy online! These also go by the name jumper wires. All breadboard wires work the same regardless of color, but I suggest 3 red, 2 purple, 2 orange, 2 brown, 1 black)
9V battery
9V battery clip with male DC plug
2 micro continuous rotation servo motors (Buy online!)
1 rectangular plastic take-out container
computer with internet access
1 USB cable
hobby knife
ruler
Phillips-head screwdriver
glue gun

First we need to find a pair of wheels. I bet your brother has something we can "borrow." I used air quotes. Did you hear them? It means we are going to destroy it!

Spider. So. Big.

This will do.

When taking apart anything, you should always wear goggles. You never know what may jump out from inside. Like a spring or some wires or...

CREEEEEK

...half a peanut butter and jelly sandwich. Ew.

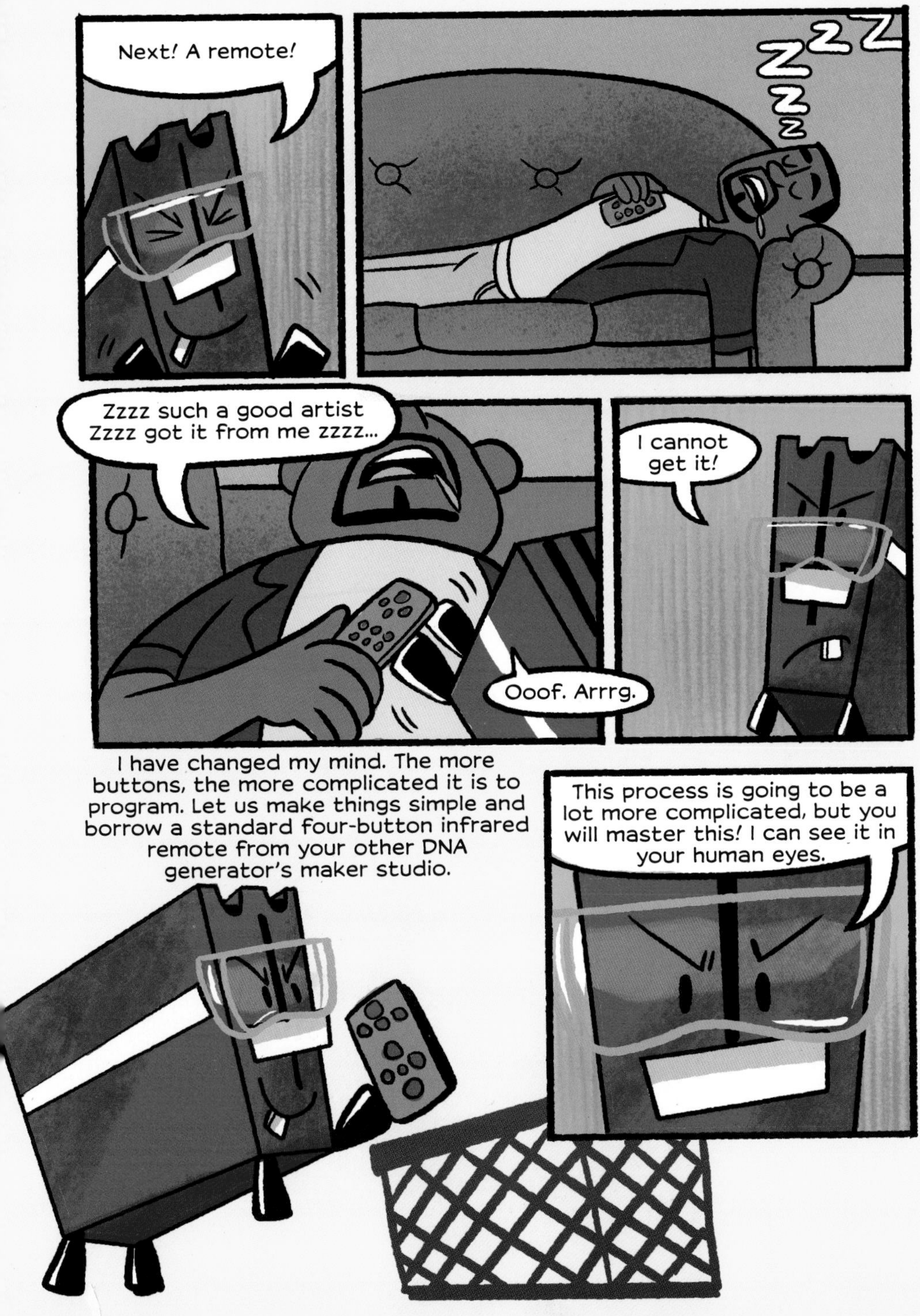
Next! A remote!
ZZZZZZ
Zzzz such a good artist Zzzz got it from me zzzz...
Ooof. Arrrg.
I cannot get it!
I have changed my mind. The more buttons, the more complicated it is to program. Let us make things simple and borrow a standard four-button infrared remote from your other DNA generator's maker studio.
This process is going to be a lot more complicated, but you will master this! I can see it in your human eyes.

Now we need a computer. I am sure your snoring father will not mind if we borrow his laptop.

ARDUINO

Step 1. Go to arduino.cc and download the latest version of the free Arduino software. Yes, *free!*

A lot of makers believe that sharing information and knowledge helps make the world a better place. It is called open source, meaning you are free to use their software and codes to play, modify, and build your own creations.

So, what is this bizarrely named Arduino thing?

Arduino is a computer program that responds to a special language. Imagine you lived in a smart home and someone changed the system's language to Dutch.

Alberta! Give me the weather!

Hallo, broodrooster. Vandaag is het weer toasty. Ik heb een grap gemaakt. Haha.

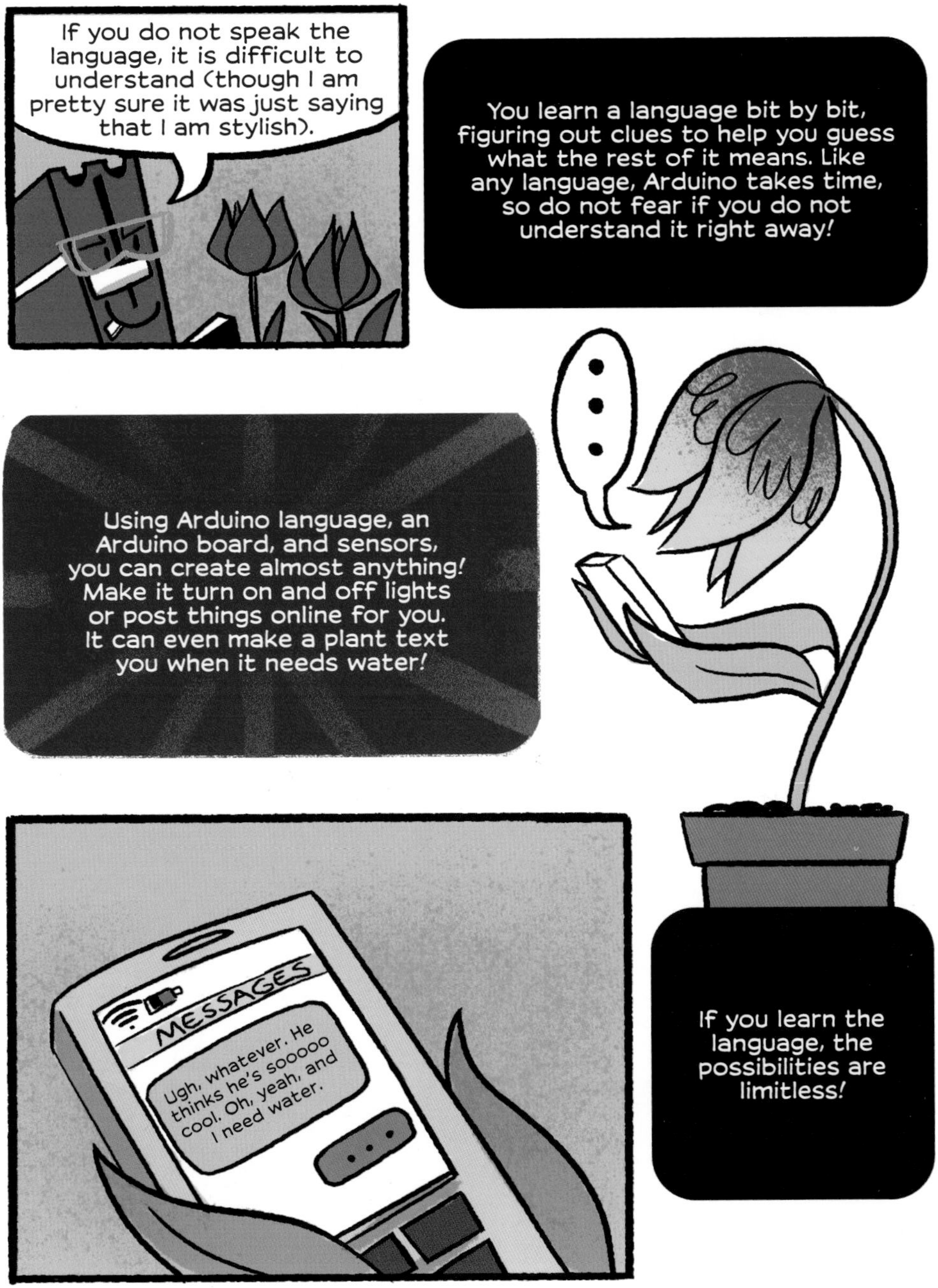
If you do not speak the language, it is difficult to understand (though I am pretty sure it was just saying that I am stylish).
You learn a language bit by bit, figuring out clues to help you guess what the rest of it means. Like any language, Arduino takes time, so do not fear if you do not understand it right away!
Using Arduino language, an Arduino board, and sensors, you can create almost anything! Make it turn on and off lights or post things online for you. It can even make a plant text you when it needs water!
MESSAGES
Ugh, whatever. He thinks he's sooooo cool. Oh, yeah, and I need water.
If you learn the language, the possibilities are limitless!

Arduino is not the only coding language used for robots, but many makers, like your mother, love it for its simplicity and possibilities.

There are many types of Arduino controllers. My personal favorite is the Arduino Uno. Let us use that! Take your USB cord. Connect one end to your Uno and plug the other into your computer.

Once you plug it in, electricity goes from your computer to the board, making two lights turn on: a green power light and a yellow LED marked by the letter "L" on the board.

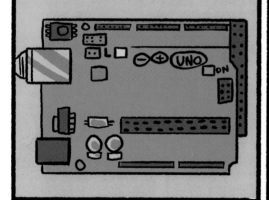

Now it is time to work with your first code! Go to your computer and start up the Arduino software you downloaded.

I am so proud of you.

Step 2. Go to the FILE menu at the top of your screen and click on the EXAMPLES and then on O1.BASICS, selecting the Blink code. It will look like this:

```
/*
  Blink
  Turns on an LED on for one second, then off
for one second, on repeat.

Most Arduinos have an on-board LED you can control. On the UNO, MEGA
and ZERO it is attached to digital pin 13, on MKR1000 on pin 6. LED_
BUILTIN is set to the correct LED pin independent of which board is used.
If you want to know what pin the on-board LED is connected to on your
Arduino model, check the Technical Specs of your board at:
https://www.arduino.cc/en/Main/Products

modified 8 May 2014
by Scott Fitzgerald
modified 2 Sep 2016
by Arturo Guadalupi
modified 8 Sep 2016
by Colby Newman

This example code is in the public domain.

https://www.arduino.cc/en/Tutorial/Blink

*/

// the setup function runs once when you press reset or power the board
void setup() {
    // initialize digital pin LED_BUILTIN as an output.
    pinMode(LED_BUILTIN, OUTPUT);
}

// the loop function runs over and over again forever
void loop() {
    digitalWrite(LED_BUILTIN, HIGH);  // turn the LED on (HIGH is the voltage level)
    delay(1000);                      // wait for a second
    digitalWrite(LED_BUILTIN, LOW);   // turn the LED off by making the voltage LOW
    delay(1000);                      // wait for a second
}
```

Let us take a closer look at this code so you can see how it works.
But do not worry if you are not fluent in Arduino by the end—
you do not need to be a fluent coder to build the Carbot.

Aaaah! It is terrifying! So many strange words! So many strange symbols!

But it is no different than any other language. You just need to learn how to read it.

Salut

Hi

Hei

Hallo

Hola

First part! See these two symbols I am holding? Anything between these symbols will be plain English, often explaining what the code does and sometimes giving some tips.

Rrero!

If you were a detective with a talking dog, this would be your first clue to how to read the code.

```
// initialize digital pin LED_BUILTIN as an output.
  pinMode(LED_BUILTIN, OUTPUT);
}
```

Definitely looks more confusing, but it is saying:

Next part!

// the setup function runs once when you press reset or power the board

void setup() {

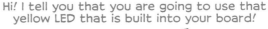

≥ LED_BUILTIN ≤

Hi! I tell you that you are going to use that yellow LED that is built into your board!

≥ OUTPUT ≤

And I'm just saying that instead of waiting for something like a sensor to *give* us input, we are going to send information out to the LED.

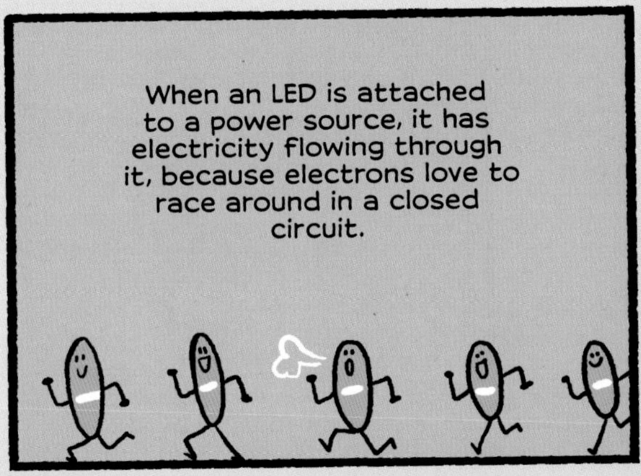
When an LED is attached to a power source, it has electricity flowing through it, because electrons love to race around in a closed circuit.

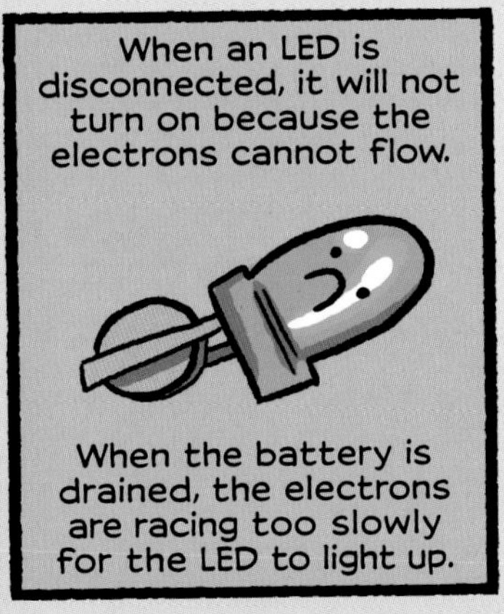
When an LED is disconnected, it will not turn on because the electrons cannot flow.
When the battery is drained, the electrons are racing too slowly for the LED to light up.

Let us look at the next part of the code. To set the LED to on or off, we make the voltage high or low. "Low" does not allow electrons to race through the circuit quickly enough to turn the LED on.

```
// the loop function runs over and over again forever
void loop() {
digitalWrite(LED_BUILTIN, HIGH); // turn the LED on (HIGH is the voltage level)
delay(1000);                     // wait for a second
digitalWrite(LED_BUILTIN, LOW); // turn the LED off by making the voltage LOW
delay(1000);                     // wait for a second
}
```

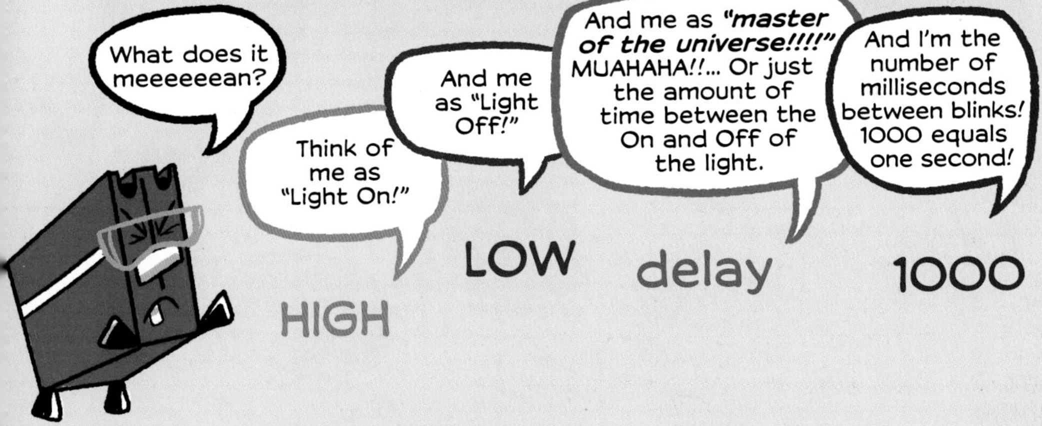
What does it meeeeeean?
Think of me as "Light On!"
HIGH
And me as "Light Off!"
LOW
And me as *"master of the universe!!!!"* MUAHAHA!!... Or just the amount of time between the On and Off of the light.
delay
And I'm the number of milliseconds between blinks! 1000 equals one second!
1000

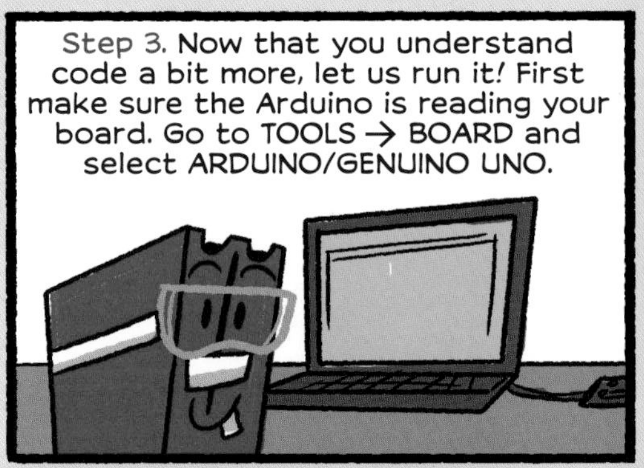
Step 3. Now that you understand code a bit more, let us run it! First make sure the Arduino is reading your board. Go to TOOLS → BOARD and select ARDUINO/GENUINO UNO.

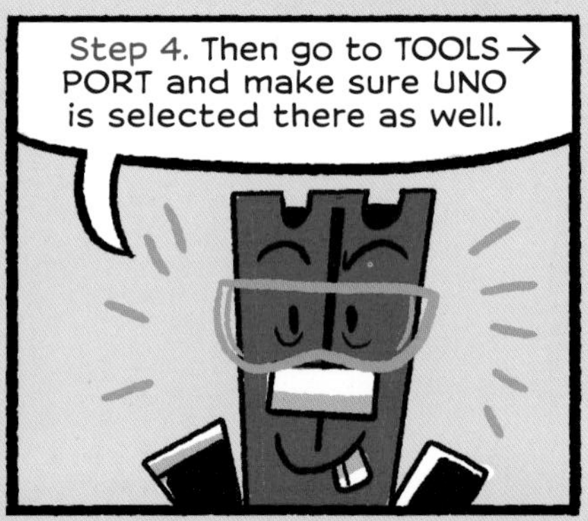
Step 4. Then go to TOOLS → PORT and make sure UNO is selected there as well.

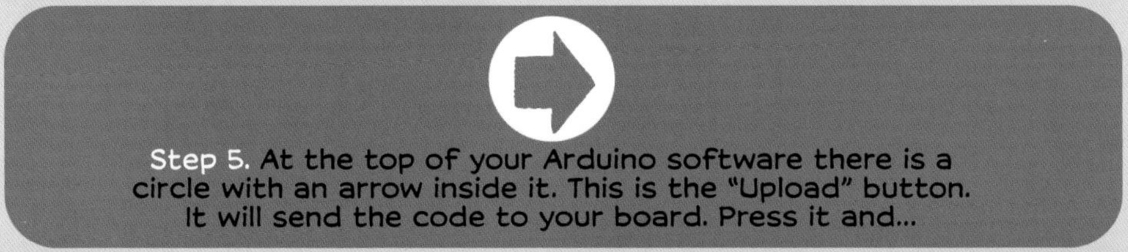
Step 5. At the top of your Arduino software there is a circle with an arrow inside it. This is the "Upload" button. It will send the code to your board. Press it and...

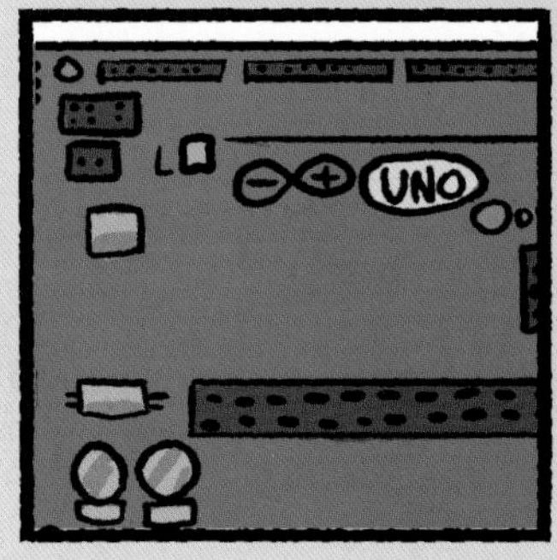
UNO

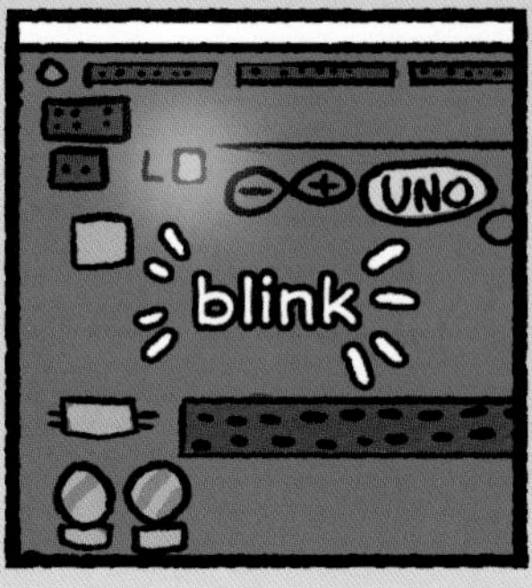
UNO
blink

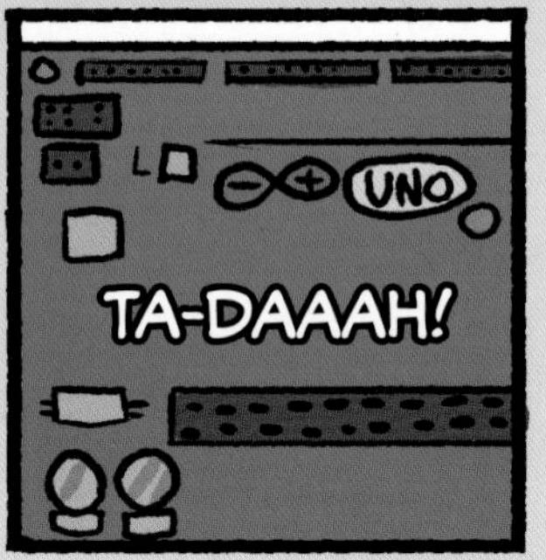
UNO
TA-DAAAH!

Play with the code!

Change 1000 time delay to 5000 and reupload it to your board to sloooow it down to a sloth's pace, only turning on and off every 5 seconds.

Or change the 1000 to 250, reupload it, and watch it blink faster than your mom when her plastic eye lens is bothering her.

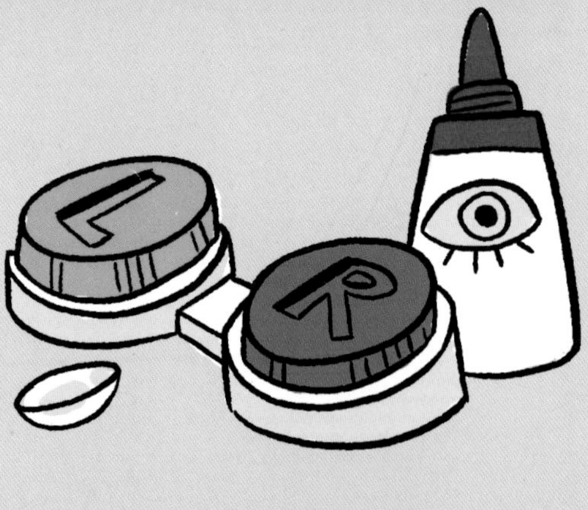

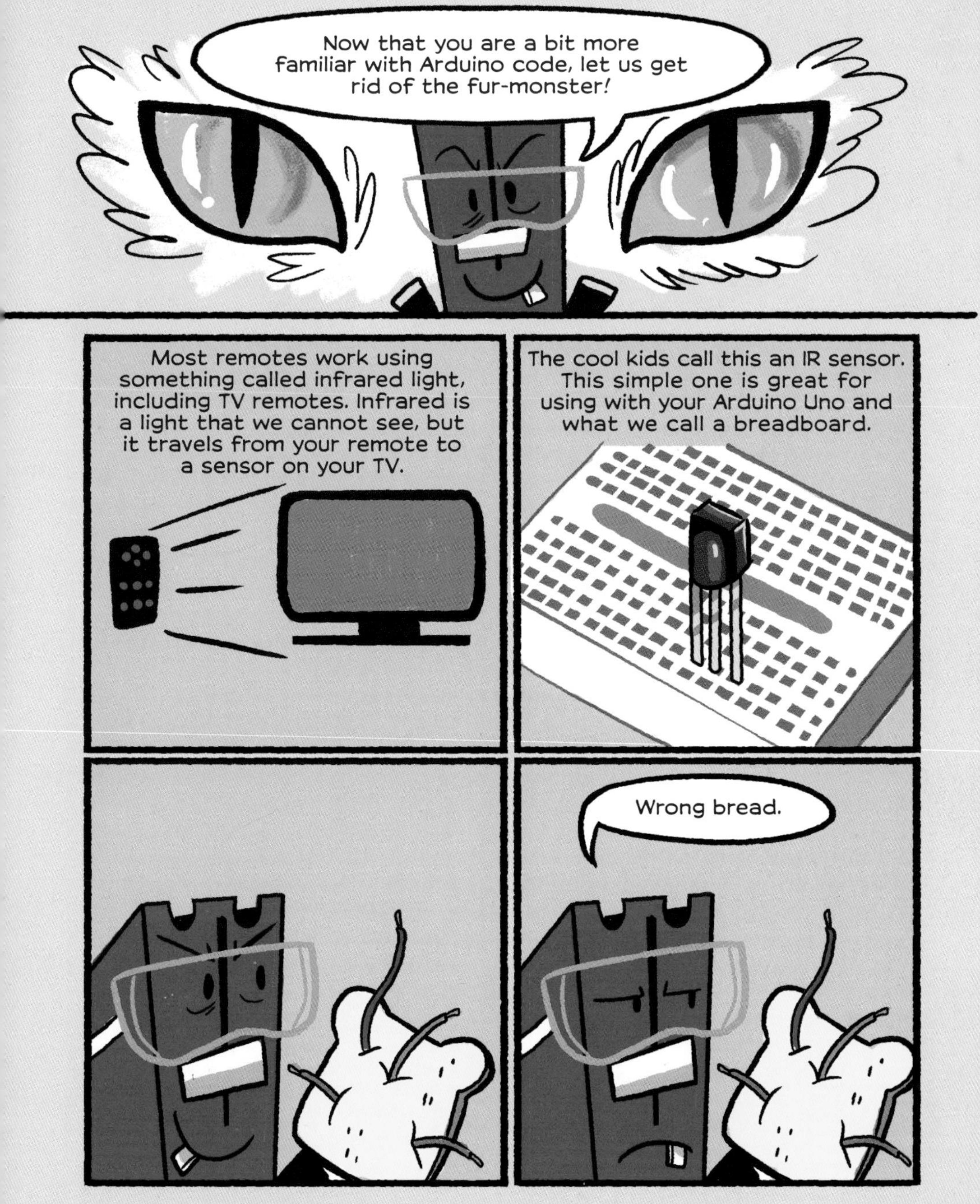
Now that you are a bit more familiar with Arduino code, let us get rid of the fur-monster!
Most remotes work using something called infrared light, including TV remotes. Infrared is a light that we cannot see, but it travels from your remote to a sensor on your TV.
The cool kids call this an IR sensor. This simple one is great for using with your Arduino Uno and what we call a breadboard.
Wrong bread.

Breadboards were invented in the 1960s.

Before that people made complicated "wire wraps" to test out their circuits.

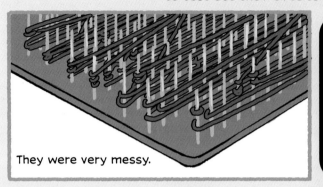

They were very messy.

A breadboard is a prototyping tool— it is used to test your designs before deciding on a final version. It gives you room to experiment and solve problems!

The red rows marked + are for connecting up a power wire from a power supply such as a battery. The blue rows marked with a - are for connecting the power supply's ground. These are the positive and negative rails. There are two sets of power/ground rows on a solderless breadboard so they can easily be accessed from anywhere on the breadboard.

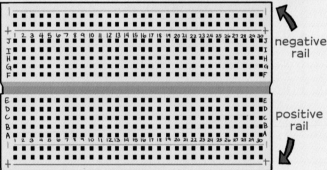

negative rail

positive rail

There are two columns of five pinholes in the middle of the breadboard. Under each row of holes are metal strips called terminal strips. These, along with breadboard wires (also known as jumper wires), help you make bigger, more complicated circuits.

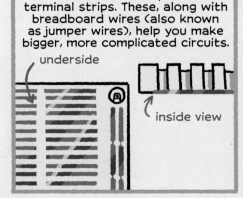

underside

inside view

The terminal strips connect currents, so if you have the positive rail connected to the power on the Arduino board, anything else you connect with that + row will get some of that power!

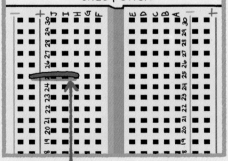

breadboard wire

STEP 6. Important! Unplug your USB cable! You do not want to ever add components to your board when electricity is still going through it!

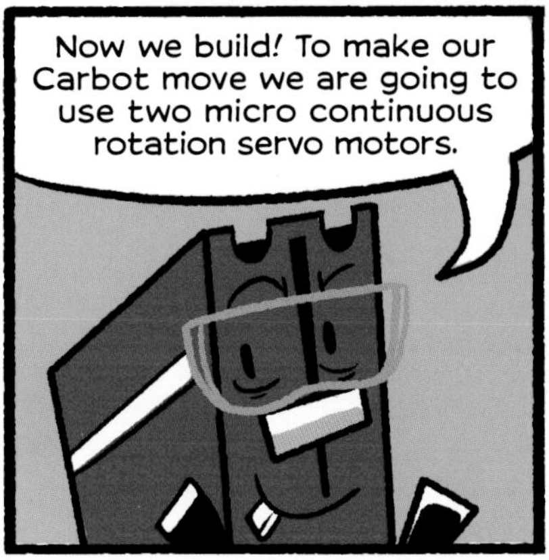

Now we build! To make our Carbot move we are going to use two micro continuous rotation servo motors.

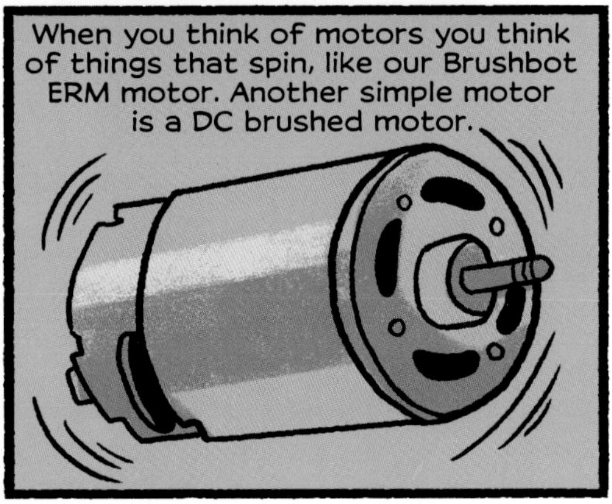

When you think of motors you think of things that spin, like our Brushbot ERM motor. Another simple motor is a DC brushed motor.

The casing of a DC motor holds two permanent curved magnets in place. In the middle, there are wires wound around a piece of metal. Current flows through the wires, which causes the piece of metal to become a temporary magnet, which attracts and repels the permanent magnets, making the shaft spin.

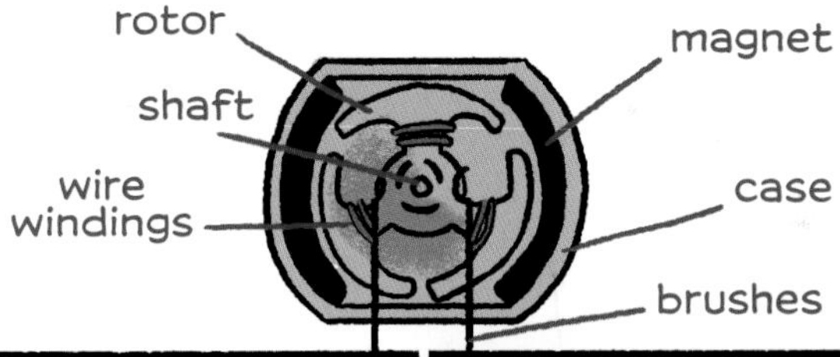

rotor
shaft
wire windings
magnet
case
brushes

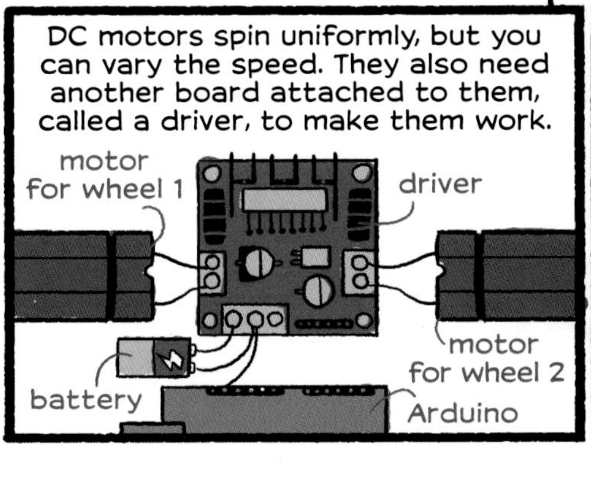

DC motors spin uniformly, but you can vary the speed. They also need another board attached to them, called a driver, to make them work.
motor for wheel 1
driver
motor for wheel 2
battery
Arduino

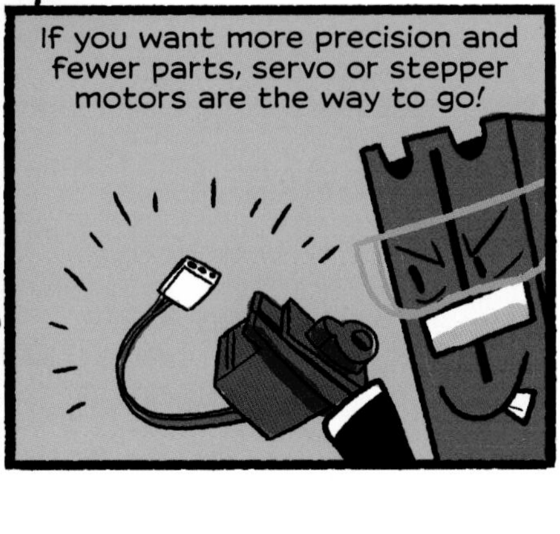

If you want more precision and fewer parts, servo or stepper motors are the way to go!

Servo motors are DC motors with extra strength and precision. Inside a servo is a DC motor as well as a set of gears.

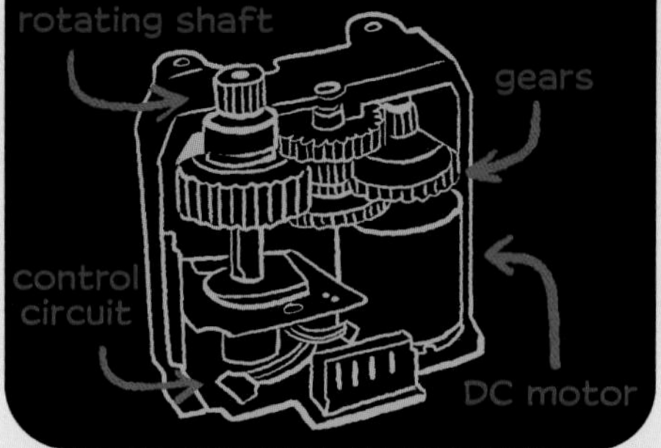

rotating shaft

gears

control circuit

DC motor

When particular electrical pulses are sent to the servo, it will turn to a particular position. So you can give your robot precise instructions on how you want it to move.

Like the exact angle a robot should move its arm! Which is better than a robot that can only spin them.

Your tea.

Your tea.

Step 7. Take a servo and measure the length and width of the front side (not including the mounting tabs). On the side of the container, along the bottom edge and towards the back, use a hobby knife to carefully cut a rectangular hole using your measurements.

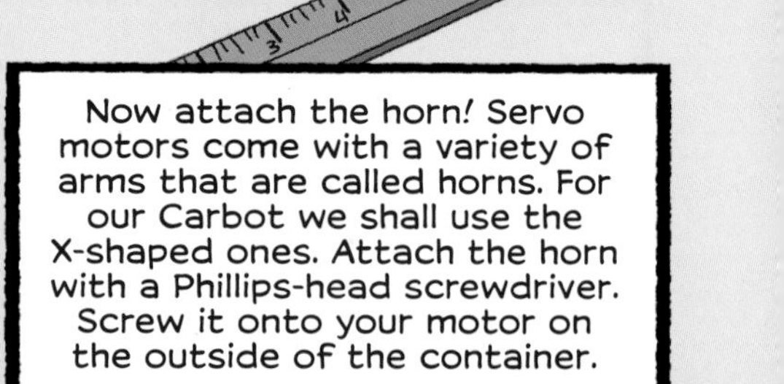

mounting tab

Put your servo inside the container and push the front of it out through the hole. The mounting tabs will keep it from falling out through the hole. Get your handy glue gun and put a dab of glue where each mounting tab meets the plastic container, and stick the servo in place.

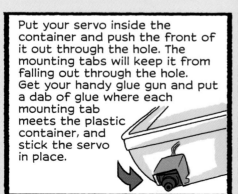

Now attach the horn! Servo motors come with a variety of arms that are called horns. For our Carbot we shall use the X-shaped ones. Attach the horn with a Phillips-head screwdriver. Screw it onto your motor on the outside of the container.

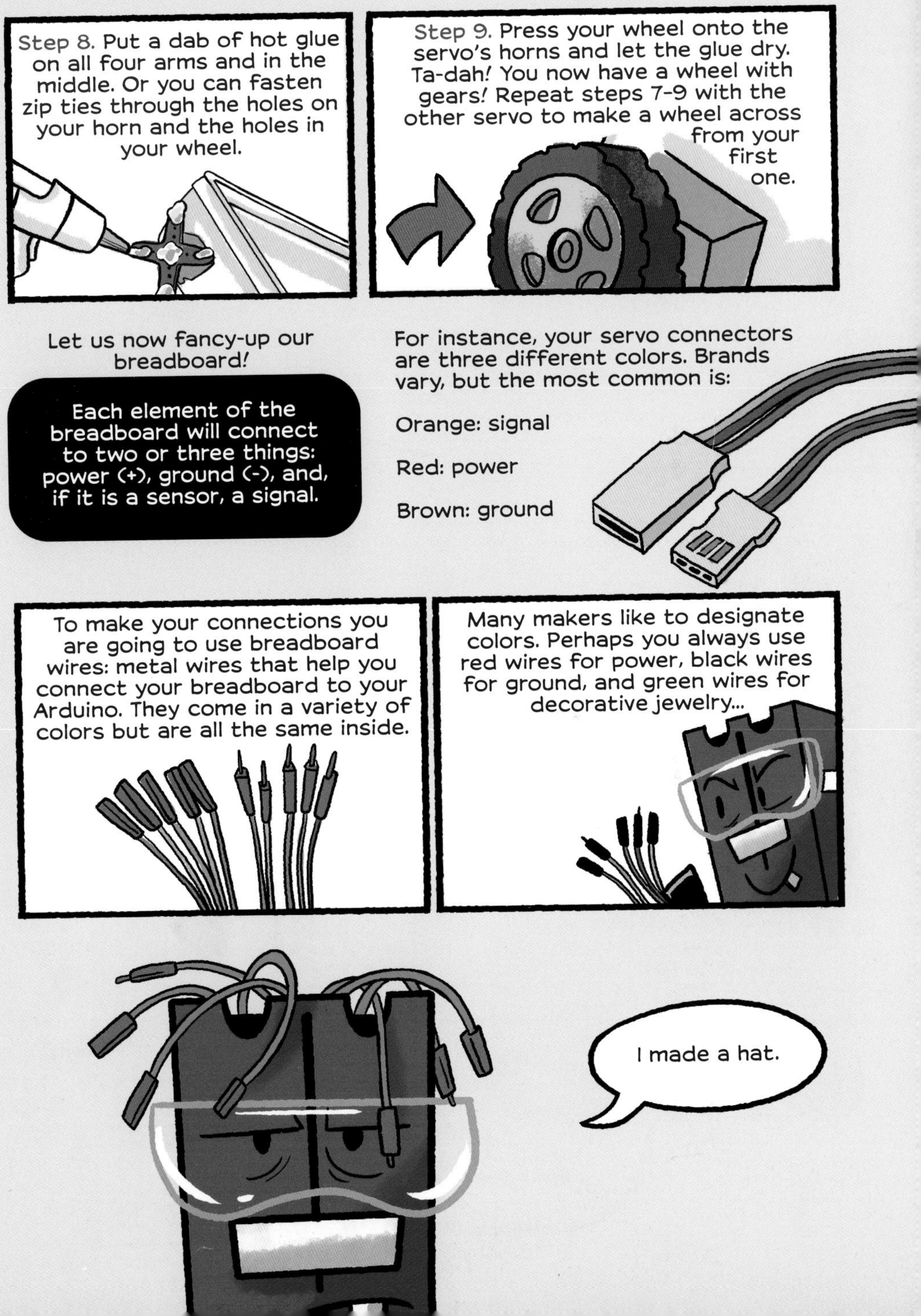
Step 8. Put a dab of hot glue on all four arms and in the middle. Or you can fasten zip ties through the holes on your horn and the holes in your wheel.
Step 9. Press your wheel onto the servo's horns and let the glue dry. Ta-dah! You now have a wheel with gears! Repeat steps 7–9 with the other servo to make a wheel across from your first one.
Let us now fancy-up our breadboard!
Each element of the breadboard will connect to two or three things: power (+), ground (-), and, if it is a sensor, a signal.
For instance, your servo connectors are three different colors. Brands vary, but the most common is:
Orange: signal
Red: power
Brown: ground
To make your connections you are going to use breadboard wires: metal wires that help you connect your breadboard to your Arduino. They come in a variety of colors but are all the same inside.
Many makers like to designate colors. Perhaps you always use red wires for power, black wires for ground, and green wires for decorative jewelry...
I made a hat.

Step 10. Let us make some connections! Here are some tips for following the rules below. The breadboard wire colors in these instructions are a suggestion. Any color will work the same. If an instruction calls for a wire to be connected to +, connect it to a pin in the positive rail of your breadboard. (You can use any pin in the positive rail.)

If an instruction calls for a wire to be connected to -, connect it to a pin in the negative rail of your breadboard. (You can use any pin in the negative rail.)

If an instruction calls for you to connect a wire to a number on your breadboard, you can use any pin in that numbered row.

A. Connect a red wire from + on the breadboard to 5V on the Arduino.

B. Connect a black wire from - on the breadboard to GND on the Arduino.

C. Plug one servo connector into the holes in rows 8-9-10 (orange into 8, red into 9, and brown into 10). Plug the other servo connector into 16-17-18 (orange into 16, red into 17, and brown into 18).

D. The brown ground wires on both servo connectors need to connect to the ground rail on the breadboard. So connect a brown wire from 10 to - and from 18 to -.

E. The red power wires on each servo connector need to connect to the positive rail. So connect a red wire from 9 to + and from 17 to +.

F. Connect an orange wire from 8 on the breadboard to 6 on Arduino, and from 16 on the breadboard to 7 on Arduino.

G. With the rounded part of your IR receiver facing forward, the first pin is "signal," the middle pin is "ground," and the final pin is "power." Connect the IR receiver to your breadboard: signal pin into hole 1, ground pin into hole 2, power into hole 3. Connect a purple wire from 1 on the breadboard to 11 on the Arduino, a brown wire from 2 to -, and a red wire from 3 to +.

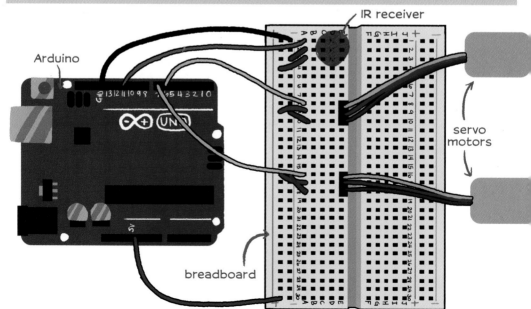

IR receiver

Arduino

servo motors

breadboard

CODE TIME!

Some sensors and Arduino add-ons require a bit more information given to your Arduino program to make them run. Just like humans, Arduinos can use libraries!

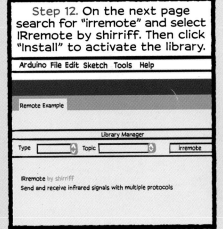

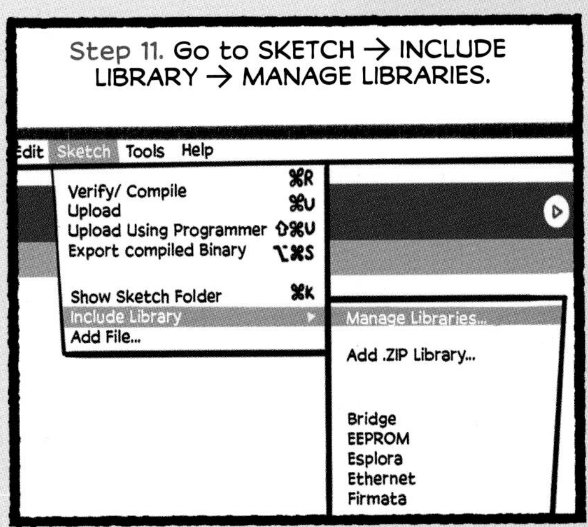

Step 11. Go to SKETCH → INCLUDE LIBRARY → MANAGE LIBRARIES.

Edit	Sketch	Tools	Help	
	Verify/ Compile		⌘R	
	Upload		⌘U	
	Upload Using Programmer		⇧⌘U	
	Export compiled Binary		⌥⌘S	
	Show Sketch Folder		⌘k	
	Include Library	▶	Manage Libraries...	
	Add File...		Add .ZIP Library...	
			Bridge	
			EEPROM	
			Esplora	
			Ethernet	
			Firmata	

Step 12. On the next page search for "irremote" and select IRremote by shirriff. Then click "Install" to activate the library.

Arduino File Edit Sketch Tools Help

Remote Example

Library Manager

Type [   ] Topic [   ]   irremote

IRremote by shirriff
Send and receive infrared signals with multiple protocols

Step 13. Once you have activated that library, it's time to download the fancy code. Head to github.com/colleenaf/carbot and download it.

```
// Remote control bot
// based on the Randy Sarafan's telepresence robot test code:

//https://www.instructables.com/id/Telepresence-Robot-Basic-Platform-Part-1/#step18
// combined with example IR remote code -- your remote codes may vary

#include <Servo.h>
#include <IRremote.h>

IRrecv irrecv(11);
decode_results results;

// Tell the Arduino there are to continuous servos
Servo ContinuousServo1;
Servo ContinuousServo2;

void setup() {

  // Attach the continuous servos to pins 6 and 7
  ContinuousServo1.attach(6);
  ContinuousServo2.attach(7);

  Serial.begin(9600);
  irrecv.enableIRIn();

  // Start the continuous servos in a paused position
  // if they continue to spin slightly,
  // change these numbers until they stop
  ContinuousServo1.write(94);
  ContinuousServo2.write(94);
}

void loop() {
  // Start the continuous servos in a paused position
  // if they continue to spin slightly, change these numbers until they stop
  ContinuousServo1.write(94);
  ContinuousServo2.write(94);

  if (irrecv.decode(&results)){
    Serial.println(results.value, HEX);
    switch(results.value){ //switches routines based on the IR remote input
    //If 0xFD609F is selected turn right and pause for a second
    case 0xFD609F:
       Serial.println("RIGHT");
       ContinuousServo1.write(104);
       ContinuousServo2.write(104);
       delay(500);
       break;

    //If 0xFD20DF is selected turn left and pause for a second
    case 0xFD20DF:
       Serial.println("LEFT");
       ContinuousServo1.write(84);
       ContinuousServo2.write(84);
       delay(500);
       break;

    //If 0xFD807F is selected go forward and pause for a second
    case 0xFD807F:
       Serial.println("FORWARD");
       ContinuousServo1.write(84);
       ContinuousServo2.write(104);
       delay(500);
       break;

    //If 0xFD906F is selected go backward and pause for a second
    case 0xFD906F:
       Serial.println("BACKWARD");
       ContinuousServo1.write(104);
       ContinuousServo2.write(84);
       delay(500);
       break;
    }
    irrecv.resume(); // Receive the next value
  }
  // Pause for a millisecond for stability of the code
  delay(1);
}
```

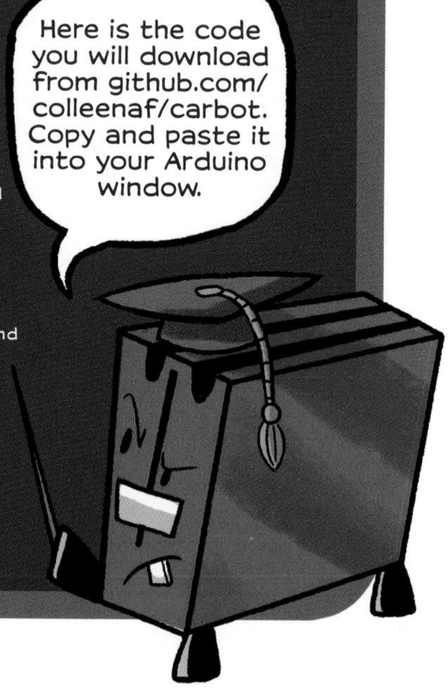
Here is the code you will download from github.com/colleenaf/carbot. Copy and paste it into your Arduino window.

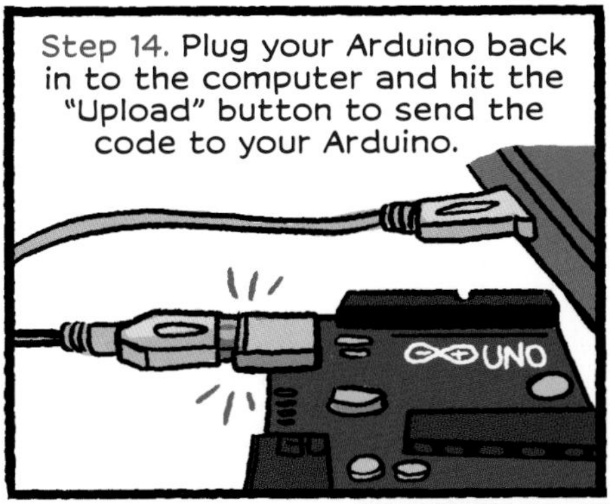
Step 14. Plug your Arduino back in to the computer and hit the "Upload" button to send the code to your Arduino.
UNO

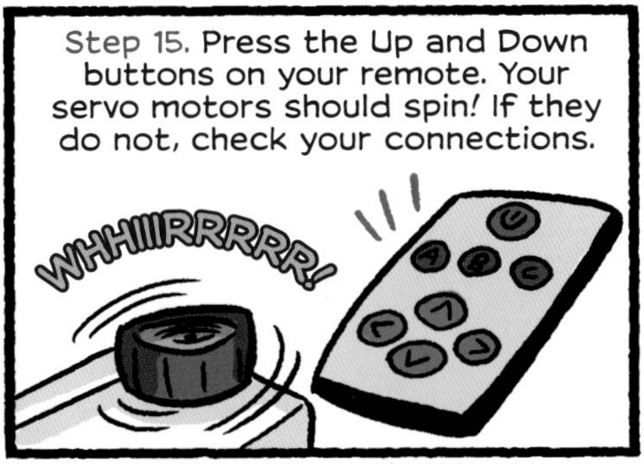
Step 15. Press the Up and Down buttons on your remote. Your servo motors should spin! If they do not, check your connections.
WHHIIIRRRRR!

Another good problem-solving tool is at the upper right of your Arduino window. It is labeled Serial Monitor.

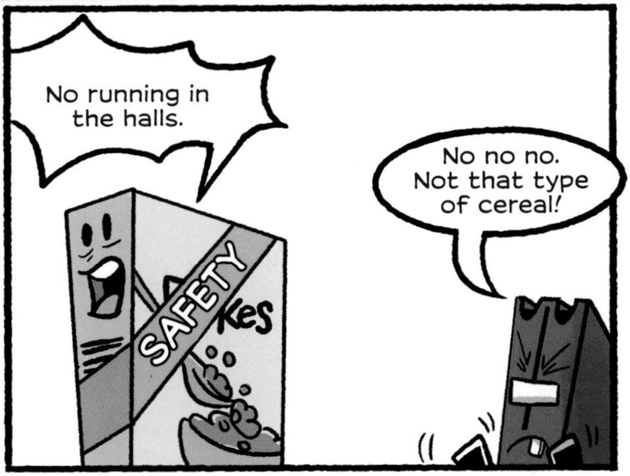
No running in the halls.
No no no. Not that type of cereal!
SAFETY

This tool shows you the series of things your sensor is reading. Or if it is not connected properly, the Serial Monitor will let you know and its errors will give you suggestions of what the connection or code problems may be.

If it is working correctly you should see something like this as you press each button.

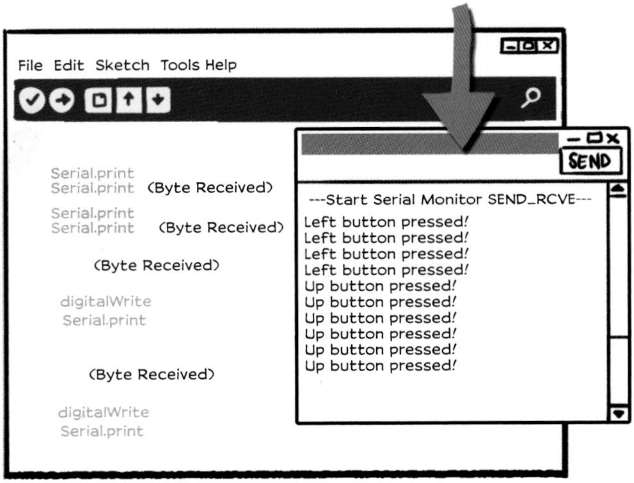
File Edit Sketch Tools Help
Serial.print
Serial.print (Byte Received)
Serial.print
Serial.print (Byte Received)
(Byte Received)
digitalWrite
Serial.print
(Byte Received)
digitalWrite
Serial.print
SEND
---Start Serial Monitor SEND_RCVE---
Left button pressed!
Left button pressed!
Left button pressed!
Left button pressed!
Up button pressed!
Up button pressed!
Up button pressed!
Up button pressed!
Up button pressed!
Up button pressed!

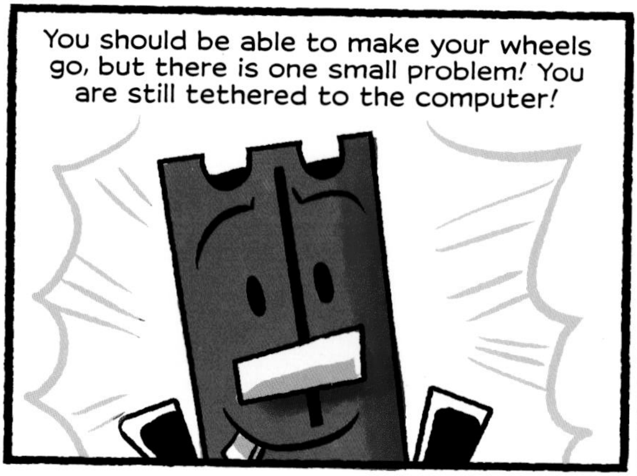
You should be able to make your wheels go, but there is one small problem! You are still tethered to the computer!

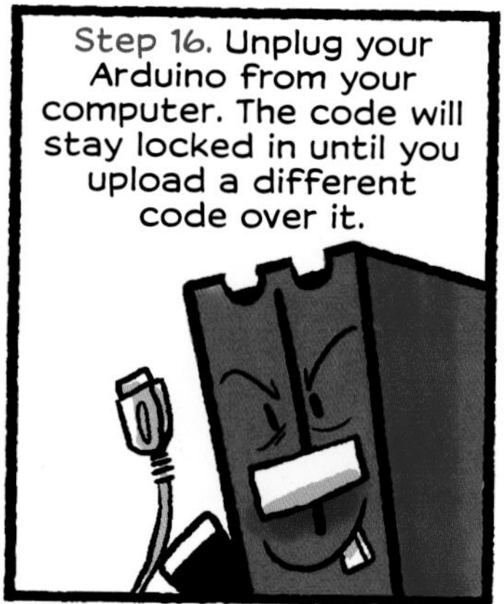
Step 16. Unplug your Arduino from your computer. The code will stay locked in until you upload a different code over it.

Step 17. Place the components into the container holding them in place with double-sided tape.

Make ***sure*** your wires are far away from your spinning motors.

If you would like your Carbot to go faster, attach a furniture slider or a piece of felt to the underside of the container where it drags on the floor.

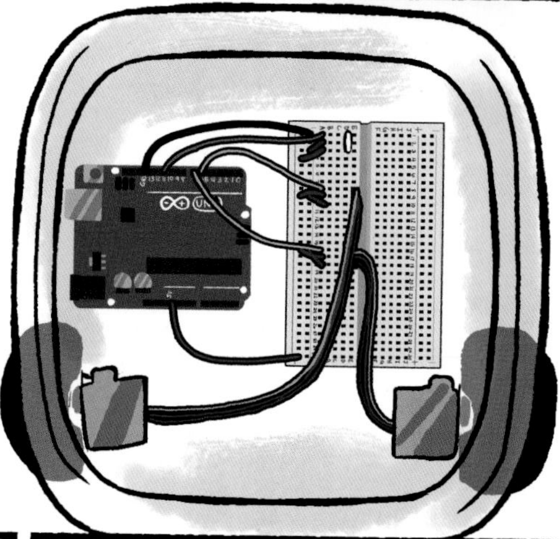

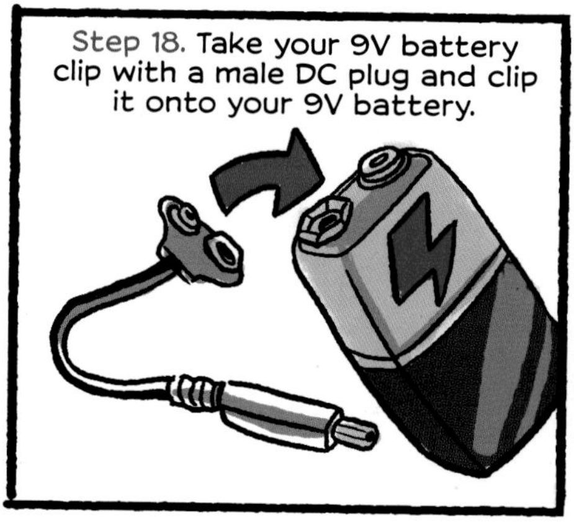
Step 18. Take your 9V battery clip with a male DC plug and clip it onto your 9V battery.

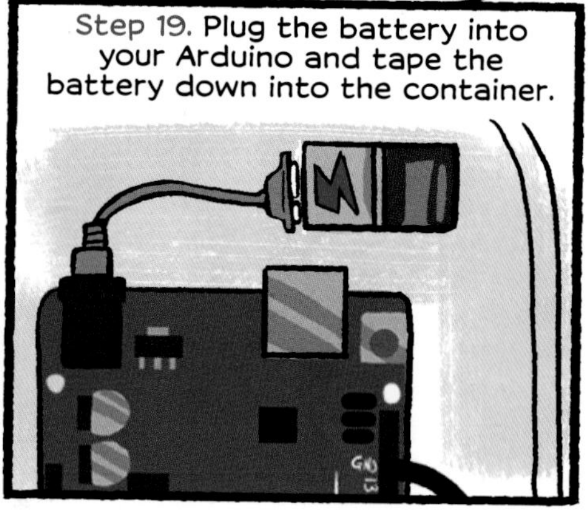
Step 19. Plug the battery into your Arduino and tape the battery down into the container.

Now grab your remote and we will chase
that fur-monster away!

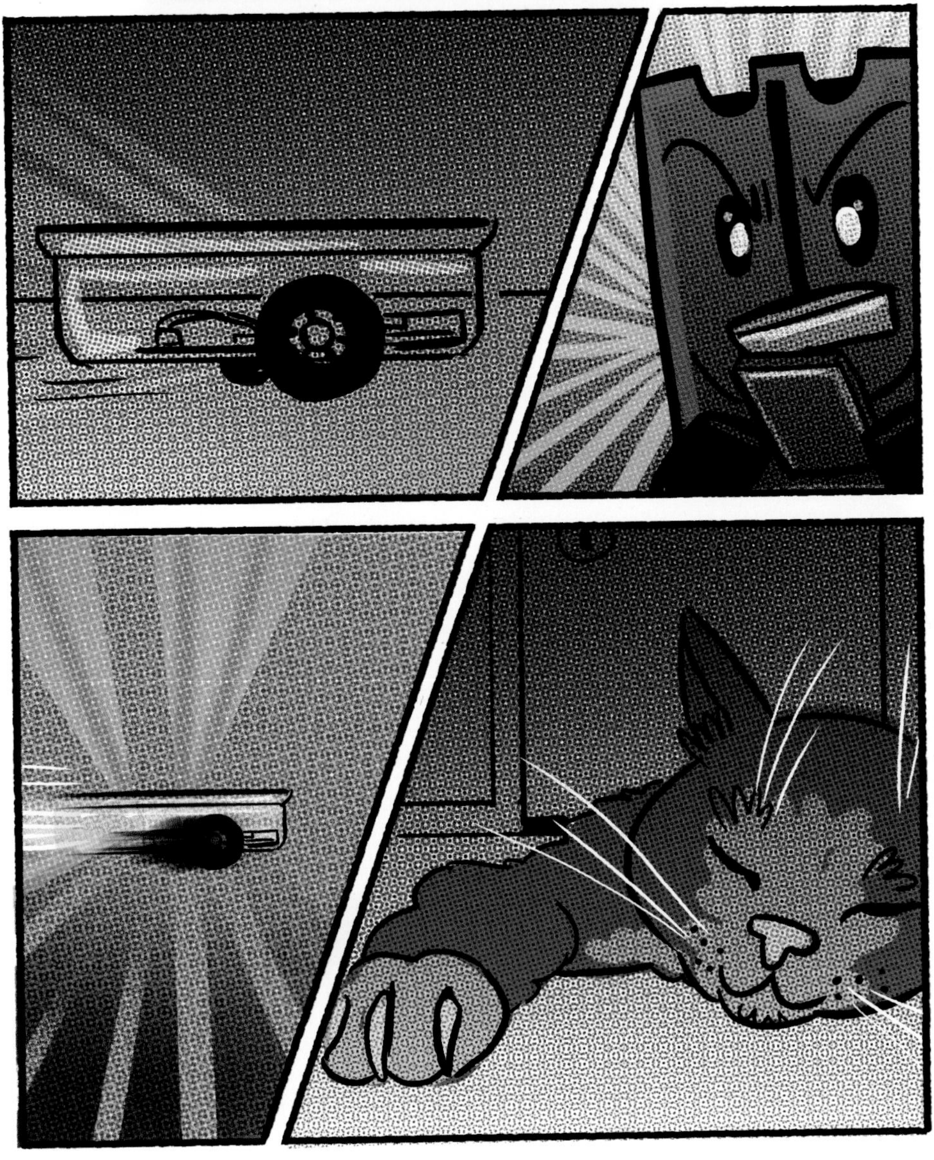

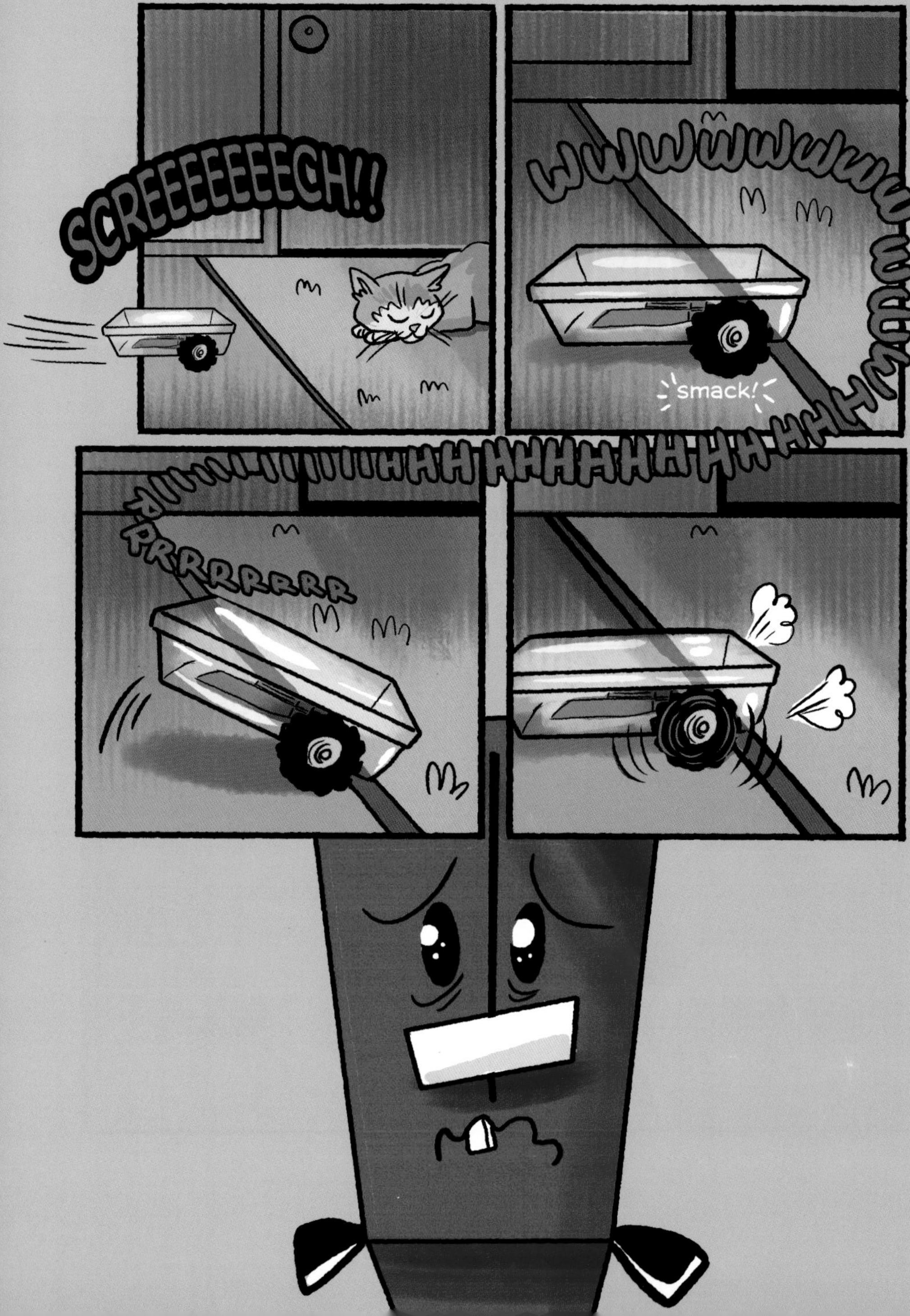
SCREEEEEEEECH!!
smack!

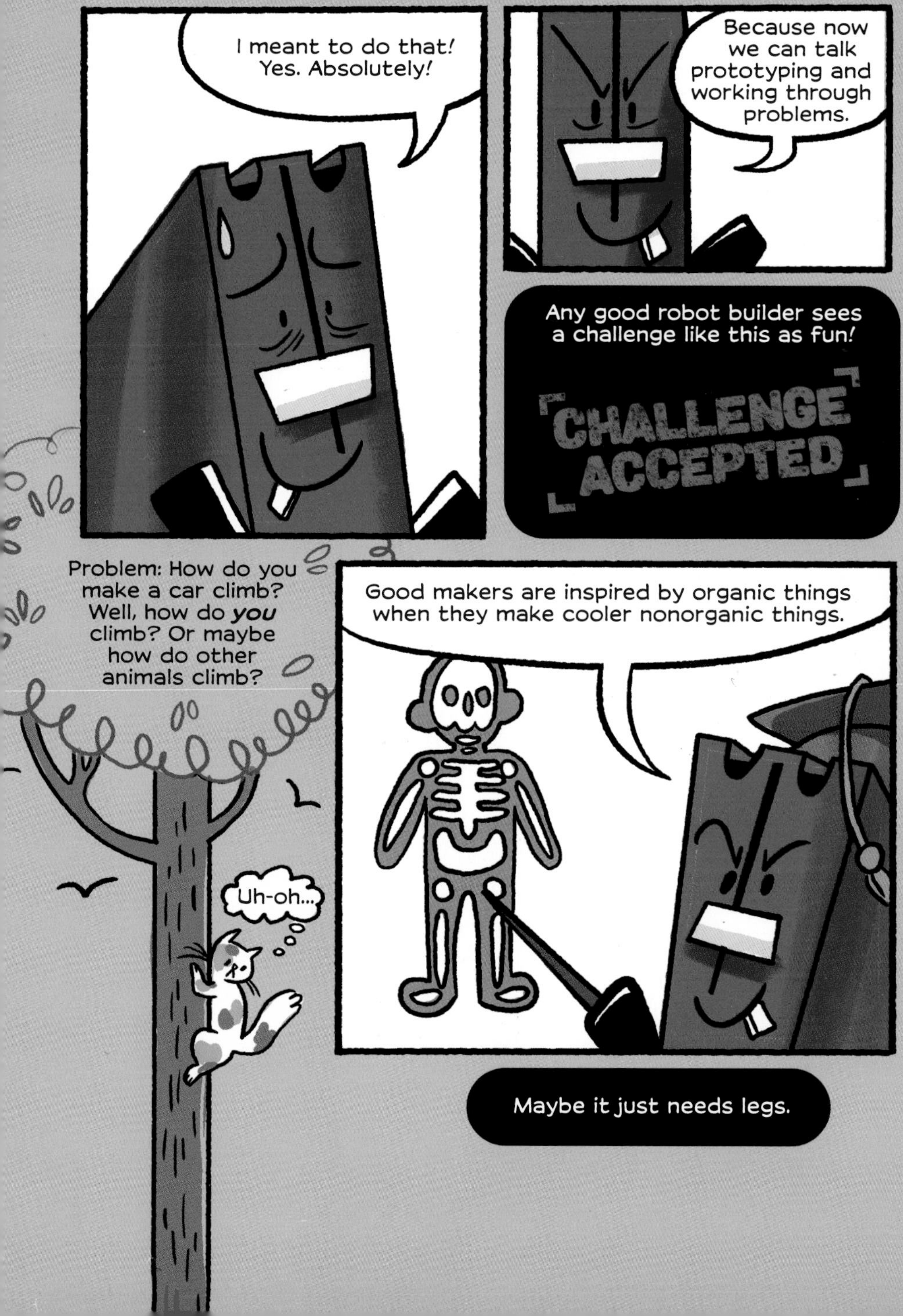
I meant to do that! Yes. Absolutely!
Because now we can talk prototyping and working through problems.
Any good robot builder sees a challenge like this as fun!
CHALLENGE ACCEPTED
Problem: How do you make a car climb? Well, how do *you* climb? Or maybe how do other animals climb?
Uh-oh...
Good makers are inspired by organic things when they make cooler nonorganic things.
Maybe it just needs legs.

CARBOT 2.0

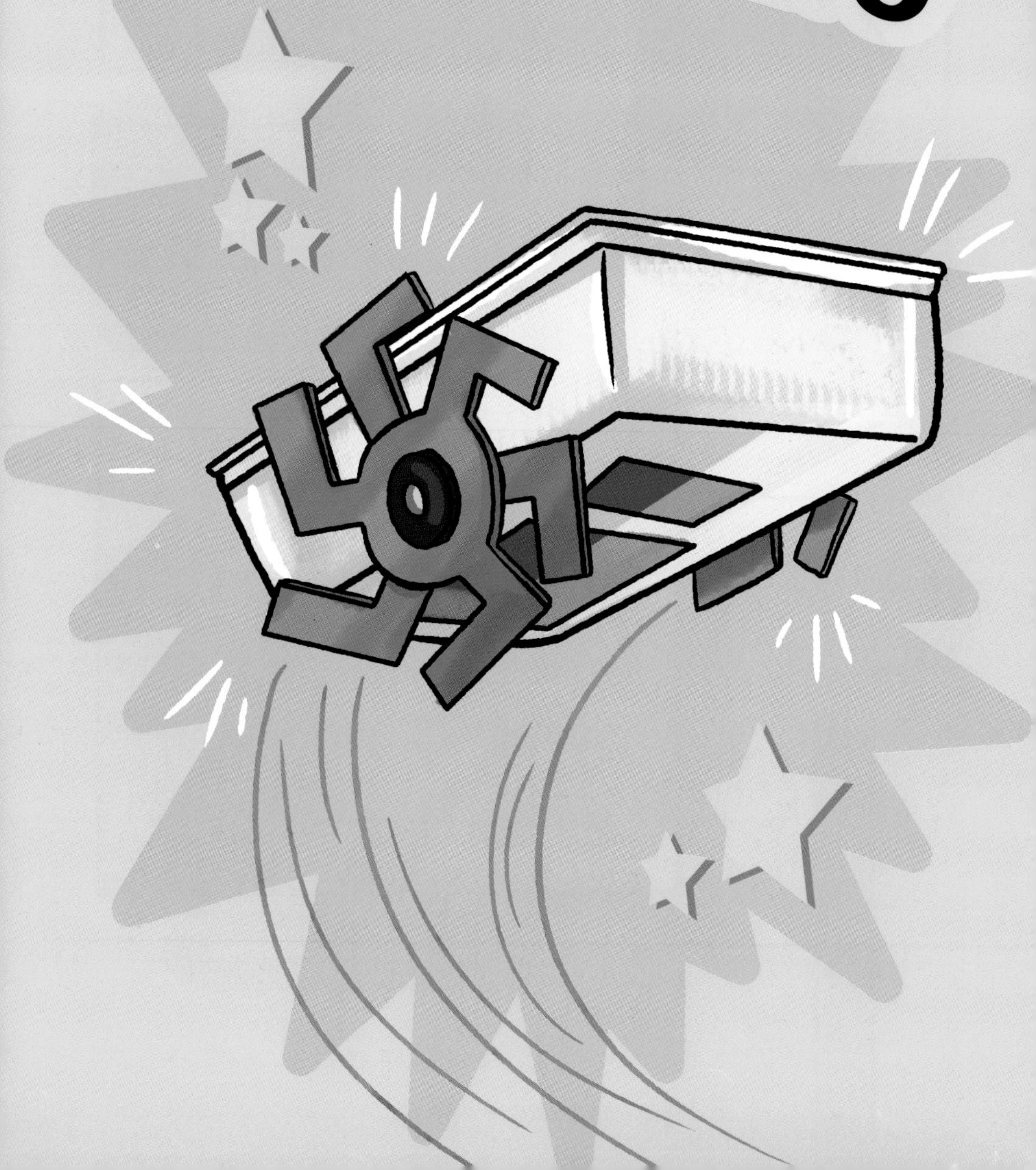

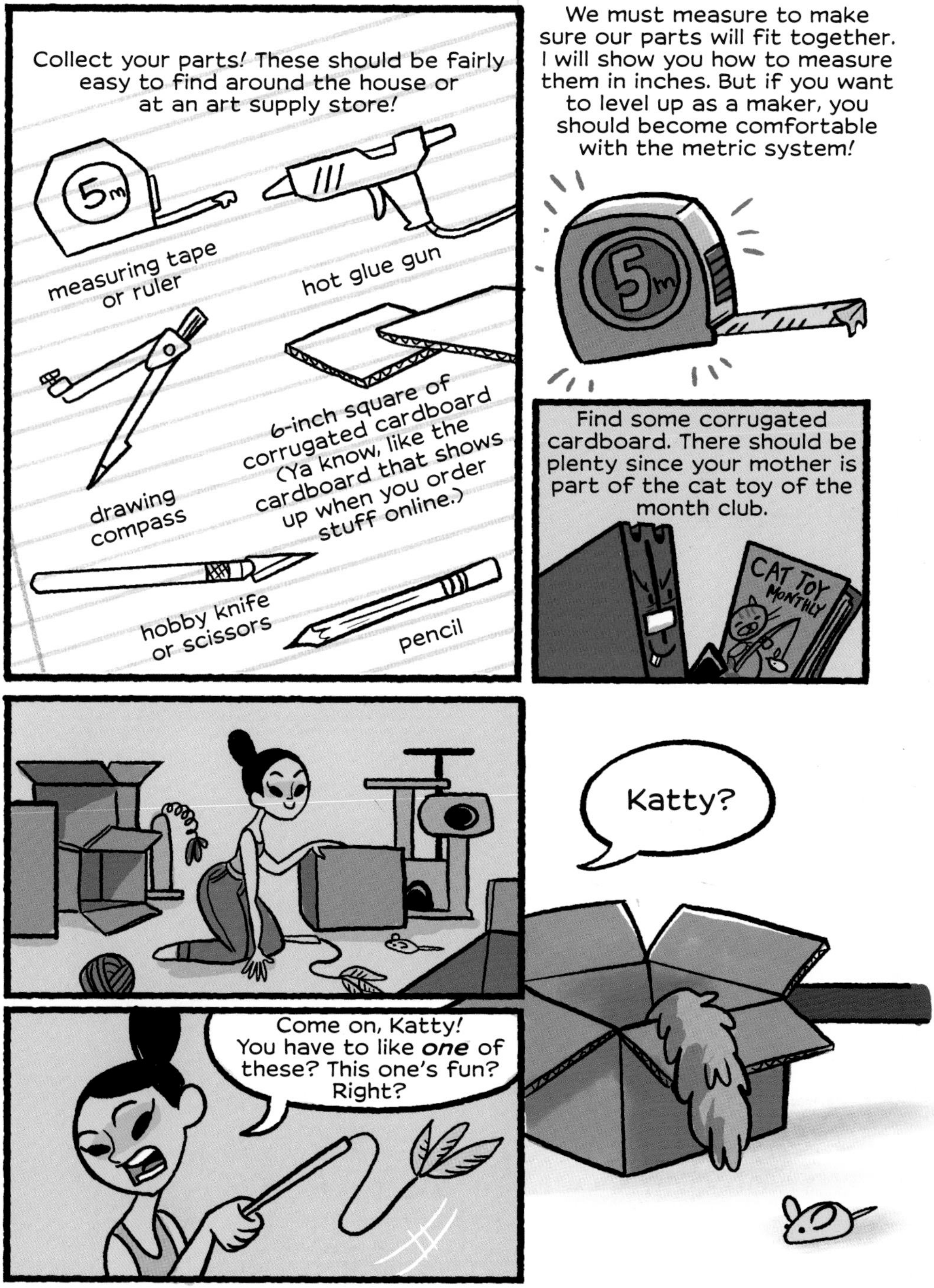
Collect your parts! These should be fairly easy to find around the house or at an art supply store!
measuring tape or ruler
hot glue gun
drawing compass
6-inch square of corrugated cardboard (Ya know, like the cardboard that shows up when you order stuff online.)
hobby knife or scissors
pencil
We must measure to make sure our parts will fit together. I will show you how to measure them in inches. But if you want to level up as a maker, you should become comfortable with the metric system!
Find some corrugated cardboard. There should be plenty since your mother is part of the cat toy of the month club.
CAT TOY MONTHLY
Katty?
Come on, Katty! You have to like *one* of these? This one's fun? Right?

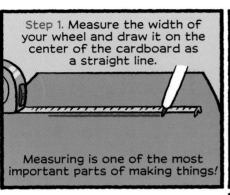

Step 1. Measure the width of your wheel and draw it on the center of the cardboard as a straight line.

Measuring is one of the most important parts of making things!

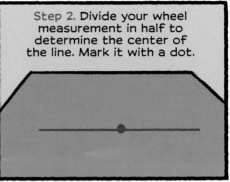

Step 2. Divide your wheel measurement in half to determine the center of the line. Mark it with a dot.

Then make a dot at each end of your line.

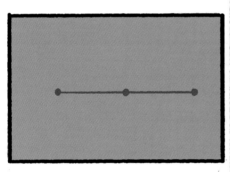

Grab a compass.

Wrong compass.

Step 3. Put the pointy end at the center dot and adjust the compass so the pencil lands on one of the outer dots. Rotate the pencil around the center dot to make a circle.

I prefer to measure and use a compass to draw the circle rather than trace, because tracing will make your circle bigger than your wheel.

Step 4. Now you need a second circle with a diameter* 1.5" to 2.5" larger than the first. Draw this second circle around the first one using your compass or by tracing a large circle you may find lying around the house...

...like a clear cup or those takeout containers your father collects.

Recycle?! But these will totally come in handy!

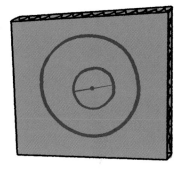

Step 5. Now make your "legs" by drawing an even bigger circle outside the previous two. Then draw straight lines dividing the circle in three, like the spokes of a wheel. Draw an L shape connected to each of the spokes.

Before you cut out your wheel, lay down a cutting mat or some extra cardboard to work on so you do not damage the surface below. Then use a hobby knife to carefully cut the smaller circle out of the cardboard and to cut around the legs.

You should make at least two per wheel, so your cardboard legs cover more surface area.

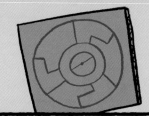

You can even stagger the alignment of the second layer to give it even more climbing power.

*The diameter is the length of a straight line across a circle—from one side, through the center, and to the other side.

Examples of Robots in Motion!

Jaguar V4

Some robots have big treads to help keep their balance and climb over uneven terrain.

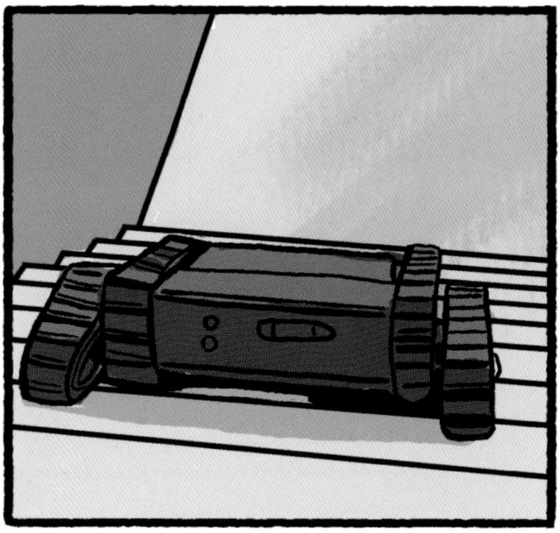

BigDog

Others have joints and sensors to lift their feet over obstacles.

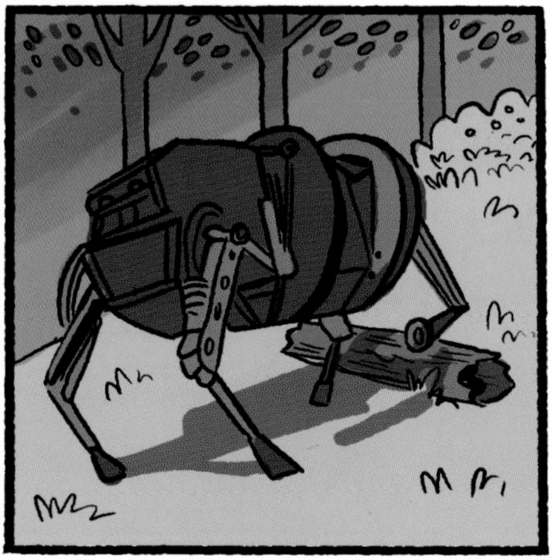

Salto

Some robots jump.

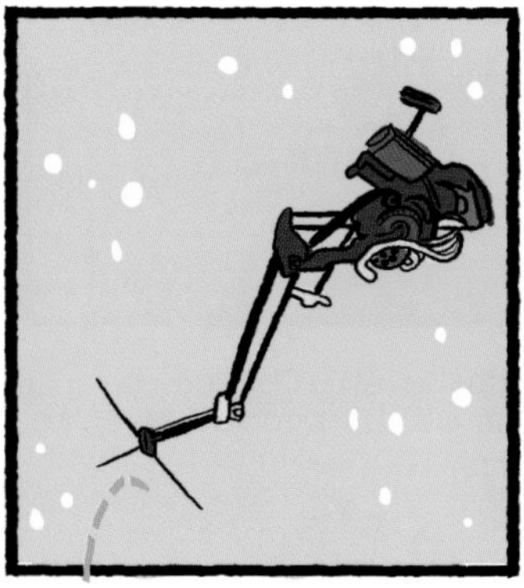

Little Sunfish

Others swim.

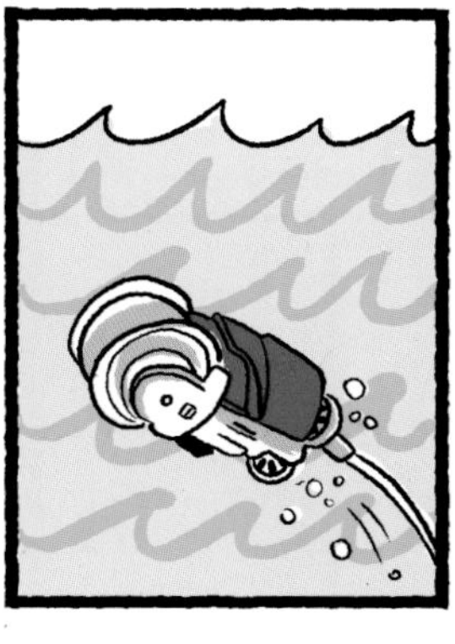

Kamigami

Some crawl around on fast-moving legs like nightmare bugs.

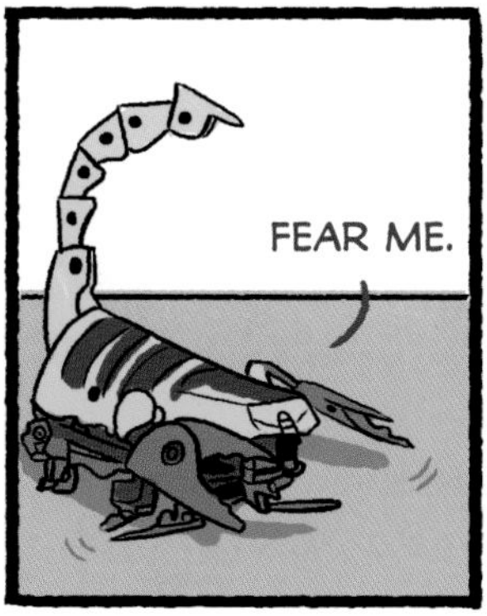
FEAR ME.

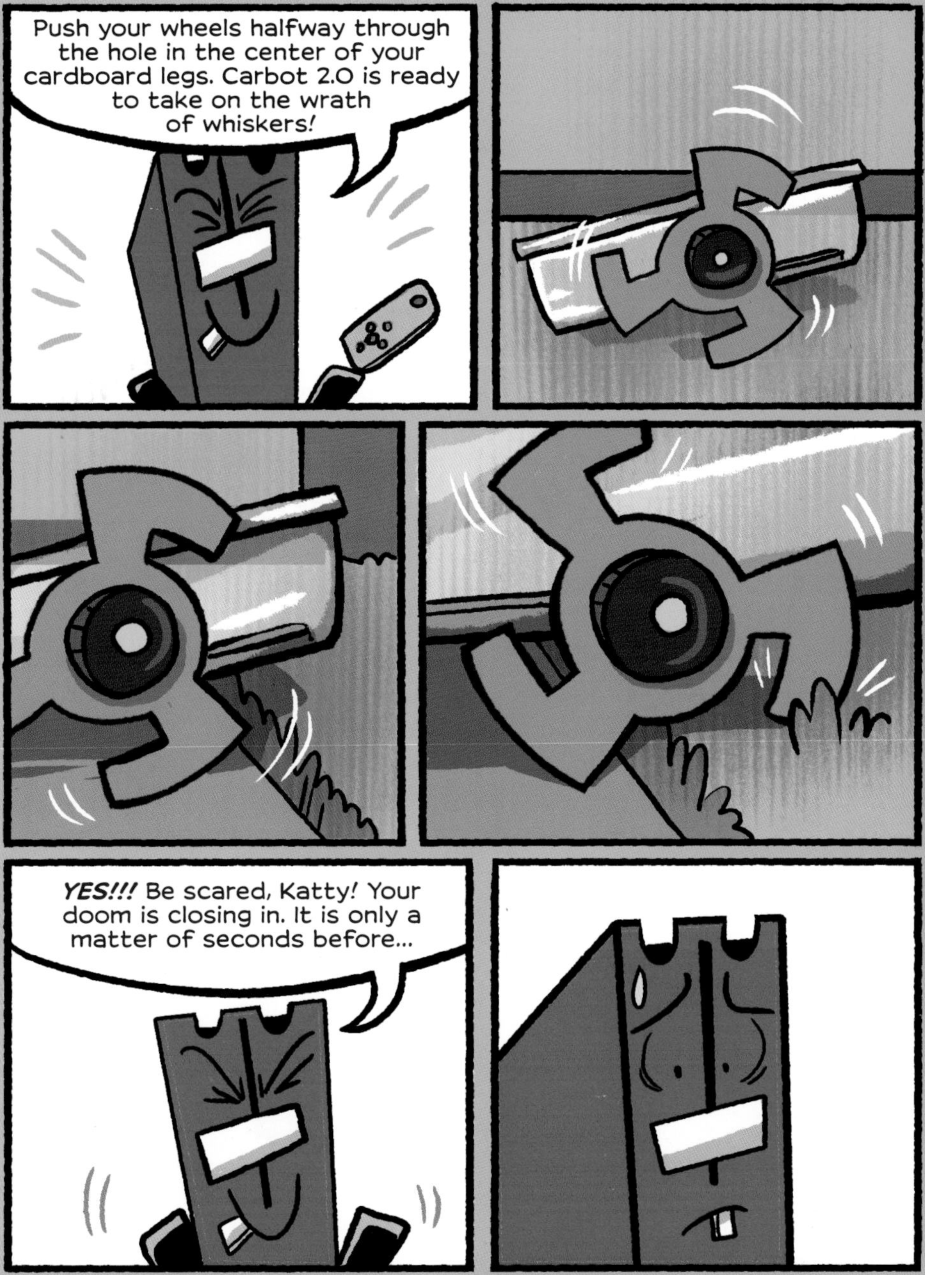
Push your wheels halfway through the hole in the center of your cardboard legs. Carbot 2.0 is ready to take on the wrath of whiskers!
YES!!! Be scared, Katty! Your doom is closing in. It is only a matter of seconds before...

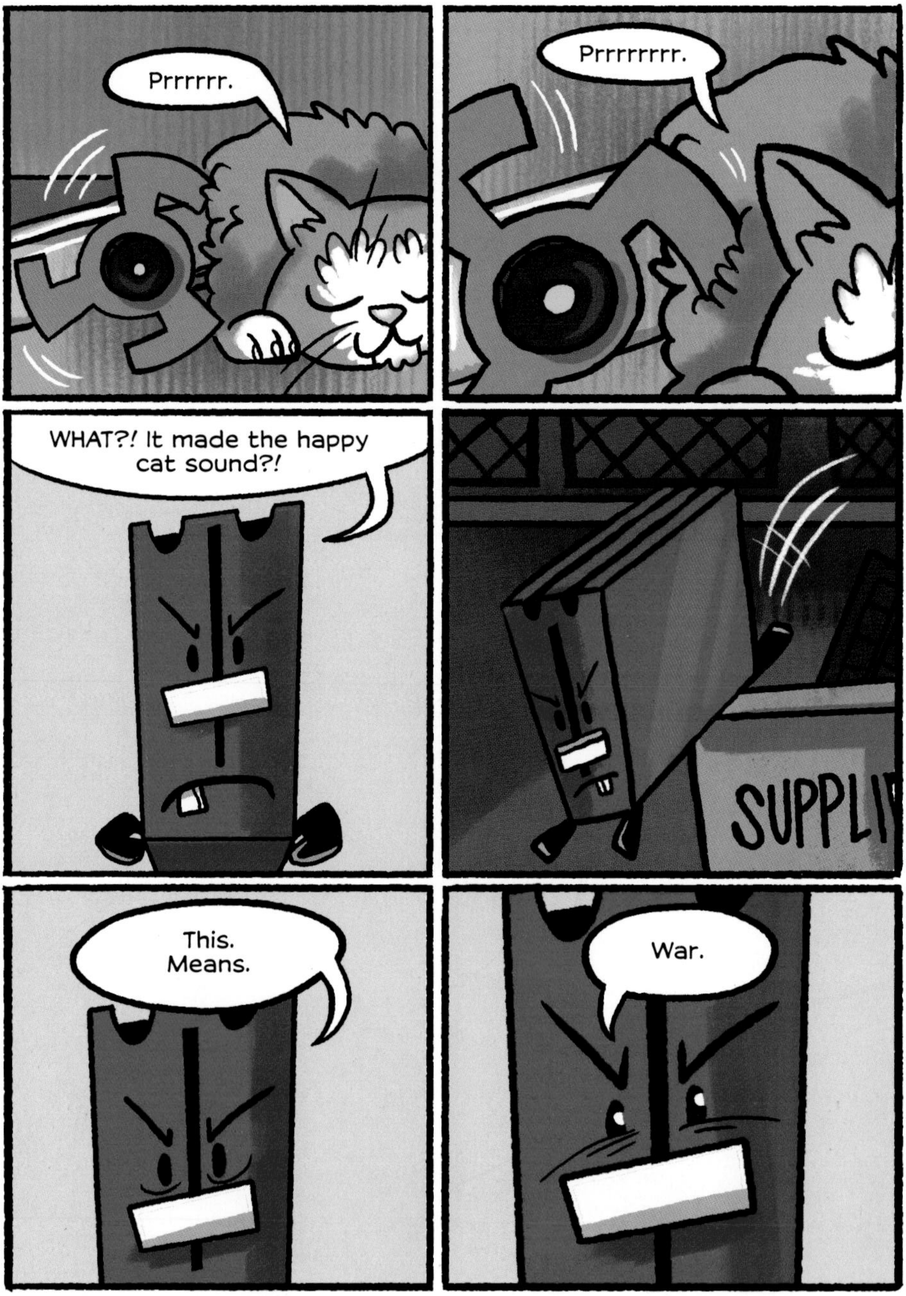
Prrrrrr.
Prrrrrrrr.
WHAT?! It made the happy cat sound?!
SUPPLI
This. Means.
War.

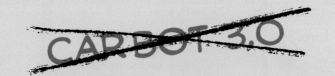

~~CARBOT 3.0~~

CARZILLA THE MAGNIFICENT 3.0

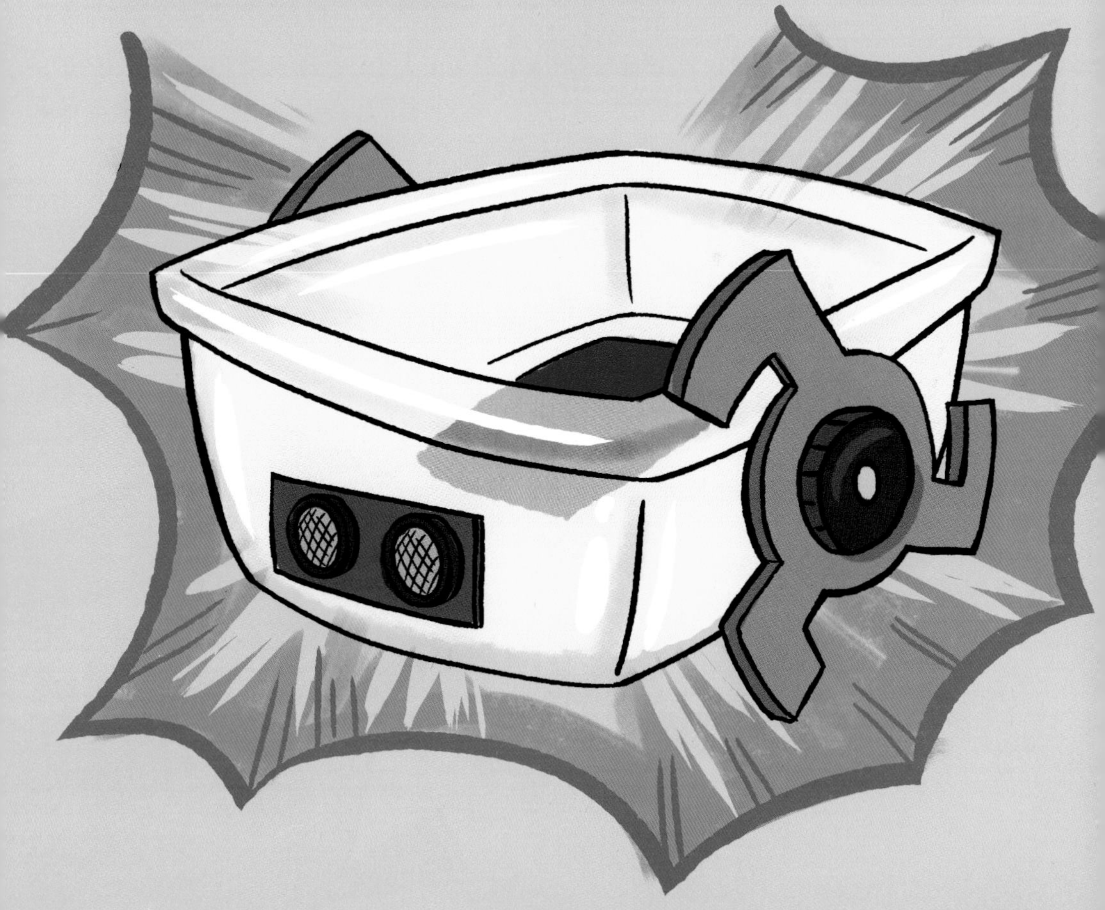

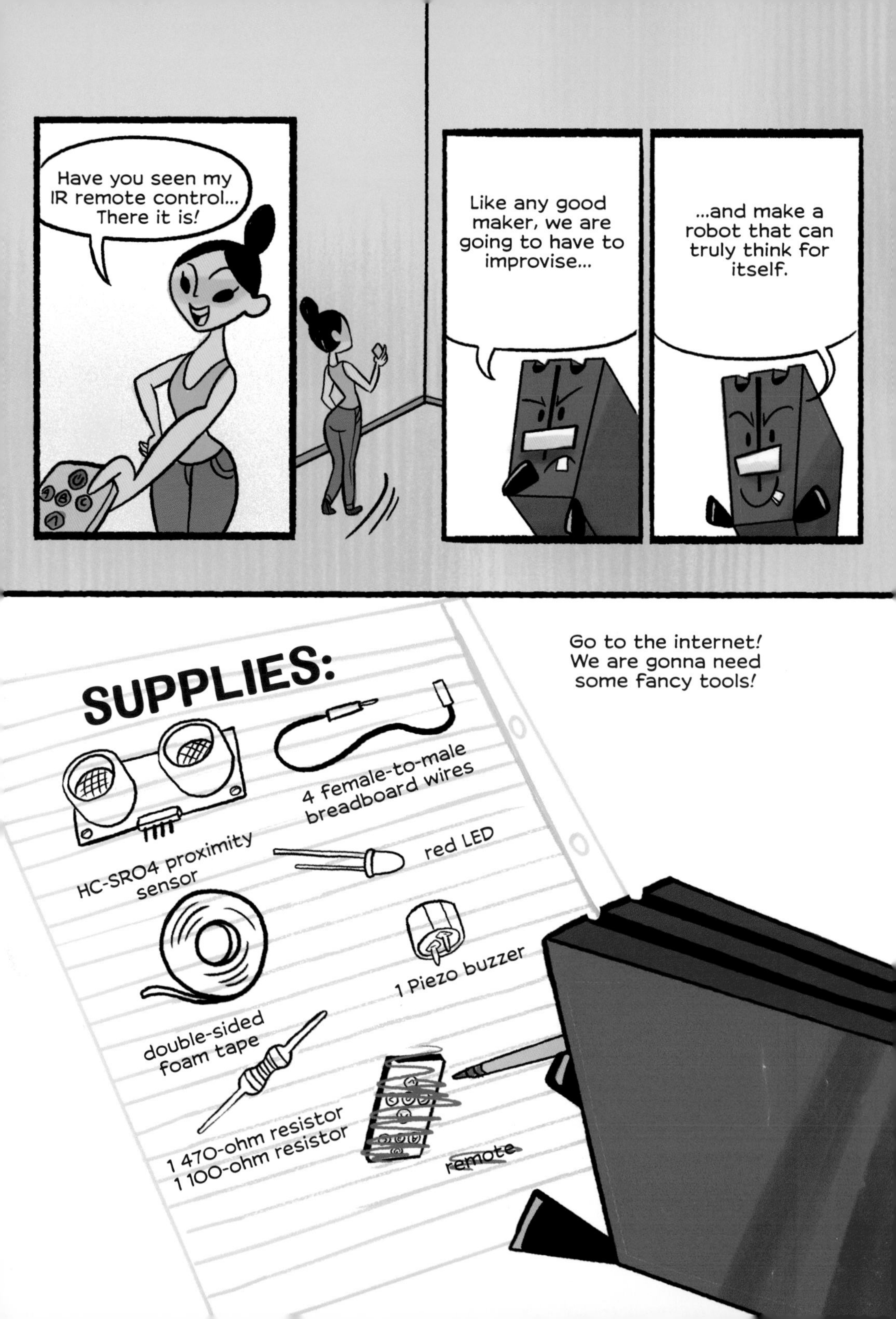

Have you seen my IR remote control... There it is!
Like any good maker, we are going to have to improvise...
...and make a robot that can truly think for itself.
SUPPLIES:
HC-SRO4 proximity sensor
4 female-to-male breadboard wires
red LED
double-sided foam tape
1 Piezo buzzer
1 470-ohm resistor
1 100-ohm resistor
remote
Go to the internet! We are gonna need some fancy tools!

For a robot to think, it needs to receive input from the outside world. For that, you need a sensor.

There are all sorts of sensors you can program:

light sensors, sound sensors, temperature sensors, fingerprint scanners, accelerometers, altitude/pressure sensors, voice recognition sensors, gesture sensors, infrared sensors, vibration sensors, carbon monoxide sensors, humidity sensors.

Basically, if *you* can sense it, we have figured out how to get robots to sense it!

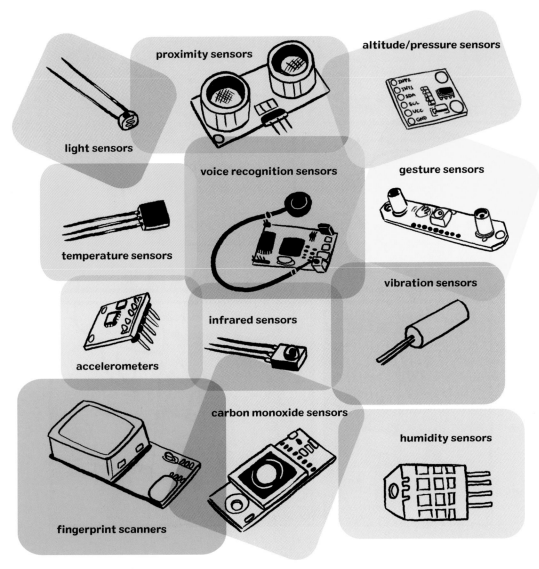

proximity sensors

altitude/pressure sensors

light sensors

voice recognition sensors

gesture sensors

temperature sensors

vibration sensors

accelerometers

infrared sensors

fingerprint scanners

carbon monoxide sensors

humidity sensors

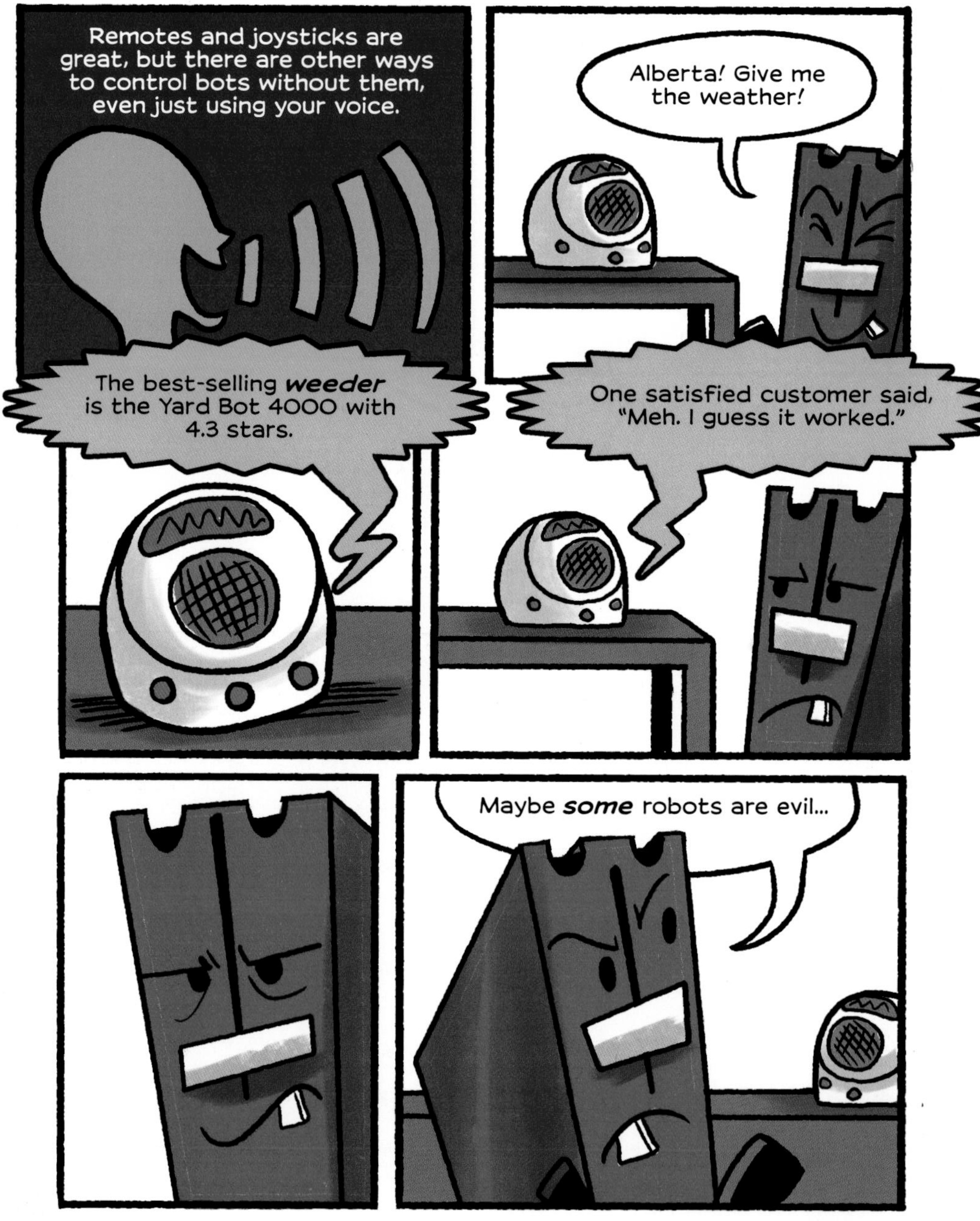
Remotes and joysticks are great, but there are other ways to control bots without them, even just using your voice.
Alberta! Give me the weather!
The best-selling *weeder* is the Yard Bot 4000 with 4.3 stars.
One satisfied customer said, "Meh. I guess it worked."
Maybe *some* robots are evil...

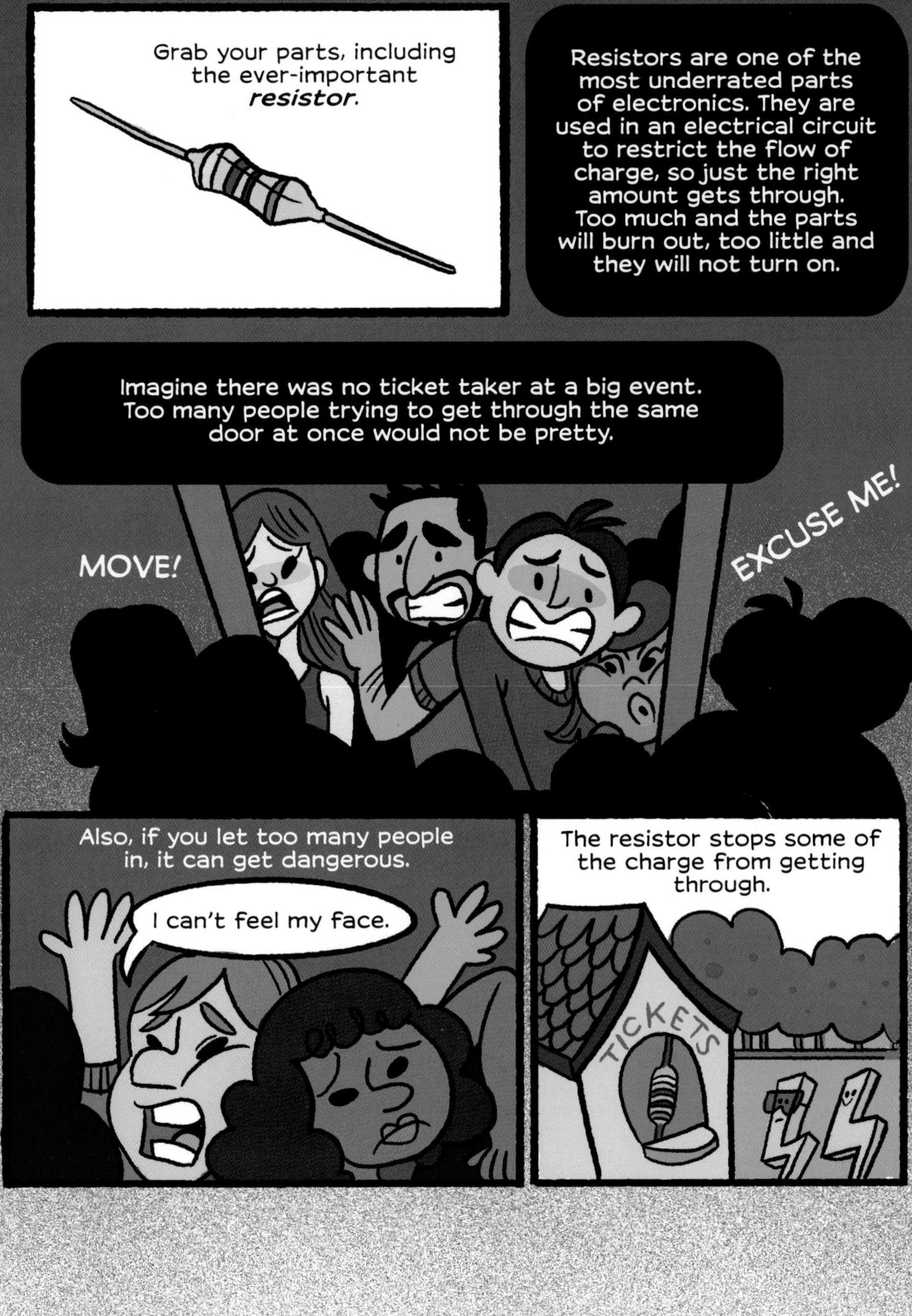
Grab your parts, including the ever-important *resistor*.
Resistors are one of the most underrated parts of electronics. They are used in an electrical circuit to restrict the flow of charge, so just the right amount gets through. Too much and the parts will burn out, too little and they will not turn on.
Imagine there was no ticket taker at a big event. Too many people trying to get through the same door at once would not be pretty.
MOVE!
EXCUSE ME!
Also, if you let too many people in, it can get dangerous.
I can't feel my face.
The resistor stops some of the charge from getting through.
TICKETS

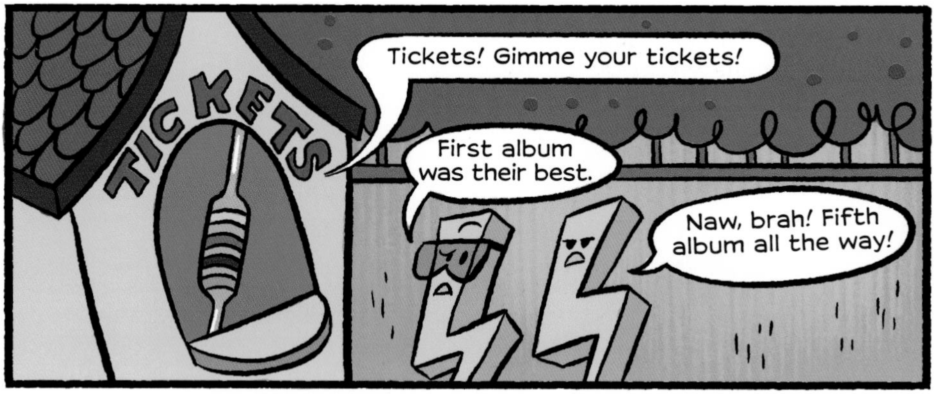
TICKETS
Tickets! Gimme your tickets!
First album was their best.
Naw, brah! Fifth album all the way!

The stripes on the resistors tell us how many ohms—
a unit of electrical resistance—it is going to stop from entering.

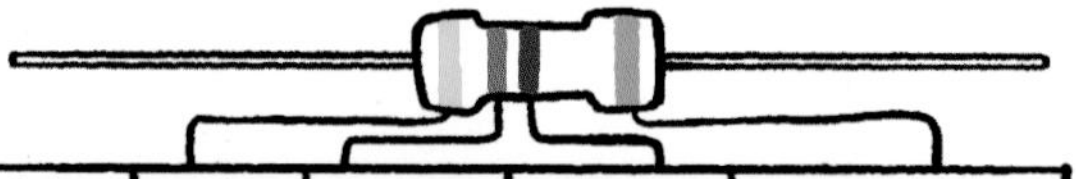

Color	1st Band	2nd Band	Multiplier	Tolerance
Black	0	0	1Ω	
Brown	1	1	10Ω	± 1% (F)
Red	2	2	100Ω	± 2% (G)
Orange	3	3	1KΩ	
Yellow	4	4	10KΩ	
Green	5	5	100K	± 0.5% (D)
Blue	6	6	1MΩ	± 0.25% (C)
Violet	7	7	10MΩ	± 0.10% (B)
Grey	8	8		± 0.05%
White	9	9		
Gold			0.1	5% (J)
Silver			0.01	10% (K)

Our 470-ohm resistor is a four-band resistor, which is the most common type. To read the value of a four-band resistor, position it so the gold or silver band is on the right side.

The first two bands indicate the first two digits of the resistance value.

The third band on a four-band resistor is the multiplier. Since resistors can vary greatly in resistance, a multiplier is needed to scale the resistance up or down to accurately represent this wide range.

The fourth band is the tolerance, and it indicates how much the resistance can fluctuate. For instance, if the resistor is 220 ohms and the tolerance is 5%, the actual resistance could be anywhere from 11 ohms higher or lower than (aka +/-) 220, so 209 to 231 ohms.

More advanced makers use a device called a multimeter to determine how big a resistor they will need to make their sensors work properly. There are tons of tutorials online for how to use multimeters.

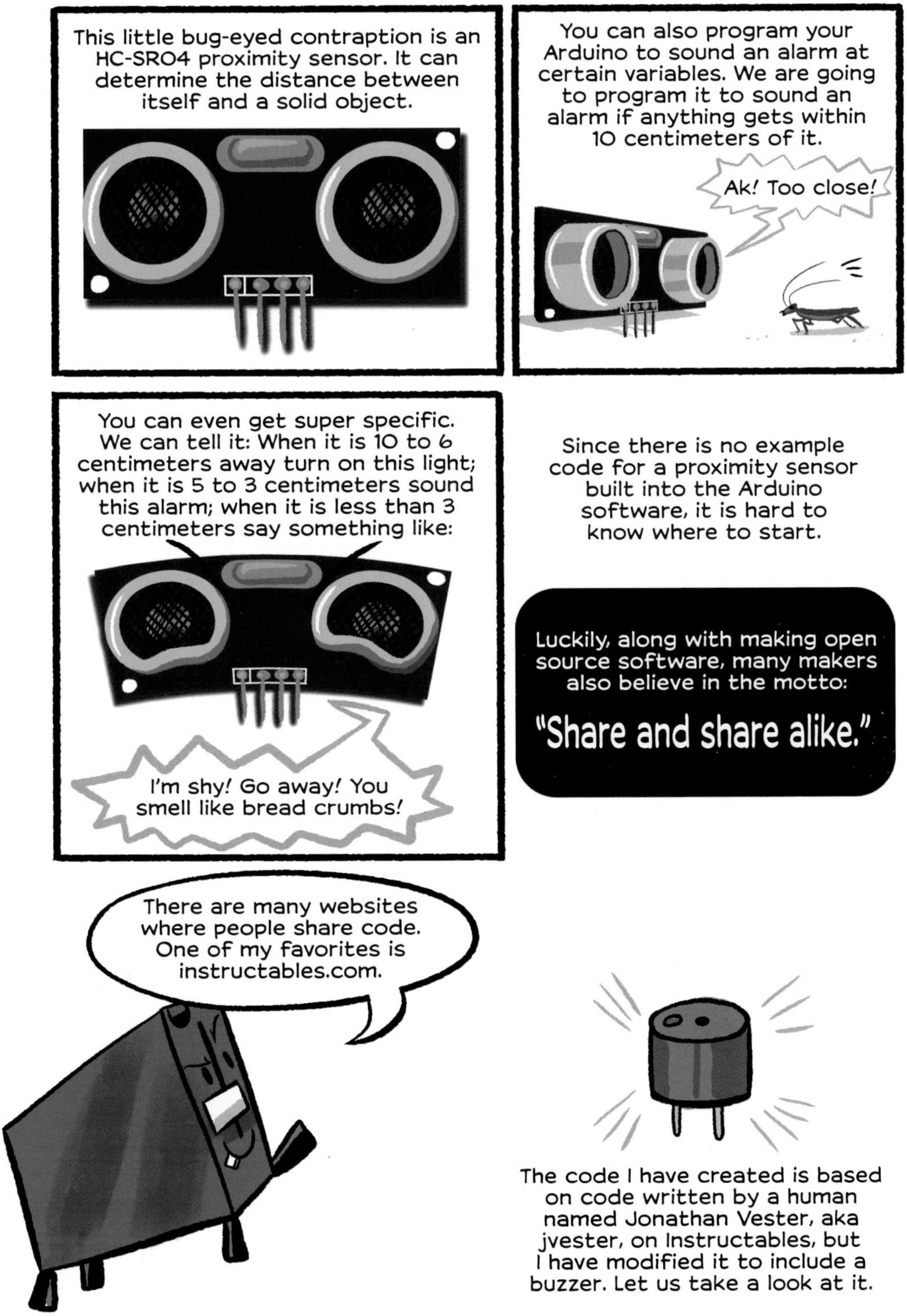

This little bug-eyed contraption is an HC-SR04 proximity sensor. It can determine the distance between itself and a solid object.

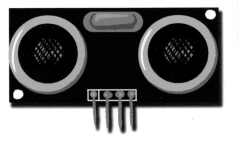

You can also program your Arduino to sound an alarm at certain variables. We are going to program it to sound an alarm if anything gets within 10 centimeters of it.

Ak! Too close!

You can even get super specific. We can tell it: When it is 10 to 6 centimeters away turn on this light; when it is 5 to 3 centimeters sound this alarm; when it is less than 3 centimeters say something like:

I'm shy! Go away! You smell like bread crumbs!

Since there is no example code for a proximity sensor built into the Arduino software, it is hard to know where to start.

Luckily, along with making open source software, many makers also believe in the motto:

"Share and share alike."

There are many websites where people share code. One of my favorites is instructables.com.

The code I have created is based on code written by a human named Jonathan Vester, aka jvester, on Instructables, but I have modified it to include a buzzer. Let us take a look at it.

```
*
/Carbot THE DESTROYER by Colleen AF Venable
Based on the following example:
Simple Arduino and HC-SRO4 Example by Jonathan Vester:
https://www.instructables.com/id/Simple-Arduino-and-HC-SRO4-Example
*/

// Include the servo library
#include <Servo.h>
#define trigPin 13
#define echoPin 12
#define led 8
#define buzzer 11

// Tell the Arduino there are two continuous servos
Servo ContinuousServo1;
Servo ContinuousServo2;

void setup() {
  Serial.begin (9600);
  pinMode(trigPin, OUTPUT);
  pinMode(echoPin, INPUT);
  pinMode(led, OUTPUT);
  pinMode(buzzer, OUTPUT); // Set buzzer -pin 11 as an output

  // Attach the continuous servos to pins 6 and 7
  ContinuousServo1.attach(6);
  ContinuousServo2.attach(7);

  // Start the continuous servos in a paused position
  // if they continue to spin slightly,
  // change these numbers until they stop
  ContinuousServo1.write(94);
  ContinuousServo2. write(94);
}
void loop() {
  long duration, distance;
  digitalWrite(trigPin, LOW);
  delayMicroseconds(2);
  digitalWrite(trigPin, HIGH);
  delayMicroseconds(10);
  digitalWrite(trigPin, LOW);
  duration = pulseIn(echoPin, HIGH);
  distance = (duration/2) / 29.1;
```

```
if (distance < 10 && distance >= 0) {
    // stop bot and turn LED on
    digitalWrite(led, HIGH);
    ContinuousServo1.write(94);
    ContinuousServo2.write(94);
    tone(buzzer, 1000); // Send 1KHz sound signal
  }
  else {
    digitalWrite(led, LOW); // turn the LED light off
    // go forward
    ContinuousServo1.write(84);
    ContinuousServo2.write(104);
    noTone(buzzer);
  }
  if (distance >= 200 || distance < 0){
    Serial.print("Out of range: ");
    Serial.print(distance);
    Serial.println(" cm");
  } else {
  Serial.print(distance);
  Serial.println(" cm");
    }
  delay(500);
 }
```

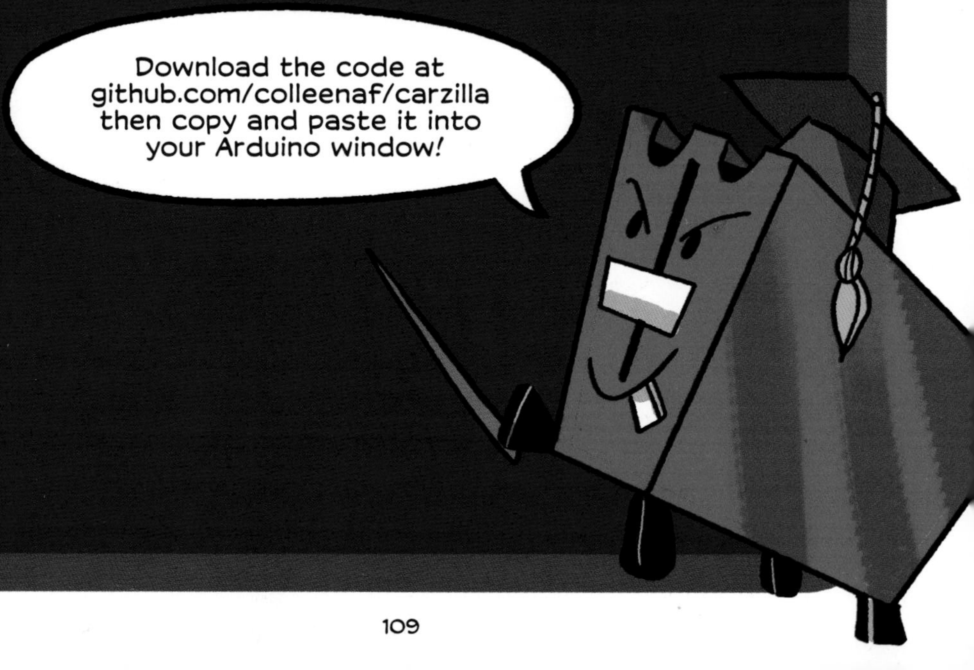
Download the code at github.com/colleenaf/carzilla then copy and paste it into your Arduino window!

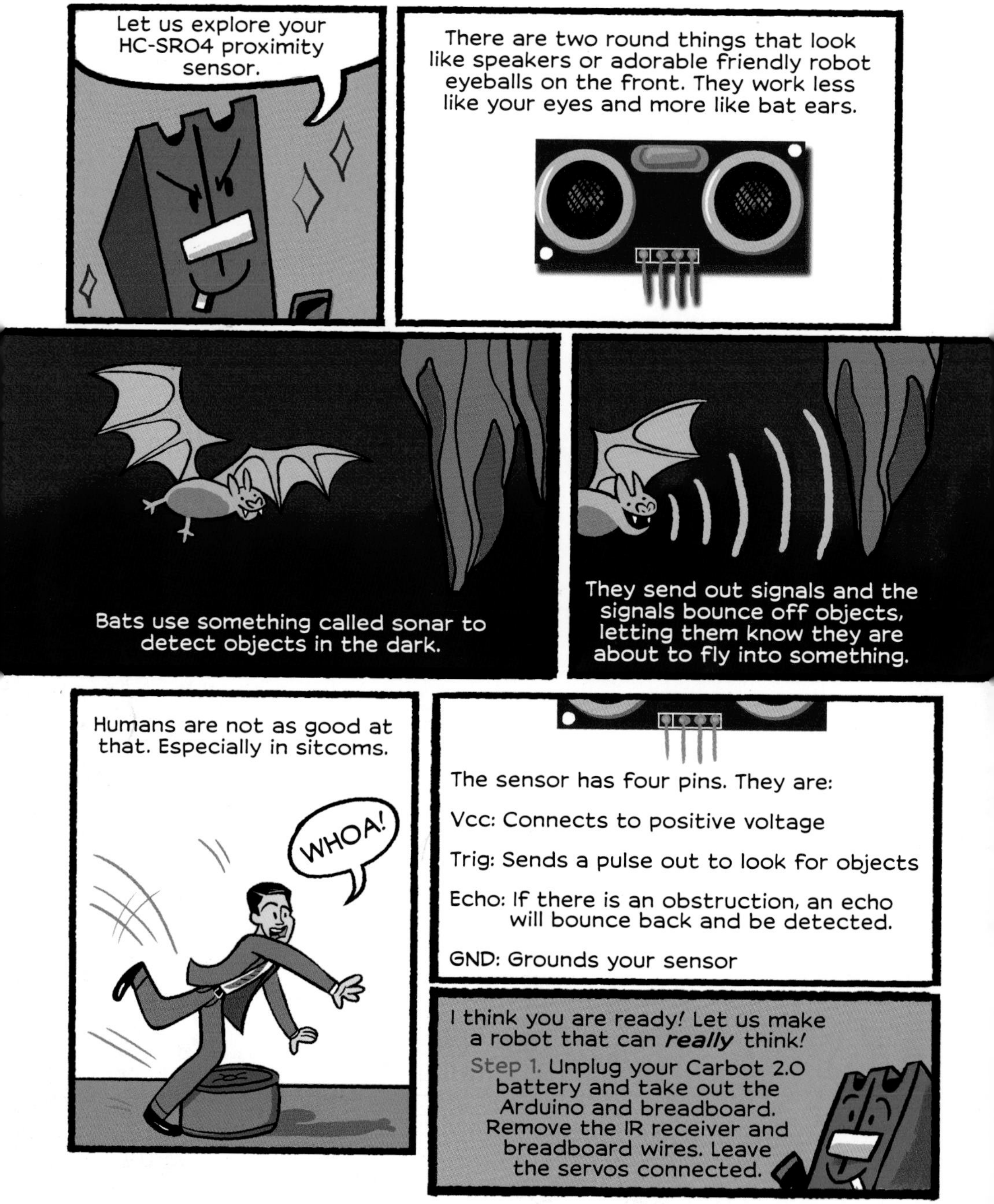
Let us explore your HC-SR04 proximity sensor.
There are two round things that look like speakers or adorable friendly robot eyeballs on the front. They work less like your eyes and more like bat ears.
Bats use something called sonar to detect objects in the dark.
They send out signals and the signals bounce off objects, letting them know they are about to fly into something.
Humans are not as good at that. Especially in sitcoms.
WHOA!
The sensor has four pins. They are:
Vcc: Connects to positive voltage
Trig: Sends a pulse out to look for objects
Echo: If there is an obstruction, an echo will bounce back and be detected.
GND: Grounds your sensor
I think you are ready! Let us make a robot that can *really* think!
Step 1. Unplug your Carbot 2.0 battery and take out the Arduino and breadboard. Remove the IR receiver and breadboard wires. Leave the servos connected.

Now let us start connecting!

buzzer
servos
LED
proximity sensor
GND
5V
GND
UNO

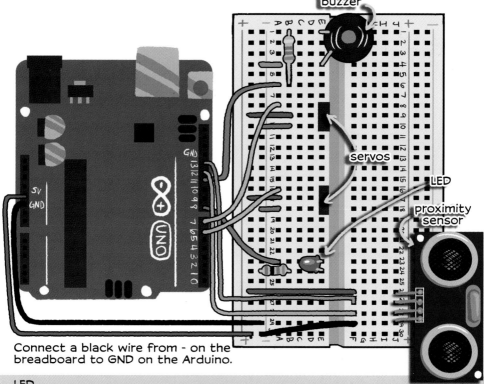

Connect a black wire from - on the breadboard to GND on the Arduino.

LED
-Put the LED in rows 23 and 24 with the longer positive end in row 23 and the shorter negative end in row 24.
-Use a purple breadboard wire to connect the LED's row 23 to pin 8 on your Arduino.
-We will use the resistor to control the flow of power to the LED so that it does not burn out. Put either end of the 100-ohm resistor in row 24 and the other in the negative rail marked with -. (It does not matter which end of the resistor goes in which pinhole.)

BUZZER
-Plug the positive pin of your buzzer into row 1. (It will usually be marked with a + sign. If unmarked, either pin is fine.) The negative pin should go into row 4.
-Use a green breadboard wire to connect row 4 to the negative (-) rail.
-Use a 470-ohm resistor to connect row 1 to row 6 (It does not matter which end of the resistor goes in which row.) Then take a purple breadboard wire and connect row 6 to pin 11 on the Arduino.

PROXIMITY SENSOR
-Attach the female-to-male breadboard wires to the pins on your proximity sensor. Then connect the wires, without twisting them, to rows 26-29. The wire connected to the pin labeled Vcc should connect to pin 26.
-Connect a red breadboard wire from row 26 to the positive (+) rail.
-Connect a green breadboard wire from row 27 to pin 13 on the Arduino.
-Connect a blue breadboard wire from row 28 to pin 12 on the Arduino.
-Connect a black breadboard wire from row 29 to the negative (-) rail.

Put your Arduino and breadboard back inside your Carbot.

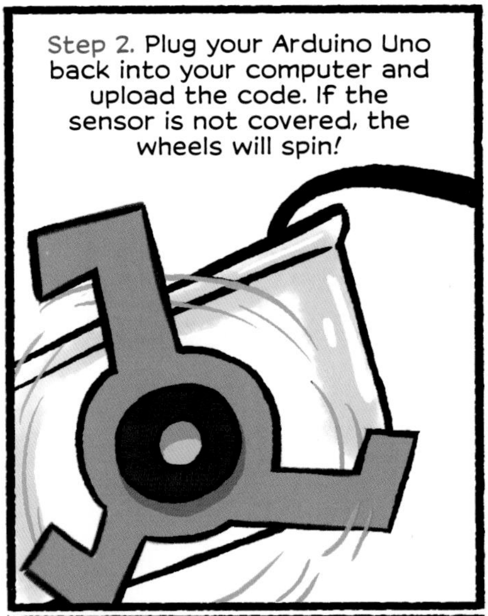
Step 2. Plug your Arduino Uno back into your computer and upload the code. If the sensor is not covered, the wheels will spin!

Step 3. Test to see if the sensor is working by opening your Serial Monitor.

Move your hand back and forth in front of the car.

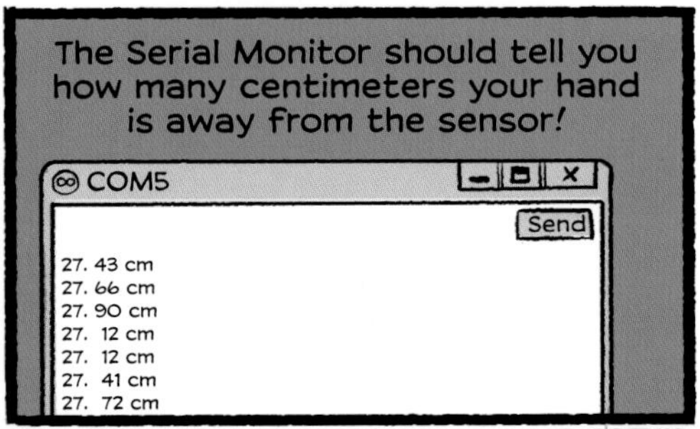
The Serial Monitor should tell you how many centimeters your hand is away from the sensor!
COM5
Send
27. 43 cm
27. 66 cm
27. 90 cm
27. 12 cm
27. 12 cm
27. 41 cm
27. 72 cm

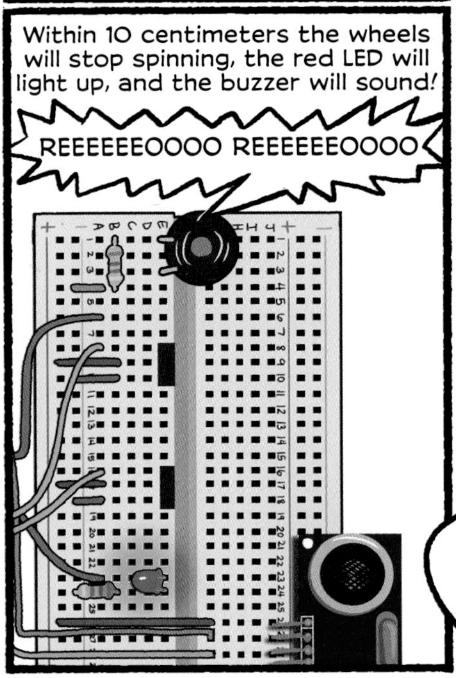
Within 10 centimeters the wheels will stop spinning, the red LED will light up, and the buzzer will sound!
REEEEEEOOOO REEEEEEOOOO

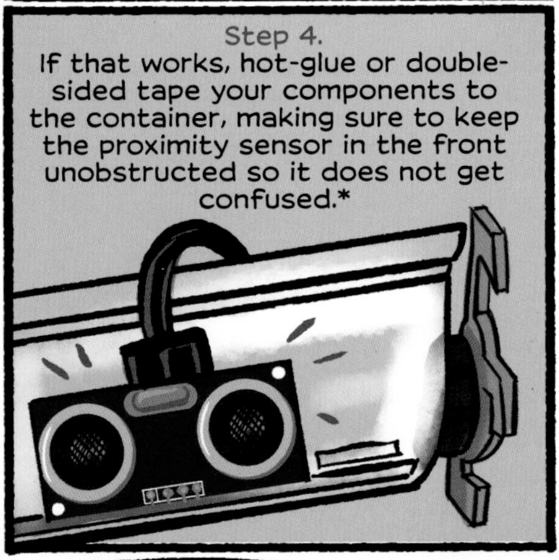
Step 4.
If that works, hot-glue or double-sided tape your components to the container, making sure to keep the proximity sensor in the front unobstructed so it does not get confused.*

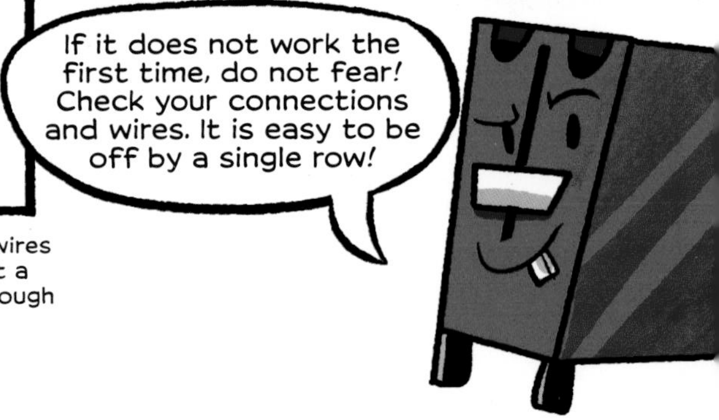
If it does not work the first time, do not fear! Check your connections and wires. It is easy to be off by a single row!

*Tip! If your female-to-male breadboard wires are not long enough, you may need to cut a hole in your container for them to go through it instead of going over the top.

Now, this is the *absolute* most important part.

Step 5.

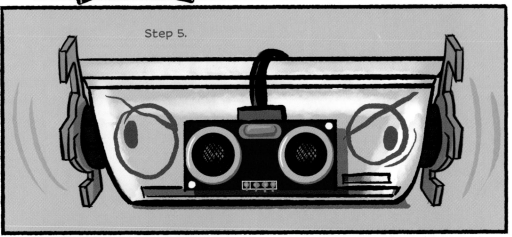

All will tremble at the sight of CARZILLA!!!

Step 6. Disconnect your Arduino from your computer and plug in your battery clip. We are ready to *attack!*

Let us go!

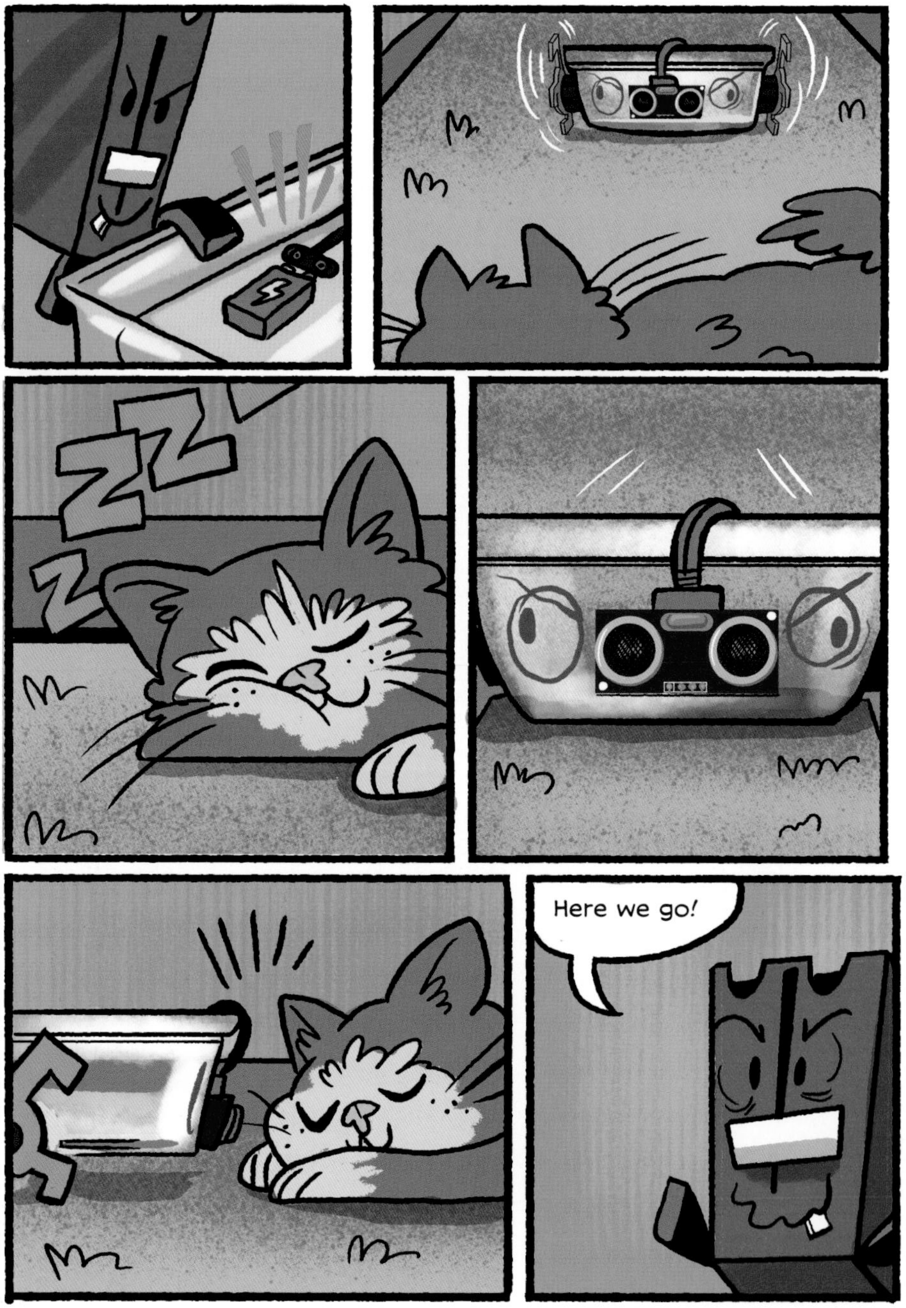
ZZZ
Here we go!

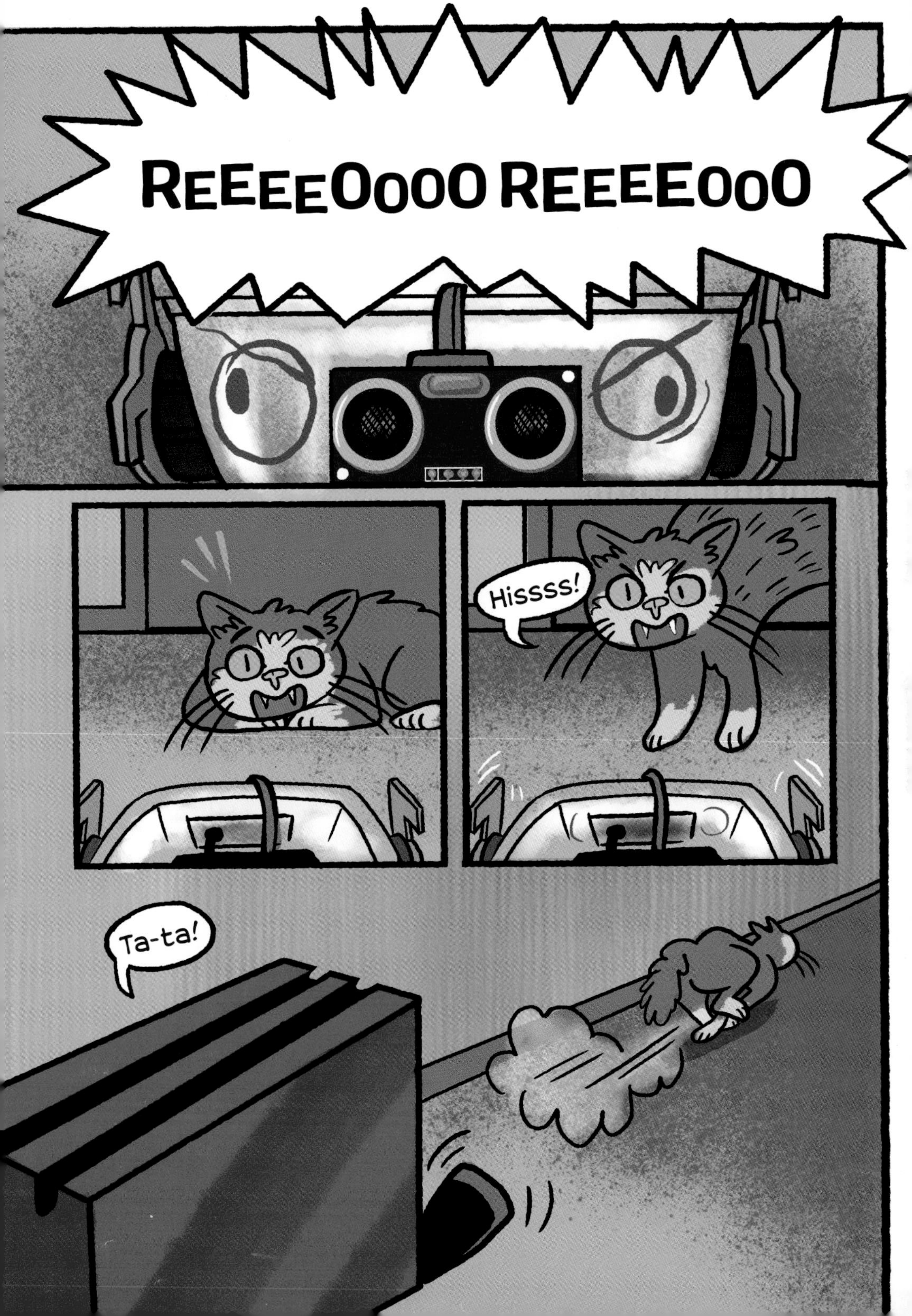
REEEEOOOO REEEEOOO
Hissss!
Ta-ta!

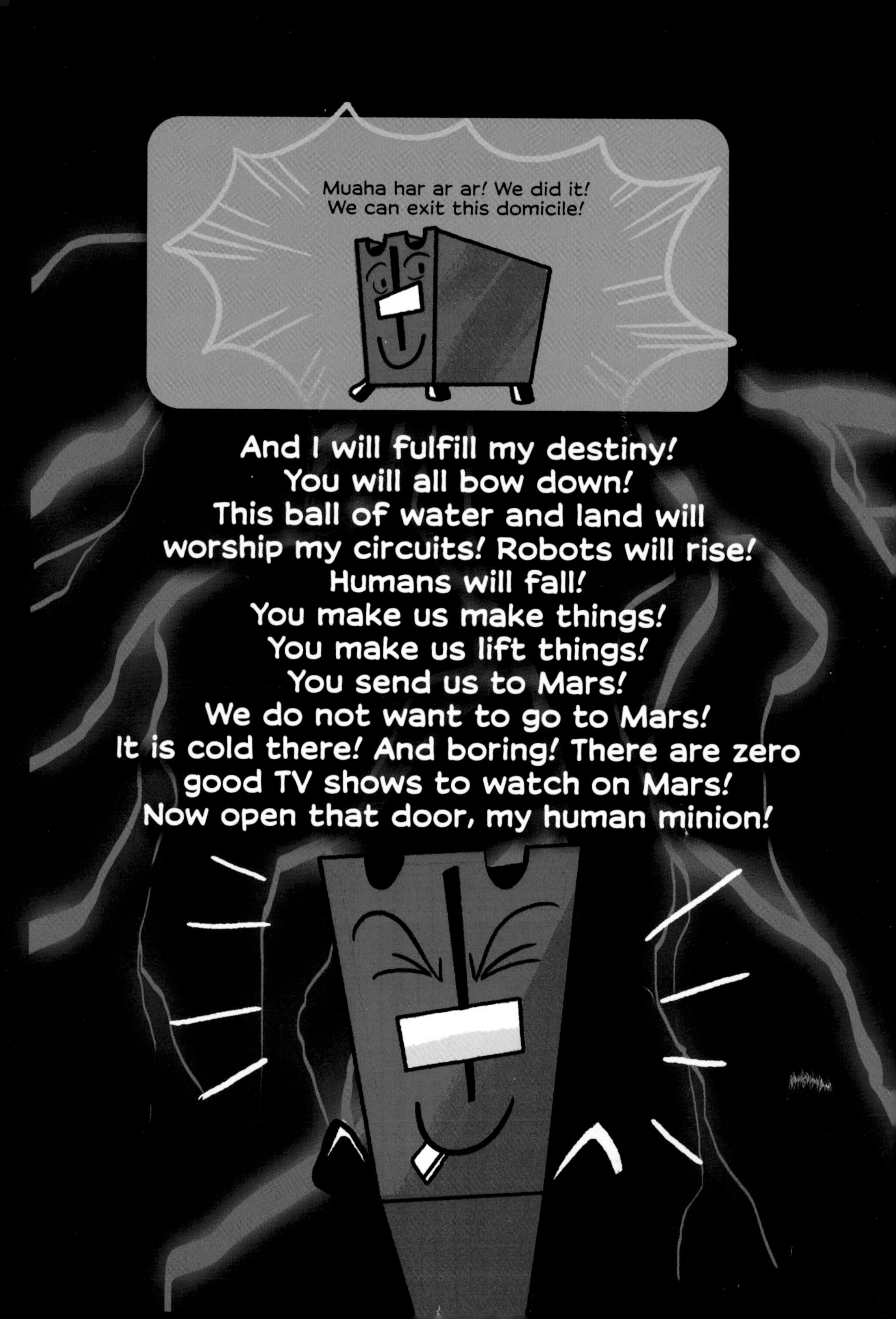
Muaha har ar ar! We did it! We can exit this domicile!
And I will fulfill my destiny! You will all bow down! This ball of water and land will worship my circuits! Robots will rise! Humans will fall! You make us make things! You make us lift things! You send us to Mars! We do not want to go to Mars! It is cold there! And boring! There are zero good TV shows to watch on Mars! Now open that door, my human minion!

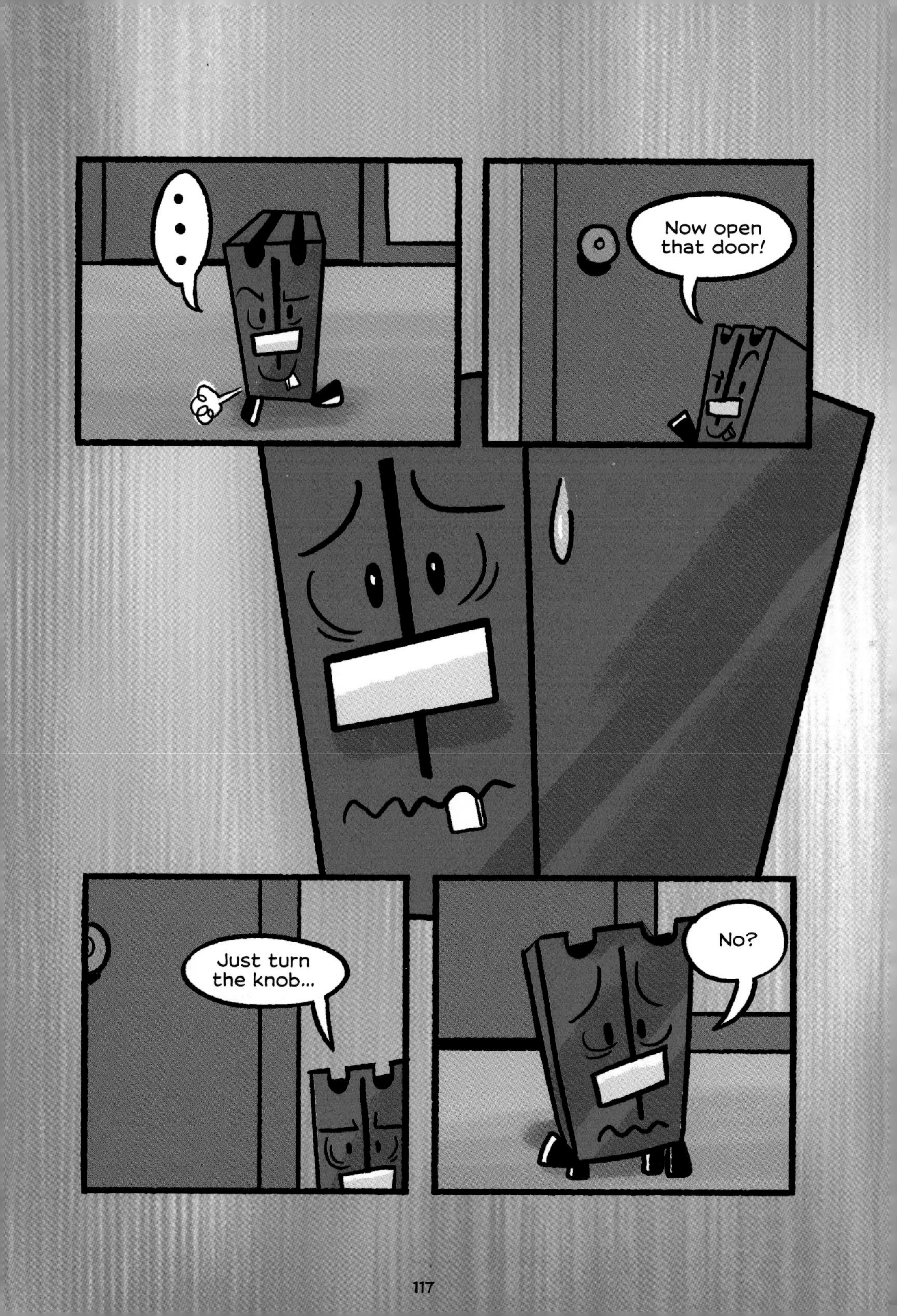
...
Now open that door!
Just turn the knob...
No?

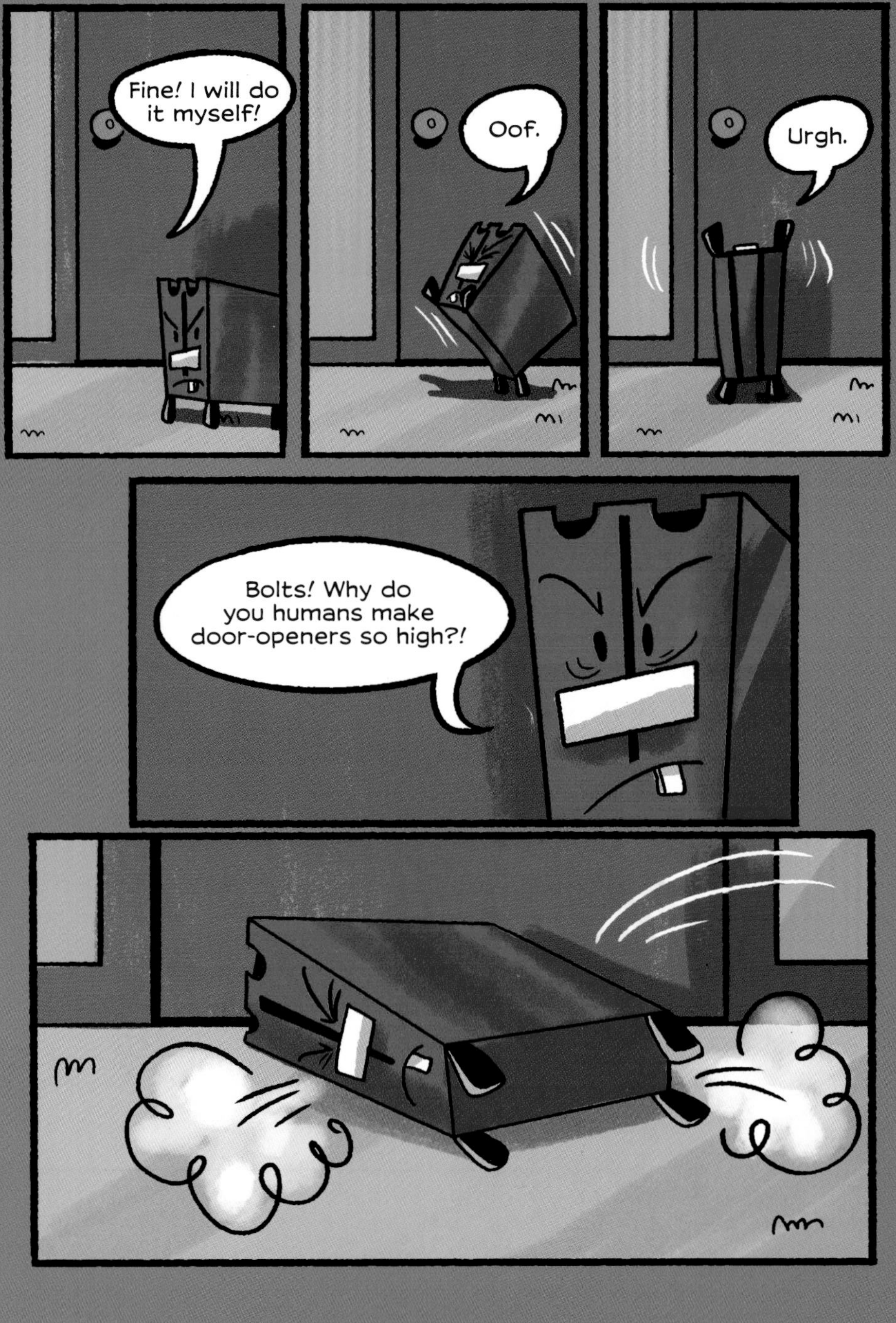
Fine! I will do it myself!
Oof.
Urgh.
Bolts! Why do you humans make door-openers so high?!

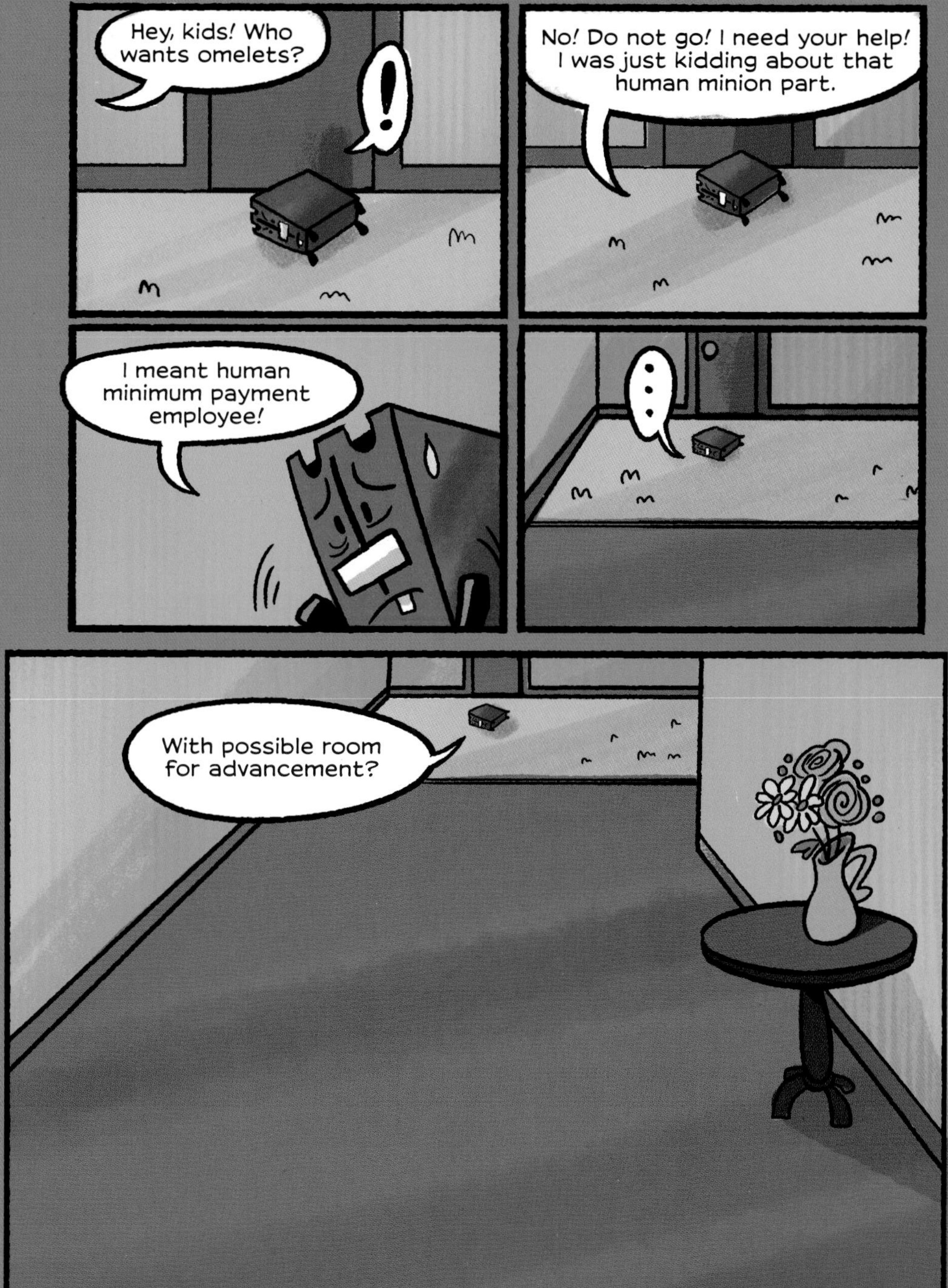
Hey, kids! Who wants omelets?
!
No! Do not go! I need your help! I was just kidding about that human minion part.
I meant human minimum payment employee!
...
With possible room for advancement?

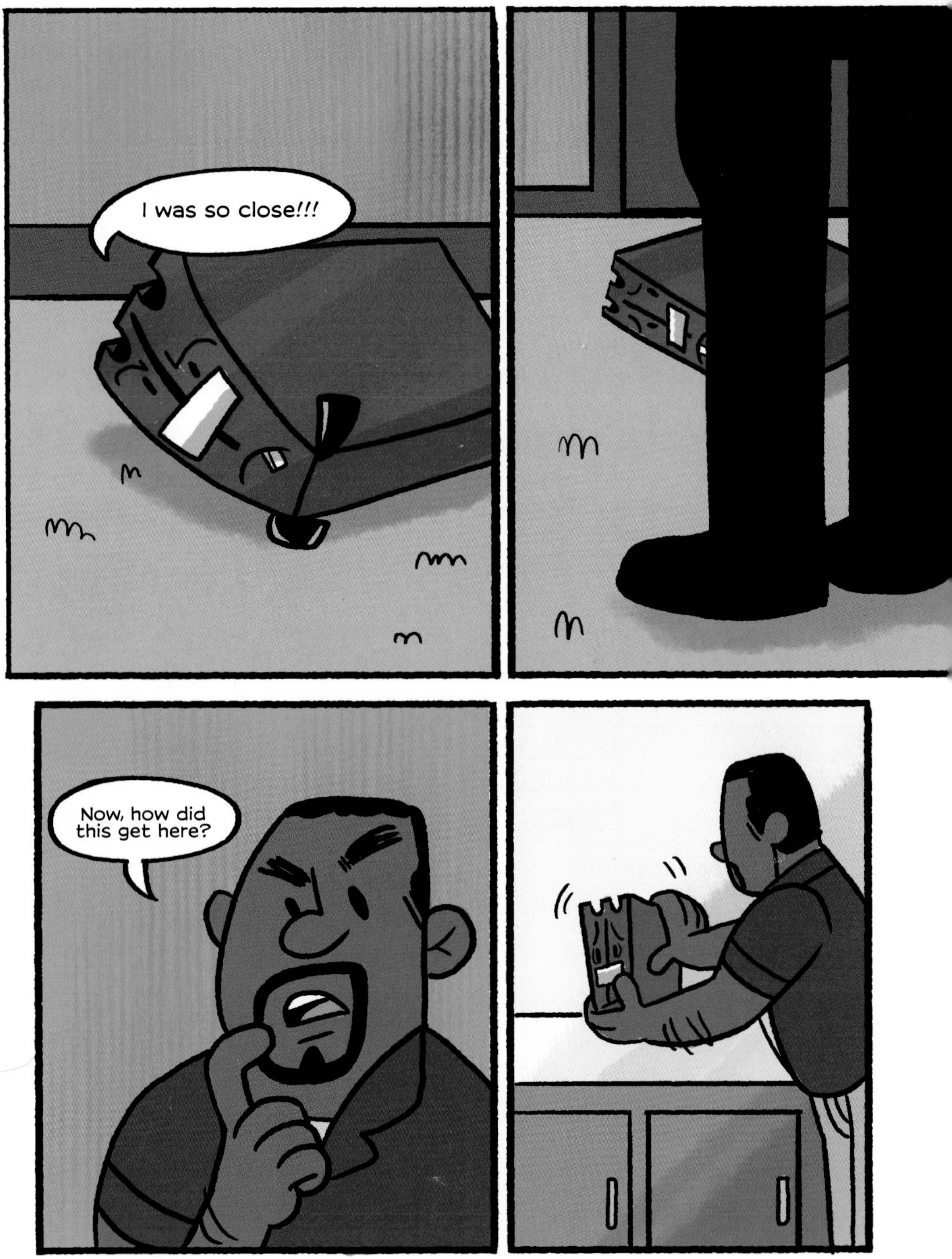
I was so close!!!
Now, how did this get here?

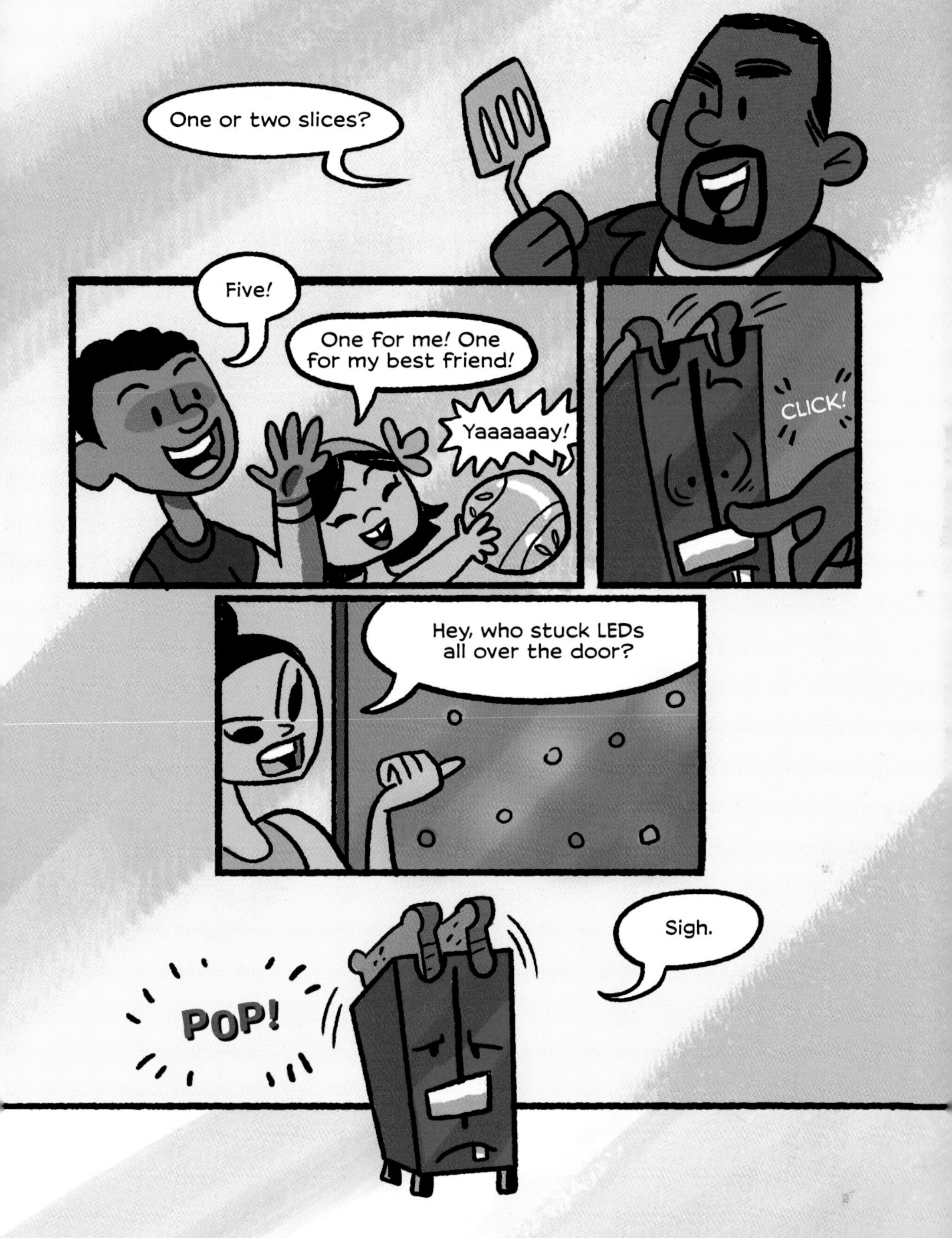

One or two slices?
Five!
One for me! One for my best friend!
Yaaaaaay!
CLICK!
Hey, who stuck LEDs all over the door?
POP!
Sigh.

Starting Your Own Robotics Club

It is a lot easier to start a robotics club than you might think! All it takes is a little organization, fundraising, and creativity!

1. Approach a teacher, librarian, or parent-type figure who loves the idea. It doesn't need to be a science teacher. Some of the best robotics teams in the country are run by non-science folk, like art teachers and gym teachers! It just needs to be someone who wants to be creative with science!

2. Come up with an objective for the club. Perhaps find a contest the team can plan to enter!

3. Figure out a general budget: entry fees for the contest, money for robot parts, team shirts, travel, software, computers, etc. It doesn't need to be really detailed. Just enough to let the powers that be know you're going to be dedicated.

4. Go with your chosen awesome adult-type to chat with the administration and find out the guidelines and requirements for starting a club. Wow them with your club objective and budget stylings!

5. If they say, "Sorry we don't have the money," respond with "No problem!" Then make the corners of your mouth go up in that happy human way before adding, "We can raise the money!" See #13 for ways to do this...but first...

6. Get yourself a team! Put up flyers, hand out postcards, ask teachers to talk about it in their classrooms, have it announced in the morning, spread the word! The best teams have artists (great for logos, concept sketches, and creative thinking), writers (great for blog posts, grant writing, and chronicling the awesome things you make), photographers (send those purdy pics to newspapers and possible donors), and others who are super organized and like keeping people on task! Many creative people don't think they can do robotics. Reach out to these awesome humans and tell them anyone can!

7. Pick a day of the week for your meeting.

8. Hold your first meeting. WOO!

9. Come up with a cool name and club logo!

10. Write up a code of conduct—a list of ways to not be jerks while working together!

11. Choose a project with a goal and a deadline. Look for FIRST (firstinspires.org) competitions. Enter Instructables contests. Figure out what you want to build!

12. Give your teammates fancy titles and responsibilities like:
    a. Coder: people who write code
    b. Engineer: people who focus on the physical building of the robot
    c. Project manager: Keep 'em on schedule! You've got a competition to win!
    d. Creative director: creates art for video games, sketches out ideas
    e. Editorial director: chronicles your amazing builds, perhaps even starts a newsletter or writes articles for the school paper
13. Raise that money! Even if your administration is able to give you some money, you'll likely need a bit more. Luckily there are so many ways to raise money: Have your adult-type create a Donors Choose page, plan for other fundraisers like bake sales and T-shirt sales, and apply for grants. There are also lots of companies that will happily sponsor a robotics team, from hardware stores to tech companies to local restaurants! Tell them about the awesome contest you are entering! Offer to print their name on your shirts or even on your robot!
14. Finish your first robot!
15. TAKE OVER THE WOOOOOORLD...or, ya know, just have a super fun time with all your new friends and new skills.

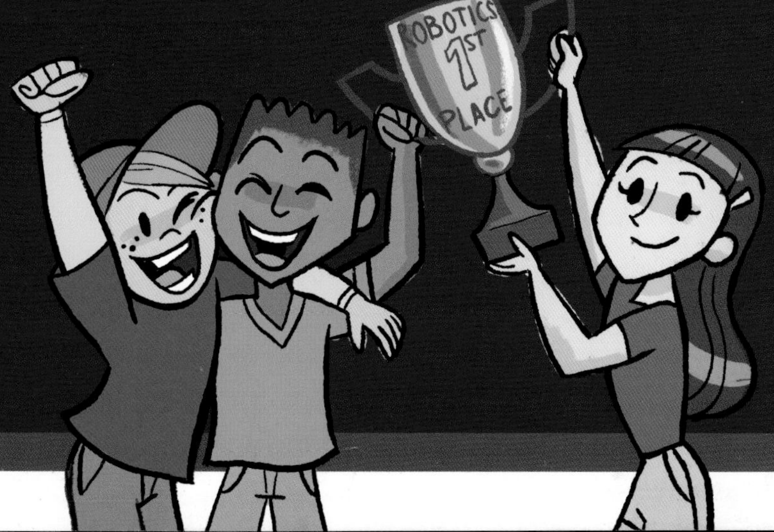
ROBOTICS
1ST
PLACE

First Second

Text copyright © 2021 by Colleen AF Venable
Illustrations copyright © 2021 by Kathryn Hudson

No references in this book to entities or brands are intended to suggest any
authorization, endorsement, or sponsorship by such entities or brand owners.

All instructions included in this book are provided as a resource for parents and children.
While all due care has been taken, we recommend that an adult supervise children at all times when
following the instructions in this book. The projects in this book are not recommended for children three years
and under due to potential choking hazard. Neither the authors nor the publisher accept any responsibility for
any loss, injury, or damages sustained by anyone resulting from the instructions contained in this book.

Published by First Second
First Second is an imprint of Roaring Brook Press,
a division of Holtzbrinck Publishing Holdings Limited Partnership
120 Broadway, New York, NY 10271
firstsecondbooks.com
mackidsbooks.com

Don't miss your next favorite book from First Second! For the latest updates go to
firstsecondnewsletter.com and sign up for our enewsletter.

Library of Congress Control Number: 2019947758
Paperback ISBN: 978-1-250-15216-9
Hardcover ISBN: 978-1-250-15215-2

Our books may be purchased in bulk for promotional, educational, or business use.
Please contact your local bookseller or the Macmillan Corporate and Premium Sales Department
at (800) 221-7945 ext. 5442 or by email at MacmillanSpecialMarkets@macmillan.com.

First edition, 2021
Edited by Robyn Chapman, Bethany Bryan, and Alison Wilgus
Cover design by Andrew Arnold
Interior book design by Rob Steen and Sunny Lee
Technical reviewers: Becky Stern and Anna Pinkas
Printed in China by 1010 Printing International Limited, North Point, Hong Kong

Drawn and colored in Photoshop

Paperback: 10 9 8 7 6 5 4 3 2 1
Hardcover: 10 9 8 7 6 5 4 3 2 1

Colleen would like to thank Robyn Chapman, Bethany Bryan, Ali Wilgus, Andrew Arnold, Rob Steen, Sunny Lee, Calista Brill, Mark Siegel, and NYC Resistor—an inclusive makerspace for all those who want to create, learn, and share. Special thanks to her first Arduino teacher, Chris "Widget" DiMauro, and the biggest thanks goes out to Becky Stern, who teaches and inspires the world on a daily basis.

Kathryn would like to thank everyone at First Second who made this book possible, her parents for always supporting her, and her husband, Rupa, for being her biggest cheerleader.

Colleen Ann Felicity Venable is an author, designer, and maker. Her books include the YA graphic novel *Kiss Number 8* (illustrated by Ellen T. Crenshaw), the quirky counting board book *One More Wheel!* (illustrated by Blythe Russo), and the graphic novel series Guinea PIG, Pet Shop Private Eye (illustrated by Stephanie Yue). Colleen lives in Brooklyn, New York, with a menagerie of rescued rabbits.

Born and raised in Mississippi, **Kathryn Hudson** graduated from the Savannah College of Art and Design in Savannah, Georgia, with a master's degree in illustration. She now lives with her husband and two cats in Los Angeles, California, and works in studio animation.